Cognitive Behavior Counseling Practice

MW00774399

Recent changes in health care continue to impact professional counseling practice. Specifically, counselors are increasingly expected to use evidence-based interventions in their work with clients. Besides being evidence-based, CBT has become more consistent with the core values of the counseling profession with its evolving focus on relationships, strengths, and cultural sensitivity.

Developing a sufficient level of competence in CBT cannot be acquired through reading an overview chapter in a counseling theories book. Counselors and counselors-in-training need additional training in this core approach and also need a CBT text that is written specifically by professional counselors for them. *Cognitive Behavior Therapy in Counseling Practice* meets that need. It is based on the core values of the counseling profession and emphasizes the client-counselor relationship, provides extensive case examples and session transcriptions, and includes an extensive list of CBT terms. Highlighted are detailed descriptions of the theory and actual practice of several CBT approaches including Strengths-Based Cognitive Behavior Therapy, Mindfulness-Based Cognitive Therapy, Motivational Interviewing, Dialectical Behavior Therapy, and Acceptance and Commitment Therapy.

Jon Sperry, PhD, is Assistant Professor of Clinical Mental Health Counseling at Lynn University and a staff therapist at the Counseling and Psychological Services at Florida Atlantic University. He has extensive training in CBT and practices, supervises, and consults on the use of CBT. He has published several articles and book chapters and is co-author of *Cognitive Behavioral Therapy of DSM-5 Personality Disorders: Assessment, Case Conceptualization and Treatment* and *Case Conceptualization: Mastering this Competency with Ease and Confidence*.

Len Sperry, MD, PhD, is Professor and Director of Clinical Training at Florida Atlantic University and Clinical Professor of Psychiatry and Behavioral Medicine at the Medical College of Wisconsin. He has practiced, taught, and written about CBT for over three decades and has had extensive formal training in CBT. Among his 1000+ professional publications are several articles, book chapters, and books on CBT, including the *Cognitive Behavioral Therapy of DSM-5 Personality Disorders*, and *Treatment of Chronic Medical Conditions: Cognitive-Behavioral Therapy Strategies and Integrative Treatment Protocols*.

"For Counseling Professionals and students of the Counseling Profession who have too often thought of cognitive-behavioral therapy (CBT) as a set of rationally oriented interventions or felt required to use it for insurance purposes, get ready to feel renewed in the heart and soul of this approach. Sperry and Sperry's *Cognitive Behavior Therapy in Professional Counseling Practice* is a tour de force of CBT models, presented in the ways they are meant to be practiced: they are relationally centered, wellness-oriented, and informed by both cultural and theoretical diversity. This is not the CBT that one settles for; it is CBT that counselors can fully embrace."

James Robert Bitter, EdD, Professor of
Counseling and Human Services,
East Tennessee State University

"Drs. Sperry and Sperry have done an excellent job of highlighting concepts and techniques of the cognitive behavior therapies for practitioners. I especially like their critique of the myths of CBT and their putting this approach into perspective. They clearly show how the therapeutic alliance is fundamental to practicing CBT effectively, and how the relationship is central in any therapy. I appreciated their overview of the 'third wave' contemporary CBT approaches, as this discussion illustrates the evolution of cognitive behavioral therapies. This is a practical book that provides a good overview of various aspects of CBT."

Gerald Corey, EdD, ABPP, Professor Emeritus of
Human Services and Counseling, California
State University, Fullerton

"*Cognitive Behavior Therapy in Professional Counseling Practice* is a book that has been hiding in plain sight for several years. Cognitive Behavior Therapy (CBT) has established a strong base of empirical support. Similarly, clinical professional counselors have, as a profession, developed substantially to the point of being one of the major growth areas in mental health practice. Sperry and Sperry have brought these two elements together in a clear, practical, and useful way. This is one more impressive volume from a well-experienced CBT therapist and teacher that has value for the counseling student or professional counselor."

Arthur Freeman, EdD., Sc.D., ABPP, LCPC,
Professor, Department of Behavioral Science,
Touro College, New York, NY

"Counselors, teachers and students of counseling, and frankly anyone working to help people enhance their mental and emotional well-being, can find their efforts immeasurably enhanced by applying insights and knowledge gained through reading this excellent and insightful book. Myths are debunked. The roots of CBT, its core principles and techniques, branches and recent off-shoots are presented. This valuable book by Jon and Len Sperry contains just about everything readers want to know about CBT, and then some!"

Dr. Debbie Joffe Ellis, Adjunct Professor of
Psychology - Department of Clinical and Counseling
Psychology, Columbia University, Psychologist, Writer, Presenter

Cognitive Behavior Therapy in Counseling Practice

Jon Sperry and Len Sperry

Routledge
Taylor & Francis Group

NEW YORK AND LONDON

First published 2018
by Routledge
711 Third Avenue, New York, NY 10017

and by Routledge
2 Park Square, Milton Park, Abingdon, Oxon, OX14 4RN

Routledge is an imprint of the Taylor & Francis Group, an informa business

Library of Congress Cataloging-in-Publication Data
Names: Sperry, Jonathan J., author. | Sperry, Len, author.
Title: Cognitive behavior therapy in counseling practice / Jon Sperry and Len Sperry.
Description: New York, NY : Routledge, 2018. | Includes bibliographical references and index.
Identifiers: LCCN 2017029280 | ISBN 9781138648661 (hardback : alk. paper) | ISBN 9781138648678 (pbk. : alk. paper) | ISBN 9781315626284 (ebook : alk. paper)
Subjects: LCSH: Cognitive therapy. | Counseling.
Classification: LCC RC489.C63 S68 2018 | DDC 616.89/1425—dc23
LC record available at https://lccn.loc.gov/2017029280

ISBN: 978-1-138-64866-1 (hbk)
ISBN: 978-1-138-64867-8 (pbk)
ISBN: 978-1-315-62628-4 (ebk)

Typeset in Sabon
by Apex CoVantage, LLC

MIX
Paper from responsible sources
FSC
www.fsc.org   FSC™ C013985

Printed in the United Kingdom
by Henry Ling Limited

Contents

Acknowledgments   vi

Introduction   1

1   The Practice and Evolution of CBT   9

2   CBT Theory and Competencies   22

3   Contemporary Cognitive-Behavioral Approaches   42

4   Processes   63

5   Cognitive-Behavioral Interventions   84

6   Diversity and CBT Practice   116

7   Evaluation   138

8   Pattern-Focused Therapy in Everyday
    Counseling Practice   155

    Glossary of CBT Terms   183
    Index   191

Acknowledgments

Besides being very grateful for the work of Albert Ellis, Aaron Beck, Alfred Adler, and many others, we want to thank our teachers, mentors, and friends who have taught us about psychotherapy and the importance of the therapeutic relationship. We are very grateful for the efforts of two students from Lynn University: Grisel Lopez-Escobar, who provided copy-editing, and Tania Alaby, who assisted with writing the CBT terms in the glossary. We also want to thank the individuals at Routledge who helped throughout the process of the creation of this book, especially George Zimmar and Lillian Rand.

I (Jon) am thankful for the relationship with my father, Len. His constant love and support throughout my life have been a true blessing. I am also grateful to my mother Patti, who taught me to have an endless amount of love and patience for all human beings. I would also like to thank some individuals who have taught me and/or been a mentor to me: Jim Bitter, Richard Watts, Paul Rasmussen, Marion Balla, Kirk Dougher, Debra Ainbinder, Mitch Rosenwald, Jon Carlson, Paul Peluso, Debbie Joffe Ellis, Gary Sullivan, Stacy Hyde, Candice Rasa, Dean Sababu, and many more.

Introduction

Recent changes in health and mental health care practice, including professional counseling, signal major shifts in the ways in which professional services will be provided in the near future. Practitioners will be expected to utilize evidence-based practice, monitor, and evaluate the services they provide. While it may be a few years before the full impact of these changes are experienced by most professional counselors, there is an increasing awareness that the professional practice of counseling will become more evidence-based, and that counselors-in-training will learn and become proficient in evidence-based approaches. Whether in mental health, marital and family, school, or rehabilitation settings, professional counselors will be expected to demonstrate the competent use of evidence-based interventions in the counseling services they provide.

Since Cognitive Behavior Therapy (CBT) is a both an evidence-based and effective treatment approach, it is likely to become more commonplace in professional counseling. Research confirms that CBT is effective in treating most mental disorders and other concerns—including cultural ones—faced by clients of all ages. It is also one of the most widely used treatment approaches in the world today (Norcross, 2005). Of particular importance is that recent developments in CBT—specifically the emphasis on client-counselor relationships and strengths—appears to be a particularly "good fit" for professional counseling practice. In short, CBT appears to have considerable utility and promise for professional counselors and those in training.

Developing a sufficient level of competence in any counseling approach—including CBT—cannot be acquired through reading an overview chapter in a counseling theories book assigned in a counseling theory course. Instead, counselors and counselors-in-training will need additional training in this core approach. They need a CBT text that is written specifically for professional counselors and counselors-in-training: one that is sensitive to the various ways counseling is provided in mental health, school, and rehabilitation settings.

While this book is both brief and practical, it is also reasonably comprehensive. In addition, it is tailored primarily to the needs and concerns of counselors. This means that it emphasizes the therapeutic relationship and includes core-counseling concepts such as social justice, strengths, wellness, and diversity (e.g., ethnicity, culture, sexual orientation, religion, gender, disability) interwoven throughout the book's content.

This book should be of value to all professional counselors regardless of settings—school, mental health or rehabilitation clinic or agency, or private practice. While it is likely to be used in graduate counseling theory and technique courses, as well as practicum and internship courses in counselor education programs, it will also be of value in undergraduate courses in counseling and human services programs. Experienced counselors may also find it helpful as they navigate the changes in healthcare and demands for documenting the use of effective, evidence-based interventions. Besides the clinical value and empirical support of the original CBT approaches such as Behavior Therapy, Cognitive Therapy, and Rational Emotive Behavior Therapy, a number of myths about these early approaches have also emerged.

Myths About Cognitive Behavior Therapy

Over the years we have noted that counselors have developed some well-defined opinions and attitudes about Cognitive Behavior Therapy and its practice. For some counselors, these opinions are strongly held but less so for others. Since we are not aware of definitive research studies on counselors' attitudes towards CBT, we can only report our own observations and conversations with counseling students, counselor educators and supervisors, practicing counselors, clinical psychology students, faculty, supervisors, and practitioners.

We have observed that early in training, counselors tend to be more receptive and positive about CBT than later in training, or even after completing training. In contrast, clinical psychology students tend to be positive about CBT as both a theory and intervention early on, and then generally remain positive about CBT as practitioners. They are also likely to be well trained in one or more CBT approaches. In contrast, counselors tend to have less formal training in CBT theory and interventions.

Undoubtedly, there are reasons for these different perspectives about CBT among counselors and clinical psychologists. We speculate that counselors are more likely to ascribe to one or more myths about CBT than psychologists with specialized training in psychotherapy. These three myths are: CBT downplays the therapeutic relationship, it must be used because it is reimbursable, and it is a rigid, manualized form of treatment.

Myth 1: "CBT Is Only Problem-Focused and Seriously Downplays or Even Eliminates the Focus on the Therapeutic Relationship."

Critics of CBT often view this approach as a problem-focused form of psychotherapy that challenges the irrational thoughts of clients. This view is not uncommonly accompanied by the belief that CBT counselors do not utilize the therapeutic relationship as the key to change or as a valuable part of the change process. This belief was demonstrated in some 1970s training videos of behavior therapists and cognitive therapists focusing on problem solving at the expense of the therapeutic relationship. This was, and remains, very problematic because, among all the mental health professions, counselors see themselves as "keepers" of the therapeutic relationship.

In fact, the counseling relationship is the "sine qua non" of the counseling profession. It should not be surprising then that 29 professional counseling organizations endorsed the *20/20: Consensus Definition of Counseling*, which states that "Counseling is a professional relationship that empowers diverse individuals, families, and groups to accomplish mental health, wellness, education, and career goals" (Kaplan & Gladding, 2011). There is no mistaking it: the counselor-client relationship is at the heart of the counseling profession!

However, since the 1990s, *all* forms of CBT—the first and second wave or conventional approaches as well as the newer third wave approaches—require the development and maintenance of an effective therapeutic relationship. It is noteworthy that Cory Newman, PhD says in his key CBT book, *Core Competencies in Cognitive-Behavioral Therapy*, that "CBT values the therapeutic relationship as indispensable to the process of treatment" (Newman, 2013, p. 48). Needless to say, his book contains two lengthy chapters on the therapeutic relationship.

"Third wave" CBT approaches (described in detail in Chapter 1) offer convincing proof of CBT's commitment to the therapeutic relationship, and that it is not just a "problem-focused" approach as so many believe. One of these third wave approaches is Strengths-Based Cognitive Behavior Therapy (Padesky & Mooney, 2012). It not only emphasizes the therapeutic relationship, it incorporates client strengths and resources in therapy. That makes this approach most compatible with the counseling profession's emphasis on strengths and prevention. Another way of saying this is that to the extent that counselors and other mental health practitioners view CBT as an approach that downplays the roles of the therapeutic relationship and a focus on strengths, they have bought into this first myth.

In his keynote presentation at the 2017 American Counseling Association annual conference in San Francisco, Irving Yalom voiced his concerns about counselors utilizing CBT simply because of its evidence-based status. Yalom criticized CBT by saying that "CBT omits the essence of psychotherapy—the interpersonal nature of the therapeutic relationship" (Meyers, 2017). The immediate and sustained audience applause suggested that many counselors who were present agreed with both his sentiment and this first myth. However, Yalom's contention that CBT is not relationship focused is both dated and inaccurate.

Competent CBT counselors are fully aware of the importance of incorporating interpersonal warmth, respect, genuineness, and empathy in the counseling process. Not only have Beck and Ellis identified the importance of the therapeutic relationship, the third wave CBT approaches all strongly emphasize the importance of the relationship in the counseling process (Ellis & Joffe Ellis, 2014; Beck, 1995). A key premise of this book is that the therapeutic relationship is an essential factor in all effective counseling approaches, including CBT.

Myth 2: "Even Though I Don't Like CBT, I'll Be Forced to Use It Because It Is Evidence-Based and Reimbursable."

This myth assumes that counselors are expected, and may be required, to use only evidenced-based strategies in their counseling even if they do not believe in evidence-based practice or do not like CBT. This myth is held by many experienced counselors but also by some who are currently in training. A recent article in *Counseling Today* (ref. November 2015 issue) suggests what it is that might be fueling this myth. The author observed that many graduate counseling students taking a counseling theories course often identified most strongly with the Adlerian approach to counseling—which is not currently listed as an evidence-based approach—but predicted that they would become CBT practitioners because CBT was an evidence-based approach, which they believe would be a requirement for reimbursement. In other words, they found the Adlerian approach to be compatible with their basic beliefs and values, whereas the traditional CBT theory was less so. Accordingly, they felt torn between an approach they liked and one that they could be paid for practicing.

We have also observed a high level of interest in the Adlerian approach to counseling and therapy among students, particularly Strengths-Based Cognitive Behavior Therapy and Acceptance and Commitment Therapy—both of which share similarities with the Adlerian approach. They may even attempt to integrate these approaches into their counseling clients during practicum or internship. These students say they appreciate the simplicity and the technological appeal of these CBT approaches.

Insurance companies and grant funders increasingly expect counselors to utilize evidence-based interventions. This expectation has led counselors to feel a push to rigidly apply CBT interventions because they are reimbursable. We mention again that the third wave CBT approaches (such as Acceptance and Commitment Therapy), many of which are evidence-based approaches, are both reimbursable and compatible with many counselors' beliefs and values.

Myth 3: "CBT Is a Treatment Manual Therapy That Means Rigidly Practicing 'Cookie Cutter' Therapy That Takes Away All the Creativity From the Counseling Process."

Many counselors are very taken with Carl Rogers's way of being with clients: his high level of interpersonal warmth, his active listening without asking too many questions, his encouraging reflections, and his genuine unconditional positive regard for the human being sitting across from him. The myth that CBT is too "cookie cutter" and that creativity is removed from the therapeutic process is understandable but not quite accurate.

This myth assumes that practicing CBT means rigidly following the protocol of practice in a treatment manual. It is true that close adherence to a treatment manual protocol is required when an approach is being evaluated in a clinical trial with a randomized control design to determine if it meets the criteria of an evidence-based approach. In this situation, creativity and deviation from the protocol are not only discouraged but disallowed. Fidelity checks are regularly done to determine how closely the protocol is followed by every counselor and therapist in the study. However, after the clinical trial is completed and it has been determined that the approach meets criteria and is listed as an evidence-based approach, then the counselor can use the treatment manual protocol as a general guide to practice and can individualize treatment to their client. That means that creativity is allowed and even encouraged. In short, this myth of rigidly following a protocol is inaccurate.

Too often novice counselors unsuccessfully utilize CBT techniques, then blame their subpar counseling results on rigid and manualized therapeutic approaches. Below is an example of a counselor using Rational Emotive Behavior Therapy in a rigid manner with a depressed client:

Joe: I've just been feeling so depressed lately, I really don't think anyone cares if I am alive or not. I know that if I died, no one would really care.

Counselor: What evidence do you have to support your thought that no one would care if you died?

Joe: Well my mother said that she doesn't want to speak with me until I forgive her for a recent fight we had, and my two closest friends actually encourage me to kill myself when

	I told them that I was feeling suicidal. I know they were just mad, but I know they aren't in my corner at the moment.
Counselor:	But your belief that "no one cares" simply isn't true!
Joe:	They seem pretty real to me based on the fact that my closest friends told me to kill myself.
Counselor:	That particular belief is called an "all or nothing thinking" belief and it is irrational. Do you think that your belief is helping you in your current situation?
Joe:	Well I don't think it is helping or hurting me because my situation sucks.
Counselor:	How much do you believe the thought that "no one would care if you died"?
Joe:	I'd say 100% based on the fact that my friends told me to kill myself and my mother said she doesn't want to speak with me.

This transcription shows a novice counselor struggling to follow the cognitive disputation intervention, arguing with the client about the validity and usefulness of his thoughts. The novice counselor held the belief that the disputation process must be followed closely, otherwise he would not be accurately applying Rational Emotive Behavior Therapy. After using this approach and achieving few positive outcomes, the counselor concluded that it was not an effective treatment and that it allowed little creativity since "it basically is just an approach designed to argue with clients about their irrational beliefs." This example shows how a novice counselor failed to provide empathy and encouragement while over focusing rigidly following the disputation process.

Overview of the Book

1. Chapter 1 describes the customary way in which CBT has been practiced, typically as Behavior Therapy, Cognitive Therapy, or a combination of both. This chapter emphasizes the history of CBT, the therapeutic alliance, identification of client strengths and resources, and sensitivity to diversity and cultural issues of these new developments in CBT.
2. Chapter 2 describes the theoretical premises common to all CBT approaches. It also emphasizes the competencies of the therapeutic relationship, integrative assessment, case conceptualization, treatment implementation, monitoring and evaluation of treatment, maintaining treatment gains, and dealing with treatment-interfering behaviors.
3. Chapter 3 describes the contemporary "third wave" CBT approaches. These include: Strengths-Based Cognitive Behavior Therapy,

Mindfulness-Based Cognitive Therapy, Schema Therapy, Motivational Interviewing, Cognitive Behavioral Analysis System of Psychotherapy, Pattern-Focused Therapy, Dialectical Behavior Therapy, and Acceptance and Commitment Therapy.

4. Chapter 4 reviews various processes in implementing CBT, including the role of the counselor-client relationship, the role of the counselor, the client's readiness to change, and the active engagement of the client.

5. Chapter 5 describes and illustrates the most commonly used CBT interventions in counseling practice. These include: behavioral activation, cognitive disputation and restructuring, emotional regulation training, empathy training, exposure, habit reversal, impulse control training, interpersonal skills training, mindfulness, problem solving training, relapse prevention, social skills training, and thought stopping.

6. Chapter 6 highlights two significant values in the counseling profession: diversity and cultural sensitivity. It illustrates the importance of sensitivity to diversity and cultural issues among various populations in different counseling settings.

7. Chapter 7 highlights research supporting the effectiveness of CBT for a wide gamut of client presentations. It emphases the monitoring of CBT interventions and counseling outcomes.

8. Chapter 8 describes Pattern-Focused Therapy as an approach appropriate for most clients in everyday counseling practice. It illustrates this third wave CBT approach with extensive case material and session transcripts.

Concluding Note

Counselors who ascribe to myths that CBT downplays the therapeutic relationship, that it must be used because it is reimbursable, and that it is a rigid form of treatment have unreasonably limited themselves from successfully utilizing its very effective interventions. Ultimately, holding on to these myths could be detrimental to their clients. Each of these myths are based on outdated information and serve as inaccurate perceptions and information of traditional CBT. The reality is that contemporary forms of CBT—called third wave approaches—undermine these myths and make it clear that these newer approaches are not only compatible with the values and beliefs of most counselors and the counseling profession, but can also greatly optimize counseling practice.

In closing, it is clear that the practice of counseling is continuing to evolve and change. Myths are giving way to new realities and positive counseling outcomes. Our hope is that this book will provide you with both new understandings and a new set of CBT interventions that, irrespective of your theoretical orientation, will enrich your professional life and practice!

References

Beck, J. (1995). *Cognitive therapy: Basics and beyond.* New York, NY: Guilford Press.

Ellis, A., & Joffe Ellis, D. (2014). *Rational emotive behavior therapy.* Washington, DC: American Psychological Association.

Kaplan, D. M., & Gladding, S. T. (2011). A vision for the future of counseling: The 20/20 principles for unifying and strengthening the profession. *Journal of Counseling & Development, 89*(3), 367–372.

Meyers, L. (2017, March). Yalom urges ACA attendees to hold fast to self-care and the therapeutic relationship. *Counseling Today.* Online Exclusive. Retrieved from http://ct.counseling.org/tag/yalom/

Newman, C. (2013). *Core competencies in cognitive-behavioral therapy: Becoming a highly effective and competent cognitive-behavioral therapist.* New York, NY: Routledge.

Norcross, J. (2005). A primer on psychotherapy integration. In J. Norcross & M. Goldfried (Eds.), *Handbook of psychotherapy integration* (2nd ed., pp. 3–23). New York, NY: Oxford.

Padesky, C. A., & Mooney, K. A. (2012). Strengths-based cognitive behavioural therapy: A four step model to build resilience. *Clinical Psychology & Psychotherapy, 19*(4), 283–290.

Chapter 1

The Practice and Evolution of CBT

Counselors tend to approach the therapeutic process differently than other mental health professionals. Specifically, counselors embrace a shared philosophy of counseling in which they attempt to de-pathologize human suffering by conceptualizing the integration of a developmental perspective with a wellness model of mental health. Additionally, they focus on prevention and early intervention, emphasize client empowerment and the therapeutic relationship, and highlight multicultural competency (Fuenfhausen, Young, Cashwell, & Musangali, 2017). Further, these values are exemplified in the American Counseling Association (ACA) definition posted on the ACA website (www.counseling.org): "Counseling is a professional relationship that empowers diverse individuals, families, and groups to accomplish mental health, wellness, education, and career goals." Given these stated values, it is not surprising that counselors tend to view Cognitive Behavior Therapy (CBT) differently than other mental health professionals.

This chapter describes the way in which CBT has been practiced over the years from the 1960s through today, and how it is likely to be practiced tomorrow. CBT has evolved over the years and we will discuss its "three waves." As noted in the Introduction, counselors today seem to resonate with the overall values of these new "third wave" approaches since they emphasize the therapeutic relationship, identification of client strengths and resources, sensitivity to diversity and culture, and client empowerment, which are deeply held values for most counselors.

This chapter will introduce these third wave approaches as well as the more traditional first and second wave CBT approaches. It begins with a thumbnail sketch of the evolution in terms of waves. Then separate sections briefly describe each of the waves: first wave, second wave, and third wave. Next, we will highlight the evidence-based support of CBT approaches and also review research on clinical outcomes in counseling. Finally, the chapter will close with a brief discussion of the therapeutic relationship and multicultural competence and sensitivity.

Evolution of CBT

For the last five decades, Behavior Therapy, Cognitive Therapy, and CBT were the treatments of choice for the psychosocial treatment of various mental health disorders. While research did not consistently support the efficacy of these traditional modalities with various disorders, it has for newer, more focused approaches such as Dialectic Behavior Therapy (DBT) and Mindfulness-Based Cognitive Therapy (MBCT). Interestingly, DBT and MBCT, along with Acceptance and Commitment Therapy (Hayes, 2004), constitute what is being called the "third wave" of Behavior Therapy (Hayes, Follette, & Linehan, 2004).

Since the 1970s, the field of psychotherapy has shifted from psychodynamically oriented, long-term psychotherapy to more problem-focused, short-term therapies such as variants of CBT. These counseling approaches—particularly Behavior Therapy, Cognitive Behavior Therapy (CBT), and Interpersonal Psychotherapy—have been shown to play a significant role in the treatment of specific psychiatric disorders (Craighead & Craighead, 2001). In fact, randomized clinical trials show them to be particularly effective as primary treatments (i.e., treatments of choice, for obsessive-compulsive disorder, panic disorder, and major depression). They are also effective as adjunctive interventions with medications for bipolar disorder and schizophrenia. In addition, they play a substantial role in educating patients about their disorders, explaining treatment rationales, and encouraging treatment compliance, especially when medication is involved (Craighead & Craighead, 2001).

First Wave

The first wave refers to traditional Behavior Therapy concepts such as reinforcement techniques and classical conditioning, which focused on modifying or replacing maladaptive behaviors. Early Behavior Therapy was a concrete, problem-focused, technical, and here-and-now approach that was markedly different than client-centered therapy, psychoanalysis, and similar approaches of the era that emphasized the therapeutic relationship and the client's inner world. Behavior Therapy researchers and clinicians initially emphasized interventions that were used to establish a scientific basis to effectively treat specific anxiety disorders.

Joseph Wolpe was one of the original developers of Behavior Therapy. His approach was based on his theory of "reciprocal inhibition" (Wolpe, 1958, 1990). Wolpe believed that if anxiety-producing stimuli occurred simultaneously with an inhibition of anxiety—such as being in a relaxed state—the bond between those stimuli and the anxious symptoms would be reduced. His primary contribution was "systematic desensitization" that was a protocol in which a hierarchy of anxiety-producing stimuli was constructed. Then, when the client was in a deep state of relaxation, each stimulus would be gradually introduced until they no longer produced anxiety. This rather time-consuming intervention would in time be eclipsed by exposure therapy. Other notable behavior therapists were Isaac Marks and Albert Bandura.

Unfortunately, when systematic desensitization was subjected to the research method known as "dismantling," the unmistakable conclusion was that direct exposure was the only behavioral intervention required for behavior change. It did not require any of the other interventions assumed by Wolpe to be necessary to achieve the goal of reduction of anxiety. Not needed were the establishment of a hierarchy, the presence of a relaxed state, or the gradualness of exposure that Wolpe claimed were necessary. In short, the conclusion was that only direct exposure was the necessary and sufficient condition for therapeutic change. As a result of these findings, Wolpe's (1958) theory of reciprocal inhibition was soon discarded. Today there is little question that exposure therapy is a treatment of choice for a number of conditions, and very few know much about systematic desensitization, except as a historical footnote. Besides exposure, there are several highly effective behavioral interventions in practice today. They include behavioral activation, behavioral rehearsal, skills training, habit reversal, and impulse control training. These and other techniques are described in detail in Chapter 5.

The first wave counseling process was not relationship focused in the way counselors typically describe it, but a concern for the client was clearly involved. A telling example of this is the use of the Subjective Units of Distress Scale (SUDS) (Wolpe, 1958), which is a self-rating scale of emotional pain and suffering in which the client is taught to rate their subjective units of distress on a 1–100 unit scale. Through ongoing self-assessment, clients increase their level of control over their symptoms. As a result of the counselor teaching this empowering method, they demonstrate a high level of regard for the client's well-being, of which clients are most appreciative. By the use of this and other behavioral methods, counselors who use this scale demonstrate sensitivity to the therapeutic relationship. Of particular note, some of the original behaviorists were not known to consider the therapeutic relationship to be a primary change mechanism in the counseling process.

Second Wave

The second wave involved the incorporation of the cognitive dimension into the counseling process. It did so by focusing on reducing depressive affects and behaviors by changing the thoughts that cause and perpetuate them (Beck, 1967; Beck, Rush, & Emery, 1979). Aaron T. Beck's work is credited as the starting point of the second wave even though others had previously developed cognitive-focused therapies. Beck called his approach Cognitive Therapy and initially it emphasized cognitive restructuring; only later were behavioral interventions such as behavioral activation added.

The incorporation of cognitive and behavioral therapies in the 1970s was not initially a cordial or conflict-free union. Today most cognitive counselors incorporate key behavioral interventions while many behaviorally focused counselors recognize the role of clients' beliefs about the consequences of their behaviors. The fact that both were problem-focused and scientifically based therapies has helped foster this union, resulting in CBT becoming the most commonly practiced treatment method in the United States since the late 1980s.

Rational Emotive Behavior Therapy (REBT) is of the first of the Cognitive Behavior Therapies, developed by Albert Ellis. This approach is still widely practiced today. REBT theory explains human suffering by identifying that negative emotions are influenced by unrealistic and inflexible beliefs and that individuals actively disturb themselves by assuming that their thoughts are the ultimate truth. *Aaron T. Beck's work on cognitive therapy was presented around fifteen years after Ellis first wrote and presented on REBT.*

Both were formally trained analysts who believed psychoanalysis was an insufficient approach to helping individuals with mental health issues and both developed very similar psychological treatment approaches that emphasized cognition as the mechanism of suffering and the mechanism of change in counseling. They were initially unaware of one another's theories and developed the approaches independently from each other.

Both Ellis and Beck credit Adler's contribution to their approaches, particularly the primacy of cognition in the change process. Ellis credits Alfred Adler, Karen Horney, and Epictetus among others as influential in his creation of REBT. Further, in a letter written to the North American Society of Adlerian Psychology (NASAP) by Aaron Beck in 1989, he respectfully declined an offer to provide a keynote lecture at the annual NASAP conference, but stated that he considers himself an Adlerian.

Alfred Adler is considered the first cognitive-behavioral practitioner based on his writing and practice of his therapy approach, Individual Psychology, also known as Adlerian Psychology (Freeman, 1981). One of Adler's many contributions included paving the way for cognitive-behavioral therapeutic approaches including Ellis's Rational Emotive Behavior Therapy and Beck's Cognitive Therapy (Mosak, 2005). Adler conceptualized maladaptive behavior to be influenced by one's "private intelligence," later called "faulty logic," which informs one's view of self as well as views and expectations of others. Freeman noted that Ellis and Beck "credit their training in Adlerian and Horneyan models as central to their formation of a cognitive model of psychotherapy" (1983, p. 1–2).

The role that Cognitive Therapy (CT) played in the evolution of CBT has already been discussed, and it is particularly noteworthy to mention that proponents of CT/REBT publish in the *Journal of Individual*

Psychology, the flagship journal of Adlerian Psychology. One such individual, Ellis (1970), stated, "Adler strongly influenced the work on Sullivan, Horney, Fromm, Rogers, May, Maslow, and many other writers on psychotherapy, some of whom are often called neo-Freudians, when they more correctly could be called neo-Adlerians" (p. 11). See Watts and Critelli (1997) for a comprehensive discussion of the influence that Alfred Adler has had on CBT and other contemporary forms of psychotherapy. Two separate issues published in the *Journal of Individual Psychology* (volume 73, 2017) contain comprehensive coverage of Adler's influence on contemporary therapeutic approaches, including CBT.

Third Wave

In the third wave approaches, treatment tends to be more experiential and indirect and utilizes techniques such as mindfulness, acceptance, dialectics, values, and spirituality (Hayes et al., 2004). More specifically, third wave approaches are characterized by "letting go of the attempts at problem solving, and instead standing back to see what it feels like to see the problems through the lens of non-reactivity, and to bring a *kindly awareness* to the difficulty" (Segal, Williams, Teasdale, & Williams, 2004, p. 55, italics added). Unlike the first and second wave approaches, which were based on a modernist assumption of human nature, first-order change (symptom reduction), and a de-emphasis on the therapeutic relationship, third wave approaches are quite different. Besides being based on post-modern assumptions, second-order change (i.e., basic change in personality structure and/or function), and a sensitivity to the client and the importance of the therapeutic relationship, they are also based on contextual assumptions including the influence of culture. Third wave approaches such as Acceptance and Commitment Therapy, Dialectical Behavior Therapy, Cognitive Behavioral Analysis System of Psychotherapy, or Strengths-Based Cognitive Behavior Therapy place a significant focus on the therapeutic relationship. These approaches are discussed below.

Acceptance and Commitment Therapy

Acceptance and Commitment Therapy (ACT) was developed by Steven Hayes. Note that it is referred to as "ACT" to emphasize action and behavior change, and not A.C.T. when speaking about the approach with acronym abbreviation. It is based on relational frame theory, which is its underlying approach to human language and cognition. ACT is also based on functional contextualism, which means that instead of viewing clients as disordered or flawed like many other approaches, it focuses instead on identifying the function and context of behavior (Hayes, 2004).

One of the goals of ACT is to assist individuals to increase their acceptance of difficult and painful experiences and to increase their commitment to action that can improve and enrich their lives. ACT assumes that suffering results from the avoidance of emotional pain rather than the experience of it. Instead of a symptom-reduction approach like other treatment approaches, the goal of ACT is to learn how to accept and detach from symptoms. Therefore, when acceptance occurs, symptom reduction is a byproduct. ACT treatment involves the use of metaphors, behavioral interventions, exercises, and mindfulness skills training. It uses mindfulness skills to develop psychological flexibility, clarify, and foster values-based living.

Dialectical Behavior Therapy

Originally developed to treat individuals diagnosed with borderline personality disorder (Linehan, 1993), Dialectical Behavior Therapy (DBT) has been modified and extended to treat individuals with other personality disorders as well as mood disorders, anxiety disorders, eating disorders, and other destructive behaviors such as self-harm, suicidal ideation, and substance use disorders (Marra, 2005; Lynch & Cuper, 2012). DBT is an extension of Behavior Therapy but is less cognitively focused than traditional CBT since DBT assumes that cognitions, per se, are less important than affect regulation. Accordingly, DBT places more emphasis on coping skills and emotion regulation rather than modifying distorted thoughts or irrational beliefs. While it recognizes that perception and cognitive processes are a factor in behavior, they are not conceptualized as a mediating factor. Further, DBT assumes that individuals are doing their best but are lacking some specific skills, thereby interfering with their capacity to manage their feelings or reactions.

Additionally, a DBT conceptualization of human suffering can be understood by

> identifying deprivational emotional states in early development that could have produced fixation or perseveration and attentional constriction that could serve as protection from threatening internal or external cues, as well as broadly examining the effects of negative reinforcement through emotional escape and avoidance strategies or inadequate psychological coping skills that could have been rewarded through the partial reinforcement effects.
>
> (Marra, 2005, p. 141)

Cognitive Behavioral Analysis System of Psychotherapy

Cognitive Behavioral Analysis System of Psychotherapy (CBASP) is a counseling approach developed by McCullough (2000) and further elaborated by McCullough, Schramm, and Penberthy (2015). Basic to this approach is a situational analysis that combines behavioral, cognitive, and

interpersonal methods to help clients monitor and understand the consequences of their behavior and cognitions, and to use problem solving for
resolving both personal and interpersonal difficulties. McCullough initially developed CBASP to treat clients with chronic forms of depression.

A basic assumption of CBASP is that clients can learn to analyze specific
life challenges and then manage daily challenges on their own. This is
done by having clients complete a coping survey questionnaire to monitor ongoing challenges such as social anxiety, and then the situation is
therapeutically processed and remediated by the counselor and client. The
basic premise of CBASP is simple and straightforward: a counselor assists
clients to discover why they did not obtain a particular goal or desired
outcome by evaluating their distorted or unhelpful thoughts and behaviors. Since there is often a mismatch between what a client wants and what
actually occurs in the client's life, CBASP can be utilized with a variety
of presenting issues ranging from relationship conflict and child behavior
problems to anxiety disorders and personality disorders, including borderline personality disorder (Driscoll, Cukrowicz, Reardon, & Joiner, 2004).

Mindfulness-Based Cognitive Therapy

Mindfulness-Based Cognitive Therapy (MBCT) was originally developed
by Segal and colleagues to prevent relapse for individuals diagnosed with
depression (Segal, Williams, & Teasdale, 2002; 2013). MBCT incorporates aspects of Cognitive Therapy with components of Mindfulness-
Based Stress Reduction (MBSR), which was developed by Kabat-Zinn
(1994). MBSR is a widely used adjunctive to medical treatment for various clinical conditions as well as a self-help technique for stress management and non-clinical conditions.

The goal of MBCT is to interrupt distressing thought processes and to
accept and observe incoming stimuli without judgment. Further, MBCT
emphasizes altering the awareness of, and relation to, cognitions and
thoughts, rather than changing thought content. It offers participants
alternative choices of living with and experiencing emotional pain and
suffering. The assumption is that cultivating a detached attitude towards
problematic thinking provides an individual with the skills to prevent
intensification of negative thinking at times when problematic thinking is common. This is known as "decentering," which helps individuals reduce self-criticism, rumination, and depressed mood that can arise
when individuals attend to negative thinking processes.

Strengths-Based Cognitive Behavior Therapy

Besides emphasizing a positive therapeutic relationship, incorporating
strengths and protective factors in CBT practice is a core value of the counseling profession. Strengths-Based CBT (SB-CBT) is a modified version

of Aaron Beck's Cognitive Therapy developed by Christine Padesky and Kathleen Mooney (Padesky & Mooney, 2012). This approach applies typical Cognitive Therapy techniques but also incorporates client strengths throughout all phases of therapy, which encourages them to fully engage in the therapeutic process. SB-CBT extends Cognitive Therapy by infusing encouragement, strengths, and client resources.

Traditional CBT includes an assessment process that seeks to determine the client's diagnosis and a case conceptualization. Both of these processes are typically focused on pathology and deficits of the client and may not include any strengths or resources that account for the resiliency. This approach emphasizes eliciting current wellness and recent coping attempts, exploring when the symptoms are not a problem, and eliciting what is going well in an individual's life at the outset of therapy. An SB-CBT counselor teaches clients that individuals often seek to feel better "for good reasons" and as a result may exhibit harmful behaviors in that process, such as drinking alcohol to reduce anxiety or cutting oneself to distract from emotional pain. SB-CBT is collaborative, here-and-now focused, strength focused, and client centered.

Evidence-Based Practice and CBT

A remarkable evolution in the theory, research, and practice of CBT counseling approaches has occurred during the past 30 years. Many, but not all, of these changes and developments are due to the accountability movement in healthcare and mental health practice and overarching policies. Increasingly, counseling has become more effective, focused, and accountable. The ACA *Code of Ethics* indicated [in Section C, Professional Responsibility] that "When providing services, counselors use techniques/procedures/modalities that are grounded in theory and/or have an empirical or scientific foundation" (2014, p. 10). Evidence-based practice can be defined as "the integration of best research evidence with clinical expertise and patient values" (Institute of Medicine, 2001, p. 147). It is broader than the concept of empirically supported treatment in that it directly considers clinical expertise and client values—that is, employing counseling skills to rapidly identify the client's health status, diagnosis, risks, and benefits of engaging in the counseling process, as well as personal values and expectations. Presumably then, competent and well-read counselors nurture and maintain strong and effective therapeutic relationships, utilize best practices literature and information, monitor clinical outcomes, and implement treatment tailored to match client strengths and challenges, personality style, and preferences (Sperry, 2010).

This next section further explicates the elements in the evidence-based practice formula in regard to client values and counselor expertise. It also describes the elements of the therapeutic relationship.

Client Values

Client values are key elements in the evidence-based practice formula. Values are used in the broad sense of client attitudes about and expectations for treatment, personality style, and needs. A meta-analysis of the dynamics accounting for change in the counseling process (Lambert & Barley, 2001) found that the highest variance accounting for change (40%) was due to extra-therapeutic factors, also referred to as "client resources" or "client factors." This finding was consistent with what was previously reported (Lambert, 1992). The factors include variables such as motivation to change, an individual's capacity for building and maintaining relationships, access to counseling services, access to a social support system, systemic and political factors, and other non-diagnostic factors. Counselors who assess and elicit clients' values and expectations and who effectively engage these identified client factors in the counseling process achieve better outcomes than counselors who do not (Lambert & Barley, 2001).

Counselor Expertise

A counselor's level of expertise is a significant element in the evidence-based practice formula. As useful as the Lambert research (1992) has been in understanding the elements that account for change in counseling outcomes, it did not account for the expertise of the counselor. Nevertheless, it is clear that some counselors are much more effective than others and terms such as "master therapist" and "therapist's therapist" have been used to describe the expertise of such counselors. More recently, levels of counseling expertise have been demarcated: beginner, advanced beginner, minimally competent, proficient, and expert. Research suggests that proficient and expert counselors are significantly more effective than those who are in the beginner to minimally competent stages (Sperry, 2010). Of particular note, proficient and expert counselors don't just use supportive and encouraging statements in their work with clients—they whole-heartedly emphasize the therapeutic relationship throughout all phases of counseling.

Therapeutic Relationship

Germane to the evidence-based practice formula is a strong therapeutic relationship. The counseling relationship has without doubt been identified as the single most important variable in the now-extensive research and literature on counseling outcomes. Lambert's (1992) meta-analysis articulated that the specific counseling techniques accounted for 15% of the variance in therapy outcomes. Even more significant, the therapeutic relationship accounts for 30% of the variance in therapy outcomes. The therapeutic relationship includes three important factors: the relational bond between client and counselor, the agreed-upon treatment goals, and a consensus about methods and tasks to achieve specific goals (Sperry, 2010).

Therapeutic Relationship in Professional Counseling Practice

Imagine walking into your counselor's office for the first session. She welcomes you to her office and immediately asks you approximately 40 personal questions about your life and presenting issues without any empathy, humor, warmth, or interpersonal engagement. Throughout the first meeting she checks her cell phone on several occasions and looks down at her wristwatch more times than you can remember. To top it off, she says, "Your anxiety is stemming from the negative view that you carry regarding yourself and other people." Then she gives you a worksheet with a list of irrational beliefs and asks you to determine which irrational beliefs you frequently engage in and you realize that you engage in all 10 of the beliefs on a regular basis. Next she tells you to write down your irrational thoughts over the next week. At the end of the session you decide that a second session with this counselor would be a terrible idea and you decide not to return. Besides being an example of terrible counseling, this scenario shows the counselor's premature implementation of CBT techniques before building any relationship with their client. All too often, clients receive evidenced-based interventions in which their counselor fails to engage them in an effective working relationship.

Counselors who are empathic, warm, nonjudgmental, and collaborative are more likely to have better outcomes than counselors who are cold, judgmental, and noncollaborative—it is basic common sense. Counselors should seek to treat clients the way they would like to be treated. With that being said, Alford and Beck (1997) identified that the therapeutic relationship needs to be a collaborative relationship and Beck even coined the term "collaborative empiricism" (1976). They suggested that clinicians must be engaging and collaborative, and that the counselor and client must work together to establish treatment goals, very much akin to the core conditions described by Carl Rogers.

More recently, advocates of second wave approaches are sounding much like advocates of third wave approaches. For example, Ellis and Joffe Ellis (2014) also identified that a strong therapeutic relationship will help clients to practice unconditional self- and other-acceptance when applying REBT in their daily lives. This demonstrates that the client and counselor need to have a "meeting of the minds" and a "meeting of the hearts" (Sperry, 2010) by agreeing on a treatment focus and also actively establishing a positive therapeutic relationship. Additionally, the incorporation of client strengths and resources are what we call the "client protective factor trifecta" when paired with a strong therapeutic relationship. Highly effective CBT counselors incorporate the client protective factor trifecta in their clinical work because they know that these factors are essential for positive therapeutic outcomes. Chapter 4 will review the client-counselor relationship in further detail.

Diversity and Cultural Issues

Professional counselors are expected to provide high-quality counseling services to individuals, families, and couples, as well as to groups from diverse nationalities, sexual orientations, gender identities, disabilities, religions, ethnic cultures, socioeconomic classes, and ages. Among all the current psychotherapies, the cognitive-behavioral approach is the most culturally sensitive, as it has been adapted to several ethnicities (Craske, 2010), including African-American and Latino (Miranda, Nakamura, & Bernal, 2003) and Asian (Hwang, 2006). The outcome studies validating the use of CBT among various cultural groups continues to grow each year. Further discussion and application of the use of CBT counseling practice among diverse client populations are covered in Chapter 6, which emphasizes Pamela Hays's model, Culturally Responsive CBT (CR-CBT).

Concluding Note

Cognitive Behavior Therapy is an empirically supported counseling approach that has seemed to be at odds with the core values of the counseling profession. However, a case can be made that the more contemporary versions of CBT are particularly well suited for counseling practice. While particularly true for third wave approaches, updated versions of first and second wave approaches are also more sensitive to the therapeutic relationship, client resources and strengths, and cultural sensitivity than their original version.

This chapter reviewed the history of CBT, the three waves of CBT, the importance of the therapeutic relationship, and sensitivity to diversity and cultural issues. The next chapter will describe the basic competencies and premises of CBT.

References

Alford, B. A., & Beck, A. T. (1997). *The integrative power of cognitive therapy.* New York, NY: Guilford Press.

American Counseling Association. (2014). *ACA code of ethics.* Alexandria, VA: Author.

Beck, A. T. (1967). *The diagnosis and management of depression.* Philadelphia, PA: University of Pennsylvania Press.

Beck, A. T. (1976). *Cognitive therapy and the emotional disorders.* New York, NY: International Universities Press.

Beck, A. T., Rush, A., & Emery, G. (1979). *Cognitive therapy for depression.* New York, NY: Guilford Press.

Craighead, W., & Craighead, K. (2001). The role of psychotherapy in treating psychiatric disorders. *Medical Clinics of North America, 85,* 617–629.

Craske, M. G. (2010). *Cognitive-behavioral therapy.* Washington, DC: American Psychological Association.

Driscoll, K., Cukrowicz, K., Reardon, M., & Joiner, T. (2004). Simple treatments for complex problems: A flexible cognitive behavior analysis system approach to psychotherapy. Mahwah, NJ: Lawrence Erlbaum Associates.

Ellis, A. (1970). Tribute to Alfred Adler. *Journal of Individual Psychology, 26*(1), 11–12.

Ellis, A., & Joffe Ellis, D. (2014). *Rational emotive behavior therapy.* Washington, DC: American Psychological Association.

Freeman, A. (1981). Dreams and images in cognitive therapy. In G. Emery & R. C. Bedrosian (Eds.), *New directions in cognitive therapy: A casebook* (pp. 224–238). New York, NY: Guilford Press.

Freeman, A. (1983). Cognitive therapy: An overview. In A. Freeman (Ed.), *Cognitive therapy with couples and groups* (pp. 1–10). New York, CA: Plenum.

Fuenfhausen, K.K., Young, S., Cashwell, C., & Musangali, M. (2017). History and Evolution of Clinical Mental Health Counseling. In J Scott Young and Craig S. Cashwell (Eds.), *Clinical mental health counseling: Elements of effective practice.* Thousand Oaks, CA: Sage Publications.

Hayes, S. C. (2004). Acceptance and commitment therapy, relational frame theory, and the third wave of behavior therapy. *Behavior Therapy, 35,* 639–665. doi:10.1016/S0005-7894(04)80013-3

Hayes, S. C., Follette, V., & Linehan, M. (Eds.) (2004). *Mindfulness and acceptance: Expanding the cognitive-behavioral tradition.* New York, NY: Guilford Press.

Hwang, W. (2006). The psychotherapy adaptation and modification framework: Application to Asian Americans. *American Psychologist, 61,* 702–715.

Institute of Medicine. (2001). *Crossing the quality chasm: A new health system for the 21st century.* Washington, DC: Author.

Kabat-Zinn, J. (1994). *Wherever you go, there you are: Mindfulness meditation in everyday life.* New York, NY: Hyperion.

Lambert, M. (1992). Psychotherapy outcome research: Implications for integrative and eclectic therapists. In J. Norcross & M. Goldfried (Eds.), *Handbook of psychotherapy* (pp. 94–129). New York, NY: Basic Books.

Lambert, M. J., & Barley, D. E. (2001). Research summary on the therapeutic relationship and psychotherapy outcome. *Psychotherapy: Theory/Research/Practice/Training, 38,* 357–361.

Linehan, M. (1993). *Cognitive-behavioral treatment of borderline personality disorder.* New York, NY: Guilford Press.

Lynch, T. R., & Cuper, P. F. (2012). Dialectical Behavioral therapy of borderline and other personality disorders. In T. A. Widiger (Ed.), *The Oxford Handbook of Personality Disorders* (pp. 785–793). New York, NY: Oxford Press.

Marra, T. (2005). *Dialectic behavior therapy in private practice: A practical and comprehensive guide*. Oakland, CA: New Harbinger Publications.

McCullough, J. (2000). *Treatment for Chronic Depression: Cognitive Behavioral Analysis System of Psychotherapy*. New York, NY: Guilford.

McCullough, J., Schramm, E., & Penberthy, K. (2015). CBASP: A Distinctive Treatment for Persistent Depressive Disorder. New York, NY: Routledge.

Miranda, J., Nakamura, R., & Bernal, G. (2003). Including ethnic minorities in mental health intervention research: A practical approach to a long-standing problem. *Culture, Medicine, and Psychiatry, 27*, 467–486.

Mosak, H. H. (2005). Adlerian psychotherapy. In R. J. Corsini, D. Wedding, R. J. Corsini, & D. Wedding (Eds.), (pp. 52–95). *Current Psychotherapies* (7th ed, pp. 52–95). Belmont, CA: Thomson Brooks/Cole Publishing.

Padesky, C. A., & Mooney, K. A. (2012). Strengths-based cognitive behavioural therapy: A four step model to build resilience. *Clinical Psychology & Psychotherapy, 19*(4), 283–290.

Segal, Z., Williams, J., & Teasdale, J. (2002). *Mindfulness-based cognitive therapy of depression*. New York, NY: Guilford Press.

Segal, Z., Williams J., & Teasdale, J. (2013). *Mindfulness-based cognitive therapy for depression* (2nd ed.). New York, NY: Guilford Press.

Segal, Z., Williams, J., Teasdale, J., & Williams, M. (2004). Mindfulness-based cognitive therapy: Theoretical and empirical status. In S. Hayes, V. Follette, & M. Linehan (Eds.), *Mindfulness and acceptance: Expanding the cognitive-behavioral tradition* (pp. 45–65). New York, NY: Guilford Press.

Sperry, L. (2010). *Core competencies in counseling and psychotherapy: Becoming a highly competent and effective therapist*. New York, NY: Routledge.

Watts, R. E., & Critelli, J. W. (1997). Roots of contemporary cognitive theories in the individual psychology of Alfred Adler. *Journal of Cognitive Psychotherapy, 11*(3), 147–156.

Wolpe, J. (1958). *Psychotherapy by reciprocal inhibition*. Sanford, CA: Stanford University Press.

Wolpe, J. (1990). *The practice of behavior therapy* (4th ed.). New York, NY: Pergamon.

Chapter 2

CBT Theory and Competencies

Effective counseling and therapy assumes that the counselor possesses a theoretical framework and a "cognitive map" of the normal process of development and functioning, a theory of how functioning goes awry and becomes maladaptive, and a theory of how maladaptive processes and patterns can be changed. Possessing such a theoretical framework guides what a counselor observes and collects as client information, how that information is observed and collected, how that information is conceptualized, and how the interventions based on that conceptualization are planned, implemented, and evaluated.

Although counselors may consider themselves to be "eclectic" in how they do counseling, research suggests that most counselors espouse at least one basic theoretical orientation and a corresponding cognitive map that informs their understanding of clients and the counseling process. This cognitive map serves to guide their therapeutic efforts in a consistent, confident, and effective manner (Binder, 2004). This chapter provides a brief overview of the cognitive-behavioral orientation and its core competencies. It begins with a brief discussion of the basic theoretical premises common to all cognitive-behavioral approaches, and a detailed description of the core competencies of Cognitive Behavior Therapy. A case example reflects these theoretical premises and illustrates these core competencies.

Cognitive Behavior Therapy: Theoretical Premises

There are several varieties of CBT including Cognitive Therapy, Behavior Therapy, Strengths-Based Cognitive Behavior Therapy, Schema Therapy, Dialectic Behavior Therapy, exposure therapy, Motivational Interviewing, Multimodal Therapy, Rational Emotive Behavior Therapy, Cognitive Behavioral Analysis System of Psychotherapy, Pattern-Focused Therapy, Mindfulness-Based Cognitive Therapy, and Acceptance and Commitment Therapy. Detailed descriptions of some of these appear in

Chapter 3. Although diverse, these various approaches share a number of commonalities. Research suggests that there are theoretical premises that are common to all CBT approaches. Based on their empirical review of the literature, Blagys and Hilsenroth (2002) found that six premises are common to all CBT approaches: emphasize cognition and behavior; focus on the present and the future; provide a treatment focus that is directive; focus on teaching skills; provide information or psychoeducation; and use homework and between-session activities. These common premises are discussed in this section.

Emphasize Cognition and Behavior

A basic premise of CBT is that emotions and behavior are influenced by cognitions and thinking. Because most emotional and behavioral reactions are learned, the goal of therapy is to help clients unlearn unwanted responses and learn new ways of responding. The process begins with assessing the client's maladaptive pattern of thoughts and behaviors. Then these thoughts and behaviors are challenged and the maladaptive pattern is modified so that clients can gain control over problems previously believed to be insurmountable.

Focus on the Present and the Future

Unlike many other approaches that focus on the past, CBT focuses on how clients' present maladaptive patterns of thoughts and behaviors impact their current and future functioning. Furthermore, skills learned in counseling sessions promote more effective future functioning.

Direct Session Activities

Cognitive Behavior Therapy is a directive approach in which counselors direct and focus the treatment process. They do this by setting an agenda, deciding and planning what will be discussed prior to the session, and then actively directing discussion of specific topics and tasks. This focus still allows counselors to actively engage clients in the treatment process and foster mutual agreement on treatment decisions.

Focus on Teaching Skills

Cognitive-behavioral counselors teach clients the necessary skills for coping more effectively with problematic situations. Dealing directly with skill deficits and excesses is essential for clients to achieve and maintain treatment gains.

Provide Information and Psychoeducation

Cognitive-behavioral counselors explicitly discuss the rationale for treatment and the specific techniques utilized. They may provide clients with specific information such as books, articles, or handouts. The purpose is to orient clients to the treatment process, to increase clients' confidence in treatment, and to enhance their ability to cope with problematic situations.

Use Homework and Between-Session Activities

The use of homework and between-session activities is another central element of CBT. These mutually agreed-upon activities provide clients the opportunity to practice skills learned in sessions and transfer gains made in therapy to everyday life. These activities also foster and maintain symptom reduction, increase confidence, and allow clients to feel more in control of their lives.

Cognitive Behavior Therapy: Core Competencies

Counseling competencies are defined as "the capacity to integrate knowledge, skills, and attitudes reflected in the quality of clinical practice that benefits others, which can be evaluated by professional standards and be developed and enhanced through professional training and reflection" (Sperry, 2010, p. 7). The terms competency and skill are often used synonymously, even though they are not synonyms. While a competency is composed of knowledge, skills, and attitudes (components necessary for professional practice), a skill is essentially a capacity acquired by training that has no knowledge or attitudinal components, nor is there an external standard to evaluate its sufficiency. Accordingly, competencies are more encompassing than skills. Training programs that focus exclusively on skills and skill training are problematic. Arguably, a counselor who is highly skilled can provide clients limited clinical value, since that counselor lacks the knowledge, attitude, and resolve to use those skills to increase the client's well-being (Sperry, 2010).

In *Core Competencies in Cognitive-Behavioral Therapy*, Newman (2013) identifies several CBT competencies. They include: form an effective therapeutic relationship; perform an integrative functional assessment; develop a case conceptualization and intervention plan; implement the treatment plan; monitor and evaluate treatment; maintain treatment gains; and deal with treatment-interfering behaviors. Each is described in this section.

Form an Effective Therapeutic Relationship

As we noted in the Introduction, the centrality of the therapeutic relationship in counseling is highlighted in the 20/20 Consensus Definition of Counseling (Kaplan & Gladding, 2011). Called by some the therapeutic alliance, the therapeutic relationship is also a central and indispensable factor in CBT practice. Newman notes "CBT values the therapeutic relationship as indispensable to the process of treatment" (Newman, 2013, p. 48).

Establishing a collaborative relationship in which the counselor is supportive, encouraging, and non-threatening can be the key to getting clients to engage in the difficult work of Cognitive Behavior Therapy. Although this alliance is not considered a sufficient vehicle for change of its own accord by CBT theorists, conveying warmth and empathy is necessary to facilitate the technical aspects of this intervention.

Cognitive-behavioral counselors strive towards a competency known as "collaborative empiricism." Collaborative empiricism is a process in which the client and counselor identify, understand, and work to solve the client's presenting issues together. Teaching clients cognitive-behavioral skills and working collaboratively can help clients feel more empowered and hopeful. While active listening and a friendly disposition are important factors in establishing a therapeutic alliance, it is more important for counselors to strive to inspire the client's confidence in the CBT process. Counselors begin to demonstrate their willingness to work to help their clients by familiarizing themselves with data from the client's intake sheet. This shows the counselor is prepared and engaged. From the first session, the counselor should discuss the client's goals and the agenda for therapy. This discussion gives the client a sense of direction and that their needs and goals will be addressed in therapy and links the empathic therapeutic response to the functional aspects of the intervention. It communicates care and collaboration and shows that the counselor is sensitive to the client's needs. Additionally, mention of the client's strengths instills the client with a sense of hope and faith in the process.

Counselors should be aware of the stages of change and be sensitive to the client's readiness and motivation for change. The counselor should not only assess the client's readiness and motivation, but should also be aware that many clients are hesitant to engage in the therapy process and may not return after the first session. Therefore, it is imperative for the counselor to explore reasons for the client's hesitation and to take the time to discuss the client's options for therapy, rather than prematurely diving into an intervention or homework assignment. The counselor must also be sensitive to the client's movement from one stage of change to the next and know how to alter treatment accordingly.

The counselor can best serve the client in the first session by establishing rapport through active listening and expression of empathy, discussing the client's goals for therapy, and showing the client how the CBT model can be used to address presenting problems. It is important to emphasize that the counselor is invested in the client and that success can be achieved. Summarizing the content of the first session and asking for client feedback helps the client connect to the counselor and formulate goals. Feedback helps the client and counselor discover how the client has benefitted from the session and how treatment can be altered or improved. The counselor must also develop distress sensitivity, meaning they must pay close attention to verbal and nonverbal cues to understand and be sensitive to the client's emotional state. The counselor should strive to understand where the client is emotionally and should ask for further clarification when needed. This allows the counselor to gauge when to move into problem solving techniques, when to back off an agenda in order to bear witness to the client's experience, and when to work with client resistance.

Once the therapeutic alliance has been established, it is important for the counselor to work to maintain it. A key factor in maintaining the alliance is the counselor's ability to work with client resistance. Resistance to change and noncompliance to treatment interventions can cause frustration in both the counselor and the client. The counselor should strive to understand the reasons for the client's resistance and ambivalence, including the difficulty in engaging in therapy and making changes, and the function of the resistance and how it relates to the client's longstanding patterns and beliefs. Resistance may reveal a type of transference or the client's generalization of beliefs onto the counselor. To understand this dynamic, the counselor should pay attention to her own emotional reactions to the client. The counselor can work with client resistance and maintain the therapeutic alliance by collaborating with the client about his concerns and the course of therapy. The counselor must consistently monitor the therapeutic alliance to repair it and make adjustments when necessary. Doing so requires practicing empathy, self-reflection, and even a self-practice of CBT for the counselor.

Perform an Integrative Assessment

A complete and thorough initial assessment, called an integrative assessment, is essential in planning and implementing effective cognitive-behavioral treatment. The integrative assessment includes four components: a diagnostic assessment, a developmental and pattern-focused assessment, a functional assessment, and a risk assessment.

Diagnostic Assessment

The diagnostic assessment involves an inquiry of the client's presenting problem and associated symptoms. Its purpose is to arrive at one or more DSM-5 diagnoses. Even though DSM-5 no longer includes the five axes framework, counselors and other mental health professionals typically assess for both symptoms disorders, previously designated as Axis I disorders, and personality disorders, previously designated as Axis II disorders.

This assessment is accomplished with a diagnostic interview in which screening questions for the major diagnostic areas (anxiety, depression, psychosis, substance use, etc.) are followed with an inquiry of specific DSM diagnostic criteria that may be present. Besides the diagnostic interview, the counselor might use self-report inventories. For example, one of the most common of these inventories is the Beck Depression Inventory-II (Beck, Steer, & Brown, 1996) for assessing the extent to which depressive symptoms are present.

Developmental and Pattern-Focused Assessment

The counselor uses open-ended questions to complete this component of the integrative assessment. It assesses the client's thoughts, feelings, behaviors, and physical symptoms relevant to the presenting problem. The counselor also elicits a personal history that helps explain the development of the current problem as well as the client's belief system, coping skills, emotional responses, strengths, and resources. The client's history of trauma, mental health issues, family history, and legal history should all be assessed during this process. This information can be gathered through both a written intake form and an in-person clinical interview. It is useful for the counselor to use information provided on the intake form to guide the course of questioning during the clinical interview. At times, the counselor may want to review the client's medical and psychological records from other professionals, for which the client must sign a release of information. The goal of this inquiry is to identify the client's basic maladaptive pattern and personality style.

The counselor observes not only the content of the client's answers to questions, but also the manner in which the client answers. For example, affect during responses should be noted, as well as affect that is incongruent with mood. The Mental Status Examination (MSE) is a good tool for assessing the client's affect and functioning during the interview. The MSE includes the following domains: physical appearance; attitude towards the counselor; motor activity; affect and mood; speech; thought content; orientation to person, place, and time; memory; attention; judgment and insight; and reliability of self-report.

Functional Assessment

While the diagnostic assessment is useful in assessing symptoms and specifying a DSM diagnosis, it has almost no value in decisions about planning and implementing treatment. An assessment of functional capacity is a critical part of the integrative cognitive-behavioral assessment. Functions represent how an individual typically acts and responds, and it is the legacy of the behavioral orientation. This type of assessment is most valuable in setting treatment goals and planning treatment for individuals. Functional assessments are essential in planning treatment with personality-disordered individuals. Six dimensions are represented in the ABCDEF model of functional capacity (Sperry & Sperry, 2016), which is briefly described here.

"A" represents the Affective dimension, which is the characteristic and predicable way in which an individual reacts emotionally to situations, particularly stressful situations. The Affective dimension has two polarities: emotional dysregulation and emotional constriction. "B" represents the Behavioral dimension, which is the characteristic and predicable way in which an individual reacts behaviorally when stressed or challenged. The Behavioral dimension has two polarities: behavioral inhibition and behavioral disinhibition. "C" represents the Cognitive dimension, which is the characteristic and predicable way in which individuals gather, perceive, think about, use, and recall information. This dimension has two polarities: rigidity or inflexibility and impulsivity. "D" represents the Distress tolerance dimension, which is the characteristic and predicable way individuals react to negative emotional states. It is the capacity to tolerate or withstand such negative emotion without engaging in impulsive behavior as well as persisting in goal-directed behavior despite distress. It has two polarities: distress intolerance and distress over-tolerance.

The assessment of these first four dimensions is on a continuum of under-modulation or under-control at one end, modulation or adequate control in the middle, and over-modulation or over-control at the other end. This differs from the continuum of the fifth [E] and sixth [F] dimensions, which are on a continuum from low to high.

"E" represents the Experience dimension, specifically failure to learn from experience. Failure to learn from experience is an error in thinking common among younger adolescents. While most adolescents grow out of it, a characteristic feature of moderate to severe personality disorders is that this failure to learn expands to all aspects of their lives. This inability to learn can be assessed and gradated on a continuum from low to high. Finally, "F" represents the Functional impairment dimension, which is the broadest of measures of an individual's overall functioning and well-being. It utilizes the *Level of Personality Functioning Scale* (LPFS) from Section III of DSM-5 (American Psychiatric Association,

2013). This scale consists of four levels for identifying an individual's current overall level of global functioning: 0 = little or no impairment, 1 = some impairment, 2 = moderate impairment, 3 = severe impairment, and 4 = extreme impairment. A determination of at least a level of "moderate impairment" reflects a diagnosis of a personality disorder.

Risk Assessment

A risk assessment for suicidal and homicidal ideations is the final component of the integrative assessment. It should be completed if client data indicates this may be of concern. The assessment can be done through a clinical interview format and utilizing questionnaires. The risk assessment should be approached with care and sensitivity and its purpose should be explained to the client in advance. The risk assessment should elicit if the client has thoughts of suicide, how often those thoughts occur, and if there is a plan, including an available method of suicide. The counselor should assess not only the client's suicidal or homicidal ideation but the extent of the client's commitment to that course of action.

The competent counselor strives to explain the integrative assessment process to the client and make the client feel safe and comfortable. The counselor organizes the assessment in a way that utilizes time wisely, allows for all relevant information to be obtained, and facilitates establishment of rapport. The counselor then writes up a professional summary of the assessment that covers all pertinent information, including presenting problem, symptoms, DSM-5 diagnosis, histories, assessment of functional capacity, and precipitating and perpetuating factors.

Develop a Case Conceptualization and Treatment Plan

Case conceptualization provides a way for counselors to link the information gathered during the integrative assessment to the treatment plan (Sperry, 2010). The initial assessment is merely a starting point, and case conceptualization gives counselors a plan and process for using client data in a constructive manner. Diagnosis itself does not provide an explanation for the development and perpetuation of client problems. Counselors must understand patterns and personality styles. Personality styles can be seen on a continuum from adaptive to disordered, and influence not only how an individual will behave but also how they will respond to therapy. For example, an individual with a paranoid style may be frequently suspicious and even vindictive, moving against people in order to feel safe.

Case conceptualization not only provides this explanatory model, but also allows the counselor to account for individual differences between clients. Client data is organized and synthesized in a way that allows the counselor to make hypotheses and explanatory inferences about the client's presenting problem and history that is then a direct line to selecting appropriate treatment interventions. Information acquired through the clinical interview, self-report questionnaires, and secondary sources may be used to formulate the initial case conceptualization, but the counselor must be aware that the conceptualization may be altered as new information arises over the course of therapy. The counselor should actively pay attention to new information that may fill gaps in the client's history and case conceptualization.

In order for a case conceptualization to be clinically useful for understanding clients and planning treatment, the counselor must incorporate and organize all elements of data in a way that forms a clear representation of the client. Historical experiences and events should be incorporated, including childhood experiences, traumas, medical problems, and other occurrences that may account for the development of the client's presenting symptoms and complaints. Schemas, automatic thoughts, and similar cognitive patterns underlying the client's vulnerabilities should be included. The counselor aims to understand how the interplay between the client's thought patterns, feelings, and behaviors contributes to the presenting problem. Similarly, behavioral, emotional, and physiological patterns must be considered, as they may not only perpetuate the client's presenting problem but also may reinforce it. Social and cultural factors and the context in which the client's problems occur should be integrated, as should the stressors and precipitants that motivated the client to attend therapy. Cultural factors can be of particular importance when the client belongs to a group that differs from the majority in regard to sexual orientation, gender identity, ethnicity, physical capabilities, etc. The counselor should also pay attention to strengths and protective factors that may be useful in facilitating the change process. Focusing on strengths conveys that the counselor is interested in the client as a whole person, aside from mere symptoms and dysfunction. Eliciting a client's strengths helps instill hope and self-efficacy, as well as allows the client to see how strengths can be generalized to other areas of functioning.

All of this information can be used to make hypotheses about appropriate treatment interventions as well as how the client is likely to respond to them. The case conceptualization's predictive power highlights not only how treatment may progress, but also potential obstacles that may arise. A good case conceptualization is completed collaboratively and shared with the client. It allows the counselor and client to set treatment goals together and agree on selected interventions as well as benchmarks to be used to assess progress. A case conceptualization can be viewed as a road map for treatment that also prepares the counselor for hazards and obstacles down the road. Sperry and Sperry (2012) provide a detailed description and case illustrations of CBT case conceptualizations.

Implement the Treatment Plan

Cognitive-behavioral counselors are urged to establish and maintain a treatment agenda. Using the treatment plan as a guide, the counselor structures and paces the course of treatment. This is facilitated when the counselor follows a specific treatment agenda. Although the counselor should be aware that digressions and silent periods can be necessary and beneficial, a therapeutic agenda keeps sessions focused and conveys that treatment is moving forward in a productive way. Sessions can be structured in a way that connects previous sessions to the current one by bringing the client back to the therapeutic focus during a session and by being mindful of time limits. Maintaining treatment focus also requires eliciting clear and relevant input from the client. Clients may not know how to answer certain questions or may be hesitant or unsure. The cognitive-behavioral counselor asks questions that foster client introspection, reflection, and problem solving, but must know how to work with clients who have difficulty answering these questions. The counselor should not accept an answer of "I don't know," but should be gentle and empathic when encouraging a client to find answers. Clear and specific answers should be elicited, to which the counselor replies with a validating response.

Specific CBT procedures and interventions can be used to teach clients to cope more effectively, understand themselves better, and solve problems more efficiently. Self-monitoring teaches clients to observe themselves and collect data in an objective, empirical way. Clients can become aware of their automatic thoughts and behavioral responses. Anti-arousal methods such as relaxation and controlled breathing can provide symptom relief, particularly for sympathetic nervous system reactions. Behavioral activation can be utilized for clients with anhedonia and lack of motivation. Traditional cognitive and behavioral techniques such as cognitive restructuring, exposure exercises, and behavioral rehearsal can be similarly useful depending on client needs.

The downward arrow technique is useful in helping clients analyze their automatic thoughts and trace them back to their underlying beliefs and schemas. After using the downward arrow technique, schemas and beliefs can be modified. Deeper work with particularly difficult or traumatic memories includes imagery reconstruction with rational responding. In this technique, clients imagine trips into their past and modify the outcomes of specific situations. Impulses and cravings can be addressed using the delay and distract technique in which the client is challenged to delay their response to an impulse and slowly increase the duration of the delay. Clients are also taught to identify ruminative and unproductive thoughts as they occur. When clients are able to identify these moments, they can replace ruminative thoughts with productive, problem solving activities.

Cognitive and behavioral rehearsal and role-playing can be particularly useful in skills training. The counselor helps the client imagine a situation and plan how to respond. Clients can try out their newly acquired skills by role-playing simulated interactions with the counselor. Clients can rehearse an important conversation they plan to have with someone. The client's negative expectations of themselves and the situation can be revealed and explored through this technique. Often, it is appropriate for the counselor to use the Devil's advocate technique in which the counselor takes the role of the client's maladaptive thoughts. This makes the client respond rationally to the thoughts, teaching him how to respond to these thoughts as they occur in daily situations. Additionally, role-playing can be used to process events, to reevaluate them in light of new knowledge, to learn more about certain experiences, and to change the course of events using imagery reconstruction. Through this process, the client finds resolution and empowerment.

Guided discovery, or the Socratic method, is used as an overall communication style in sessions and helps the client ponder thought-provoking questions. The client learns to think more flexibly and constructively. Guided discovery can be especially useful when the client jumps to negative conclusions in order to cut a therapeutic discussion short, and when the client has difficulty identifying or describing thoughts and experiences. When the counselor identifies a client's maladaptive belief, guided discovery may be more useful than a more forceful contradiction by the counselor. Similarly, the counselor may have a message or answer for the client that would be more productive if the client were able to generate it himself. Guided discovery can be used in this case to guide the client to identifying the message or solution himself.

Regular use of homework has been tied to positive treatment outcomes and gives the client an opportunity to test the skills they learn in therapy in daily life. CBT tools introduced in sessions can be used as homework assignments. Ideally, homework assignments are generated collaboratively between counselor and client and construct a win-win situation in which the client either successfully applies therapeutic techniques or discovers information that can deepen and expand the case conceptualization. The counselor should clearly explain homework assignments and tie them to work done in session. The counselor encourages the client and expresses empathy about their concerns about homework assignments. The client should be encouraged to complete homework during the week between sessions but should be made to understand that they will not be punished for not completing the assignment. Homework assignments should not appear random or pointless. Instead, they should be individualized, clearly explained, and offer the client a chance at success. A client's failure to complete homework is not necessarily a reason to refrain from future assignments. The counselor can use scaling questions to determine the client's level of confidence and motivation to do homework.

Monitor and Evaluate Treatment Outcomes

Although counselors may be tempted to assume they are helping based on subjective observations of clients, it is important that they regularly use several objective methods of tracking client treatment outcomes. These can include feedback from the client and related third parties, observations, and self-report inventories. Treatment monitoring should be collaborative between counselor and client and used to update treatment plans. Failure to accurately assess treatment progress can lead to early dropout, failure to achieve therapy goals, and worsening of symptoms.

The counselor should assess the degree to which the client continues or ceases to meet DSM-5 criteria and should elicit the client's input. Collaboration between the counselor and client is essential not only for monitoring improvement, but also for maintaining the therapeutic relationship. Sometimes, the client and counselor may have different opinions about the client's status and progress. In this case, a discussion should ensue to foster increased understanding and consensus.

Empirically based self-report inventories are an efficient way of collecting data on client progress. These measures should be used periodically throughout the course of treatment so the counselor can compare multiple data points. For example, a client may be given the Beck Depression Inventory-II at intake and again several weeks into treatment. Comparing scores on these measures can help the counselor gauge the client's progress and provide talking points about the course of treatment. The counselor should not only address areas of concern but also highlight positive outcomes. A worsening of symptoms constitutes an urgent talking point, which allows the counselor to assess whether this decline is temporary as well as the contextual reasons accounting for it.

Perhaps the two most commonly used brief self-report inventories by mental health professionals throughout the world are the Session Rating Scale (SRS) (Duncan et al., 2003) and the Outcomes Rating Scale (ORS) (Miller & Duncan, 2000). The SRS is a four-item measure of therapeutic alliance that the client fills out near the end of each counseling session. The ORS is a four-item measure of outcomes and functioning that the client fills out immediately before a session. Both of these scales are described in detail in Chapter 7.

Because there is evidence that clients who learn to use self-help cognitive-behavioral methods make significant therapy gains and maintain those gains, it is important for counselors to assess the client's learning and use of these methods. Counselors can observe a client's ability to recognize and restructure their own irrational thoughts as well as frequency. Some self-report and observational questionnaires may also prove useful in assessing the client's ability to apply CBT principles. Assignment and evaluation of client homework also provide an opportunity to practice and assess the client's use of self-help skills.

Counselors can use third-party observations to gauge client progress. Of course, counselors must be mindful of confidentiality issues, and acquiring consent from the client to speak to third parties is imperative. Third-party observers can either provide feedback to support the counselor's assessment of client progress or can provide information contrary to the counselor's assessment. This can be particularly useful in complex cases. Additionally, feedback from other healthcare professionals can be beneficial to treatment monitoring.

The counselor should complete a treatment update plan periodically after repeated assessments of client progress. This tool is essential to tailor treatment to the individual and continue to provide effective therapy as treatment progresses. Therapy goals and their measurable benchmarks should be reviewed and included in the updated plan. The counselor must discuss treatment progress and the treatment plan update with the client in a supportive, direct manner. The counselor and client can collaborate on their review of client progress and discussion of therapy goals and roadblocks to achieving them. At this point, some diagnoses may no longer qualify, some provisional diagnoses may be ruled out, and additional diagnoses may be included.

Supervisors play a critical role in client monitoring. Supervisors should take care to inquire about the status of a client and elicit all relevant details. Sessions may even be recorded for supervisors to monitor the success of their supervisees and their respective clients. Collaboration between the counselor and supervisor is essential for progress monitoring.

In assessing client outcomes, counselors must be aware that symptoms often do not disappear entirely and may recur at some point. This, however, is not necessarily an indicator of relapse or failed treatment. Rather, assessment of the durability and maintenance of treatment gains is the central focus. Clients can learn to identify and manage relapse triggers using self-help CBT skills and may return for booster sessions or continued therapy as necessary.

Maintain Treatment Gains

A key step in helping clients maintain treatment gains is proper preparation for termination. The counselor and client should collaborate to anticipate future stressors and rehearse how the client will respond to and cope with these obstacles. The client can become aware of possible situations and related effective coping skills. The client is encouraged to keep a log of items generated in treatment, including coping skill cards, automatic thought records, and journal entries from therapy sessions. These can be reviewed by the client and used to respond to difficult situations. Furthermore, the counselor can assist the client in writing a to-do list for future gains using acquired CBT skills. The client is also encouraged to conduct self-CBT sessions to continue therapeutic activity outside of sessions.

Practitioners should collaborate on the duration of therapy with clients and ensure sufficient time is available for clients to learn self-help strategies. Counselors should openly discuss the treatment timeline as well as measures that will be used to assess progress and update the treatment plan. The client should not only be made aware that therapy is time limited, but should also be consistently encouraged to envision use of techniques in life post-therapy. The counselor should also address thoughts and concerns the client may have about termination.

Practitioners can also plan to continue several rounds of therapy with a long-term client. Certain disorders, particularly those with more organic origins, may require longterm therapy. Therefore, therapy should be planned over the course of time to include booster sessions and further exploration.

Sometimes clients suddenly terminate therapy before achieving their treatment goals. Premature termination is linked to poor outcomes, so counselors should be careful to follow up with these clients, explore their reasons for termination, and attempt to re-engage them in therapy.

Counselors must learn to assess when termination is premature and abrupt as well as when continuing therapy is non-productive. While it is important to set time limits, the counselor should be mindful of the client's progress when considering termination. When assessing when termination should occur, the counselor should assess not only the severity of the client's problem, but also client risk factors and progress made. Finally, counselors should be sensitive to the sense of loss that clients may feel when discontinuing therapy. Termination may be a profoundly emotional experience for some clients and counselors should respond empathically.

Deal With Treatment-Interfering Behaviors

Numerous factors, known as treatment-interfering behaviors, can interfere with the course of treatment. These can include environmental factors, counselor mistakes, and the client's interfering behaviors. Environmental factors can include difficult living situations and counselor mistakes often include being overzealous or too eager to restructure the client's irrational thoughts.

Disengaged and silent clients may be particularly challenging. Not all clients are willing to engage in collaborative discussions and may remain silent and rigid. To deal with this behavior, the counselor may address the client's silence. The counselor might suggest some hypotheses as to why the client is hesitant to engage. This demonstrates professionalism and models good behavior under stress. It also gives the client a new opportunity to engage.

Sometimes, unexpected crises can alter the course of treatment. When this crisis is increased suicidality, the counselor must be careful to put aside the therapy agenda to complete a risk assessment. The counselor can anticipate such crises through regular progress monitoring using observation and self-report measures. The timing, context, pertinent thoughts, schemas, and precipitating factors are all clues that can improve the client's case conceptualization. The counselor can help the client turn crises into learning experiences. The client can gain insight into schemas and become more motivated to use CBT self-help skills to prevent future crises. This work imbues the client with the idea of thriving and flourishing as opposed to merely surviving and shows the client how he can become more resilient and an agent of change.

Illustration of CBT Competencies: Case of Jared

Jared is a 21-year-old male college student who comes to therapy seeking help dealing with a relationship that ended badly. He reports feelings of depression and anxiety and an increased reliance on food as a way to cope with his emotions. Jared looks sullen and quiet and says he wishes there were a better way to deal with his emotions. The counselor initially focuses on building rapport. She expresses empathy and conveys that she understands how difficult this situation must be for Jared. Jared goes on talking about all of his friends' relationships and the things they are doing with their significant others. He tells the counselor a story about his friends inviting him to go to the beach over the weekend. He reluctantly went but felt depressed since all of his friends are in relationships. He recounts that his friends told him he was being "too soft" about his break-up and needed to "man up." He became so angry he left and coped by eating an entire quart of ice cream when he got home. "I know I messed up. I'm so pathetic." The counselor reflects back what Jared said to convey that she is listening and understanding. "It sounds like it was too much to handle, seeing everyone happy as a couple, and you wish your friends could have been more understanding." "Yeah!" he says, "That's exactly right." Jared feels heard and understood and the therapeutic relationship begins to form. The counselor says she noticed Jared listed his participation in church on his intake form and she asks if that is a source of support for him at this time. She continues to convey her care, understanding, and empathy.

In the second half of the session, the counselor discusses Jared's goals for therapy. He says he wants to "be stronger." She asks him to clarify that and continues to summarize and reflect what he says, asking for his feedback to make sure she is understanding him correctly. Together, they collaborate on goals for therapy. "I'm always doing things for people but no one ever returns the favor," Jared says. Together they decide that adequate goals for therapy are helping Jared set boundaries, improving his coping skills, and helping him find more effective ways to meet his own needs. The counselor explains the premises of CBT to Jared and he agrees to give it a try. He reports feeling more hopeful after the first session because of the counselor's understanding. "I came in thinking no one would understand me," he says.

Next, the counselor completes an integrative assessment of Jared. She uses information from the intake sheet to guide some of her questioning. After asking Jared more about his symptoms of depression and anxiety, she is able to rule out both major depression and generalized anxiety disorder. She has Jared complete an Outcomes Rating Scale (ORS) so she can gauge his progress as well as a Beck Depression Inventory-II (BDI-II). Jared scores 12 on the BDI, indicating mild depressive symptoms. Through asking open-ended questions, the counselor finds out that Jared is a caring person who aspires to go into a career in the helping professions. Spirituality is very important to him and he finds a sense of community in his church. Jared expresses his family life is of utmost importance and he reveals that he spends much of his time doing things for his family. He drives his mother to and from work, does all the grocery shopping, picks his little brother up from school, cleans the house, and more. He says he does not always want to do these things but he wants to "be a good son" and does not want to let anyone down. The counselor inquires as to whether Jared behaves this way with people other than his family. He says he treated his now ex-girlfriend this way. "I did everything for her. I even put her slippers on her feet every morning." The counselor expresses that this is a very sweet gesture and asks if his girlfriend insisted he do that. "No, she never asked me to but I just did it. But I also did things for her that I didn't want to do, like drive her everywhere," he says.

The counselor asks if he thinks he has a pattern of going out of his way to care for others. Jared thinks about this for a minute and agrees that seems to have been his pattern since he was a boy. In the rest of the session, Jared reports no history of trauma and his mental status is appropriate. He is oriented to person, place, and time. He is well groomed and maintains sufficient eye contact, though he seems very shy. On the ABCDEF Functional Assessment Map, Jared is in the lower end of the modulated range in Affect, Behavior, and Cognitive, but slightly in the under-modulated range of Distress Tolerance. Experience and Functioning are in the average range, consistent with a DSM-5 Level of Personality Functioning Scale of 1 = Mild Impairment (American Psychiatric Association, 2013). This functional assessment suggests that while Jared is easily distressed (i.e., mild distress intolerance), his coping capacity is reasonably adequate. Accordingly, he appears to be a reasonable candidate for talk therapy with both cognitive and behavioral interventions.

The counselor uses all of this data to develop a case conceptualization. She identifies his pattern as consistent with the dependent personality style, as evidenced by his response to the loss of a relationship as the precipitant, and his presenting symptoms of depression and anxiety. Jared's pattern is perpetuated by his continued self-sacrificing behavior and limited self-management and relational skills. Jared also reports that he exercises regularly and has kept up his workout routine despite feeling sad and anxious. When asked about lifestyle changes, Jared proudly stated that he had participated in a smoking cessation program on the advice of his physician and that he has not smoked in three years. The counselor points out this strength (exercise) and this protective factor (ongoing success at smoking cessation) and integrates it into the case conceptualization.

The counselor collaborates with Jared to develop a treatment plan. She indicates that therapy is time limited but they will work together to reach his goals and will update the treatment plan as needed. She previews how therapy will proceed. Sessions are structured and the counselor will compare Jared's just-filled-out ORS with his ratings of functional status on each of the four areas with ORS ratings from previous sessions. Then they will review their mutually agreed-upon homework, progress, and difficulties. She will also connect Jared's present concerns with issues discussed in the previous session, work with him on developing needed skills, and engage him in specific therapeutic interventions. Near the end of each session, homework or between-session activities will be discussed. Finally Jared will fill out a Session Rating Scale (SRS) and discuss his ratings of their therapeutic relationship and how the session might have gone better.

In sessions 2, 3, and 4, she introduces and follows up on behavioral activation. She also has Jared keep a log of automatic thoughts. After he completes this for two weeks, she has him begin generating alternative thoughts for each automatic thought. The counselor also regularly gives Jared homework assignments. For one assignment, Jared had to set some time aside for himself instead of doing things for other people. He decides to spend an afternoon playing basketball but is not able to complete the assignment. He worries the counselor will be upset with him. He reveals that he felt too guilty to take time for himself because his mother had a cold. The counselor responds, "It sounds like in this assignment you found out that you are a very caring person and it is hard to care for yourself when others are vulnerable." She turns the failure to do the assignment into a learning experience and when Jared returns the following week, he happily proclaims he was able to spend an afternoon playing basketball.

The counselor applauds him for this and mentions that his ORS scores have been improving, indicating that he is not only feeling better but functioning much better. She asks for Jared's feedback and he confirms he does indeed feel better. He also reports a success in setting boundaries. "My mother always wants me to clean the cat's litterbox. I hate doing it after I already showered and I have told her that. So the other night she asked me to clean it after I came out of the shower. I said no and that I would do it the next day. She didn't like it but she understood." The counselor congratulates Jared and they discuss how treatment is progressing.

She has him fill out another BDI-II and notes that his score is now a seven. They discuss his improvement and how to update the treatment plan. Jared says he is doing better with his goal of improving his coping skills by using exercise and his church as support. He states he would mostly like to focus on the goal of meeting his own needs more effectively. Jared and the counselor include this in his treatment plan update.

Therapy continues with an increased focus on Jared applying CBT self-help skills to challenge his automatic thoughts. In session, the counselor asks him to generate a list of things he would like to do. "I don't really know," he says. The counselor encourages him to take some time to think about it in session. He struggles but she continues in this guided discovery. Eventually, Jared is able to think of two things: go to an NBA game and take a cooking class. He continues to generate more items for this list as part of a homework assignment. The counselor then has him choose something from this list to do for himself. He decides he wants to buy himself a new pair of basketball shoes. He does so and reports that he feels excited that he can take care of himself. "I realize I don't have to make everyone happy and wait for them to take care of me in return. I can take care of myself! I bought myself these shoes and I can do more things for myself." They explore Jared's new sense of empowerment and talk about how this can be applied to different areas of his life. The counselor mentions that Jared's pattern is beginning to change.

After eight weeks of therapy, the counselor discusses upcoming termination with Jared. No therapy-interrupting behaviors occurred. He agrees that he is doing better but admits he is afraid of ending therapy. "It's sad because you understand me so well and I'm worried I will fail if I'm out on my own." The counselor empathizes with Jared and acknowledges how difficult it must be. They role-play how to apply some of his newly learned tools to other situations and obstacles that may come up. The counselor also enlists Jared to set up a behavioral experiment.

They begin by increasing the amount of time between sessions. Jared returns three weeks later and says his worst fear, of not being able to keep up what he learned in therapy, did not come true. "I was able to keep taking care of myself and setting boundaries even though you weren't there," he says. They agree to terminate after one more session.

Jared returns for two booster sessions six months later. He reports he is doing well and is actually reconsidering his career choice. "Everyone told me I should be a nurse because I am so caring but now I realize I want to go into business," he says. They discuss how Jared's pattern change is leading to different behaviors in all areas of his life. The counselor congratulates Jared and tells him the door is always open should he choose to return to therapy.

Concluding Note

The six theoretical premises common to all cognitive-behavioral approaches were briefly described at the beginning of this chapter. Seven core competencies of CBT were then described. The case of Jared illustrated both these premises and the core competencies. The fact that the counselor elicited and incorporated Jared's strength (exercise) and protective factor (ongoing success at smoking cessation) into the case conceptualization is the mark of a well-trained counselor who recognized that Jared's prognosis for a positive outcome of relatively brief therapy was quite good. It is also very consistent with the American Counseling Association's focus on strengths-based counseling (Ungar, 2006). The positive therapeutic outcomes are rather typical of therapy provided by a licensed mental health counselor with a moderate level of training and experience in providing CBT.

References

American Psychiatric Association. (2013). *Diagnostic and statistical manual of mental disorders* (5th ed.). Alexandria, VA: Author.

Beck, A., Steer, R., & Brown, G. (1996). *Manual for the Beck depression inventory-II*. San Antonio, TX: Psychological Corporation.

Binder, J. (2004). *Key competencies in brief dynamic psychotherapy: Clinical practice beyond the manual*. New York, NY: Guilford Press.

Blagys, M., & Hilsenroth, M. (2002). Distinctive activities of cognitive-behavioral therapy: A review of the comparative psychotherapy process literature. *Clinical Psychology Review, 22*, 671–706.

Duncan, B., Miller, S., Parks, L., Claud, D., Reynolds, L., Brown, J., & Johnson, L. (2003). The session rating scale: Preliminary properties of a "working" alliance measure. *Journal of Brief Therapy, 3*, 3–12.

Kaplan, D. M., & Gladding, S. T. (2011). A vision for the future of counseling: The 20/20 Principles for unifying and strengthening the profession. *Journal of Counseling & Development, 89*, 367–372.

Miller, S. D., & Duncan, B. L. (2000). *The Outcome Rating Scale.* Chicago: Author.

Newman, C. (2013). *Core competencies in cognitive-behavioral therapy: Becoming a highly effective and competent cognitive-behavioral therapist.* New York, NY: Routledge.

Sperry, L. (2010). *Core competencies in counseling and psychotherapy: Becoming a highly competent and effective therapist.* New York, NY: Routledge.

Sperry, L., & Sperry, J. (2012). *Case conceptualization: Mastering this competency with ease and confidence.* New York, NY: Routledge.

Sperry, L., & Sperry, J. (2016). *Cognitive behavior therapy of DSM-5 personality disorders: Assessment, case conceptualization, and treatment* (3rd ed.). New York, NY: Routledge.

Ungar, M. (2006). *Strengths-based counseling with at-risk youth.* Thousand Oaks, CA: Corwin- Sage.

Chapter 3

Contemporary Cognitive-Behavioral Approaches

The newer cognitive-behavioral approaches are called contemporary or third wave approaches. The first and second wave approaches were briefly described in Chapter 1 and they will be noted throughout the rest of this book. They are still very much alive and being practiced throughout the world. However, this chapter and subsequent chapters will emphasize the third wave approaches. Why? Because these newer approaches are highly compatible with the core values, ideals, and practices of the counseling profession; these newer cognitive-behavioral approaches are a natural "fit" with the way many, if not most, counselors think and practice. Overall, these contemporary approaches emphasize the importance of developing and maintaining a strong therapeutic relationship, building on strengths, fostering mutual collaboration, and respecting individual and cultural differences.

This chapter describes eight of these third wave approaches: Strengths-Based Cognitive Behavior Therapy, Schema Therapy, Dialectical Behavior Therapy, Mindfulness-Based Cognitive Therapy, Cognitive Behavioral Analysis System of Psychotherapy, Motivational Interviewing, Acceptance and Commitment Therapy, and Pattern-Focused Therapy.

Each approach is described in terms of theory and practice. A case example illustrates its application in counseling practice. Then key references are provided for further details and applications.

Strengths-Based Cognitive Behavior Therapy

Theory

Strengths-Based Cognitive Behavior Therapy is an intervention developed by Christine Padesky and Kathleen Mooney that incorporates the tenets of positive psychology with CBT. While CBT has traditionally been used to help clients overcome challenges by altering their distorted cognitions, this intervention aims to use cognitive-behavioral interventions to help clients identify their existing strengths and cultivate resilience.

Strengths-Based CBT is a four-step approach that allows clients to construct personal models of resilience, which they can use to manage future events and obstacles. Padesky and Mooney (2012) consider resilience to be a process rather than a trait and define it as the ability to cope with adversity and resume positive and adaptive functioning despite stressors.

Strengths-Based CBT is a highly collaborative process between counselor and client in which the client is helped to explore his/her existing resilient beliefs and behaviors. The authors posit that "many pathways" can be taken to discover a client's strengths because competence in this area can be exhibited in many ways. The four-step Strengths-Based CBT model consists of the following steps: 1) Search for Strengths; 2) Construct a Personal Model of Resilience; 3) Apply the Personal Model of Resilience; 4) Practice Resilience. Once the counselor and client identify the client's strengths and ways these strengths can be used to help the client remain resilient in light of adversity, the client is encouraged to see challenging situations as opportunities to be resilient (Padesky & Mooney, 2012).

Practice

The four-step Strengths-Based CBT model is outlined as follows:

Step 1: Search for Strengths

In the first step, the counselor and client collaborate on a search for the client's beliefs, abilities, and strategies that promote resilience. The counselor is encouraged to take the "many pathways" approach by looking for strengths in different domains of the client's life. Instead of teaching a client new skills, the therapist's focus is on helping the client identify existing skills. Strengths should be searched for in areas of the client's life that are not linked to presenting problems. The counselor should also explore the client's day-to-day activities and experiences. It is thought that identifying strengths in day-to-day activities may illuminate abilities the client has overlooked (hidden strengths), and can identify how the client already overcame obstacles, assuming the client maintained these tasks over a long period of time despite obstacles and interferences. The counselor helps the client describe strengths using vivid imagery and metaphors, so they are easy to remember and use when needed (Padesky & Mooney, 2012).

Step 2: Construct a Personal Model of Resilience

In the second step, the counselor and client work together to create a Personal Model of Resilience (PMR). The counselor explains resilience and illustrates how the client has been resilient in his/her life from the information gathered in Step 1. The counselor and client work to frame strengths as tools to be used during stressful situations. The client should write the PMR in his/her own words and include imagery and metaphors as much as possible.

Step 3: Apply the Personal Model of Resilience

In the third step, the client is encouraged to think of ways the PMR can help him/her be resilient during difficult situations. In dialogue with the counselor, the client is helped to apply the model to their everyday situations.

Step 4: Practice Resilience

In the final step, the counselor and client work together to design behavioral experiments that allow the client to practice the PMR. Unlike experiments in traditional CBT that focus on outcomes and resolutions to challenges, these experiments are focused on staying resilient during challenges. The quality of the PMR is tested and the client can make predictions about his/her resilience. Difficult situations can then be reframed as opportunities to practice resilience and modify the PMR (Padesky & Mooney, 2012).

Case Example

Denise is a 31-year-old mother of two who comes to therapy because she is struggling to balance her family, work, and school obligations. She reports feeling overwhelmed and defeated at times. Step 1: the counselor works with Denise to conduct an inventory of her strengths. At first, Denise cannot think of many strengths but the counselor helps her explore her passions, hobbies, and day-to-day tasks. Denise realizes that she has never failed to make lunch for her children to take to school. The counselor helps her see that her ability to maintain this task even when she is stressed out or busy shows that she has several strengths. Denise then mentions she is good at organizing and even enjoys helping her friends organize their closets, pantries, etc. Denise identifies her strengths as: staying organized, planning things out, helping people, and making things run smoothly.

Step 2: The counselor works with Denise to construct her PMR. Denise describes and writes out her PMR using imagery and uses the metaphor of Super-Planner to characterize herself. She imagines herself as a superhero figure whose superpower is planning and organizing. Step 3: The counselor asks Denise to imagine situations in which the PMR can be applied. Denise stated that when her children are sick, her entire schedule becomes disrupted and she often feels she is failing. Step 4: Denise thinks of ways her PMR can help her be resilient in the face of stressors. Inevitably, one of her children has to stay home with a stomachache. Denise feels overwhelmed but recalls her PMR and her image of Super-Planner. She is able to see this occurrence as an opportunity to use her strengths. She regroups, calls a friend to drive her other child to school, and rearranges her day so she can both do her schoolwork and take care of her sick child. Denise begins to see herself as more effective and resilient after this experience.

Key References

Mooney, K. A., & Padesky, C. A. (2000). Applying client creativity to recurrent problems: Constructing possibilities and tolerating doubt. *Journal of Cognitive Psychotherapy: An International Quarterly, 14*(2), 149–161.

Padesky, C. A., & Mooney, K. A. (2012). Strengths-based cognitive-behavioural therapy: A four-step model to build resilience. *Clinical Psychology & Psychotherapy, 19*(4), 283–290.

Schema Therapy

Theory

Originally called Schema-Focused Therapy (Young, 1990), Schema Therapy was developed by Jeffery E. Young (1990, 2003). It is derived primarily from Cognitive Therapy. It aims to correct a client's maladaptive schemas and poor coping styles. This third wave approach combines both cognitive-behavioral and experiential methods. Schema Therapy is well suited for clients who did not respond to traditional CBT interventions, typically those with personality disorders and severe problems with emotional regulation and interpersonal relationships. While used most often with these disorders, particularly borderline personality disorder, it is also useful for treating chronic depression, post-traumatic stress disorder, eating disorders, and obsessive-compulsive disorders (Cockram, Drummond, & Lee, 2010; Simpson, Morrow, & Reid, 2010; Malogiannis et al., 2014; Thiel et al., 2016).

Schema Therapy is based on the premise that adverse childhood experiences and a lack of emotional needs met in childhood lead to the development of maladaptive schemas. Schemas are defined as patterns of beliefs, thoughts, and feelings about the self and others that form in early childhood and remain stable through the lifespan. Maladaptive schemas are ones that trigger painful emotions and lead to the development of poor coping strategies that are not conducive to self-regulation or interpersonal functioning. Eighteen maladaptive schemas have been identified: Abandonment/Instability, Mistrust/Abuse, Emotional Deprivation, Defectiveness/Shame, Social Isolation/Alienation, Dependence/Incompetence, Vulnerability to Harm or Illness, Enmeshment/Underdeveloped Self, Failure, Entitlement/Grandiosity, Insufficient Self-Control/Self-Discipline, Subjugation, Self-Sacrifice, Approval-Seeking/Recognition-Seeking, Negativity/Pessimism, Emotional Inhibition, Unrelenting Standards/Hypercriticalness, and Punitiveness (Young, Klosko, & Weishaar, 2003).

For example, an individual with the Abandonment/Instability schema is likely to perceive that significant others and those one relies on for support are unreliable and unstable. Young found that activated schemas and associated coping mechanisms can be combined into states called modes. Whereas schemas are considered traits, modes are considered states and can shift. Four categories of modes are identified by Young: dysfunctional child modes, dysfunctional parent modes, dysfunctional coping modes, and healthy modes (Fassbinder, Schweiger, Martius, Brand-de Wilde, & Arntz, 2016).

The goal of Schema Therapy is to help clients understand their emotional needs and learn strategies for getting these needs met in an adaptive way, as well as effectively cope with stressors and frustrations. The counselor helps the client undo ingrained patterns of thinking, feeling, and behaving. Cognitive, behavioral, and experiential strategies are used to replace dysfunctional modes with healthier, more functional ones.

Practice

Counselors can use the therapeutic relationship as a way to correct emotional experiences. Through limited re-parenting, the counselor simulates a positive parental relationship while maintaining proper boundaries. Limited re-parenting allows for corrective emotional experiences that alter maladaptive schemas and modes. The counselor also models behavior for emotional regulation and interpersonal behavior. Through empathetic confrontation, the counselor challenges the client's avoidance of experience and emotions to foster more positive coping modes (Fassbinder et al., 2016).

The counselor uses cognitive techniques including psychoeducation and identification and analysis of schemas. The counselor validates that the client's maladaptive coping mechanisms once served a purpose of helping the client avoid emotional pain but helps the client learn to become aware of schemas and modes. The counselor helps the client evaluate the functionality of these schemas and modes and decide on a course of action that improves long-term functioning. Behavioral strategies aim to alter rigid, ingrained patterns using behavioral experiments, role-play, problem solving, and skills training. Experiential techniques allow for processing emotions and negative childhood experiences. Emotional restructuring facilitates changes in schemas through chair dialogs, imagery exercises, and role-play (Fassbinder et al., 2016).

Case Example

Sally is a 41-year-old female seeking therapy for borderline personality disorder. Sally reports a history of childhood abuse and movement to many different foster homes. She has not had success with traditional person-centered or cognitive-behavioral techniques. After establishing a therapeutic relationship with Sally, the counselor identifies her maladaptive schemas to include abandonment and mistrust. The counselor helps Sally see that she copes with these schemas and her emotional responses to them with her impulsive substance abuse and fits of rage. The counselor validates that Sally's coping mechanisms may have worked when she was younger when trying to avoid emotional pain but now they do not help her regulate her emotions or maintain interpersonal relationships. Sally begins to see that her coping mechanisms are not conducive to achieving her long-term goals. The counselor comforts Sally and helps her identify opportunities to model positive coping mechanisms. The counselor has Sally keep a journal of her thoughts and feelings and helps her see how her feelings are connected to maladaptive schemas that formed during her childhood. Eventually, the counselor helps Sally reprocess some of her adverse childhood experiences through experiential techniques. Sally learns coping and problem solving skills and begins to implement these instead of her old nonfunctional coping mechanisms.

Key References

Young, J. E. (1990). *Cognitive therapy for personality disorders: A schema-focused approach*. Sarasota, FL: Professional Resource Exchange.

Young, J. E., Klosko, S., & Weishaar, M. E. (2003). *Schema therapy—a practitioner's guide*. New York, NY: Guilford Press.

Dialectical Behavior Therapy

Theory

Dialectical Behavior Therapy (DBT) was developed by Marsha Linehan (Linehan, 1993). Initially it was primarily used with chronically suicidal clients. Today, it is the most widely used and studied intervention for borderline personality disorder. It is also effective with bipolar disorder, bulimia nervosa, and post-traumatic stress disorder (Fassbinder et al., 2016). The core feature of DBT is the dialectic between acceptance of thoughts, behaviors, and emotions and the need for change in these areas (Linehan & Wilks, 2015). Change focuses primarily on regulating emotional responses, coping with distress, and improving interpersonal relationships. DBT draws on cognitive and behavioral techniques to foster emotional regulation and adaptive functioning. The intervention is delivered in four modules: mindfulness, emotional regulation, interpersonal effectiveness, and distress tolerance.

Mindfulness is embedded in all DBT skills. The practice includes traditional mindfulness skills such as observing one's emotions and thoughts without judgment or reaction. "Wise mind" is a component of this skill set that allows clients to make better, more informed decisions with the understanding that one's internal response to stimuli is based on ingrained patterns. Emotional regulation is taught through psychoeducation on emotions as well as problem solving skills and reality testing. Individuals are helped to become aware of how vulnerabilities effect emotions and are taught to identify triggers and to purposely behave in ways opposite to the individual's tendencies. Interpersonal effectiveness teaches clients to reach goals and express themselves effectively, while maintaining one's values and self-respect. Distress tolerance teaches clients to deal with unpleasant emotions through distraction, radical acceptance, and self-soothing. Distress tolerance skills are taught to decrease self-destructive avoidance of emotions (Linehan, 2015).

Practice

Dialectical Behavior Therapy is delivered through four components: a skills training group, individual psychotherapy, phone coaching, and a therapeutic consultation team. The skills training group is co-facilitated by two counselors using a manualized treatment protocol. The individualized therapy component consists of weekly sessions that begin by reducing self-injurious and life-threatening behaviors and move towards a process of finding meaning and purpose. Individual sessions may include validation, dialectical interventions, cognitive restructuring, problem solving, and skills training. Clients can use phone sessions and coaching to guide them through applying their new skills during crises. Finally, the individual and group counselors must conduct weekly consultations in order to focus and coordinate sessions (Linehan, 2015).

Case Example

Jenny is a 21-year-old female diagnosed with borderline personality disorder. She enters a partial hospitalization program to partake in a course of Dialectical Behavior Therapy. Jenny attends weekly group sessions facilitated by two counselors. Group sessions focus on teaching the DBT skills—mindfulness, emotional regulation, interpersonal effectiveness, and distress tolerance. Jenny learns problem solving skills and how to make more effective decisions. She also participates in weekly individual therapy sessions where these skills are discussed and practiced further. Jenny learns skills to cope with her emotions and make better decisions. At one point, Jenny receives an upsetting phone call from her mother and calls her counselor to help her deal with her emotions. Jenny states she feels the impulse to "go get drunk and maybe meet someone at a bar." Her counselor talks her through her crisis and helps her practice distress tolerance and emotional regulation as opposed to her self-destructive, emotionally avoidant behavioral tendencies. Jenny progresses through the program and her symptoms gradually improve. The therapy team meets regularly to discuss and coordinate her treatment.

Key Reference

Linehan, M. M. (2015). *DBT skills training manual* (2nd ed.). New York, NY: Guilford Press.

Mindfulness-Based Cognitive Therapy

Theory

Mindfulness-Based Cognitive Therapy (MBCT) was derived from Mindfulness-Based Stress Reduction Therapy and formulated by Zindel Segal, Mark Williams, and John Teasdale (Segal, Williams, & Teasdale, 2013). While this intervention has shown promise for treating substance abuse disorders, its primary use is for preventing relapse of depressive episodes in individuals with major depressive disorder. MBCT combines traditional Cognitive Therapy with mindfulness interventions. It is typically conducted in an eight-week group setting in which clients receive psychoeducation about depression and are introduced to mindfulness strategies such as detached awareness, decentering, and nonjudgment. Clients are engaged in meditation practices to increase their nonjudgmental awareness of thoughts, emotions, and sensations, and are expected to practice these exercises between sessions (Kuyken et al., 2010). MBCT can also be modified as an individual therapy. In this case, the duration is an eight-week intervention with each session lasting 60 minutes. Exercises may be shortened to fit this time frame (Schroevers, Tovote, Snippe, & Fleer, 2016).

The premise of MBCT is that clients who have experienced a major depressive episode are likely to revert back to negative patterns of thinking and feeling that help lead to relapse of depressive episodes. Research studies support the assumption that patients recovered from depression revert to a previously formed depressed information processing style, activating old patterns of negative thinking, when faced with stressors or the onset of low mood states (Segal, Williams, & Teasdale, 2002). Clients recovered from depression who engage in habitual, old negative thinking patterns have the highest relapse risk within an 18-month period. Therefore, MBCT's primary aim is to reduce the likelihood of the patient's reactivation of these thinking and feeling styles.

Mindfulness skills are utilized to help the client recognize distressing thoughts and become more accepting and nonjudgmental of them. Mindfulness practice's focus is on becoming aware of thoughts and emotions, and accepting their presence, without active engagement with or judgment of these experiences. It is thought that practicing detached awareness, nonjudgment, and self-compassion can disrupt negative associations and thought networks. MBCT teaches clients to pay attention to thoughts and experiences without engaging in them and to practice self-compassion through traditional mindfulness meditation practices, including body scan and mindful breathing. Clients learn to identify habitual thought patterns as well as their own negative judgments of thoughts and feelings. The client learns to meet negative thoughts with kindness and empathy, interrupting self-perpetuating cycles of depressive thinking (Segal et al., 2002).

Practice

The counselor first meets with the participating client to discuss the client's experience with depression and associated thinking and feeling patterns. The client is oriented to the group and its basic premise. Through the eight group meetings, clients are taught about negative thinking and feeling patterns and cycles of depressive episodes. Clients are engaged in mindfulness exercises such as body scan and mindful breathing and are encouraged to become aware of moment-to-moment experiences (Kuyken et al., 2010). The group facilitator instructs participants to not engage in negative thoughts or judge themselves for negative feelings. Rather, participants are encouraged to view these as objective experiences. Clients are taught to consistently redirect themselves to the objective noticing of experiences without judgment or engagement. Clients are taught to practice kindness and empathy towards themselves when negative thought and feeling patterns arise. The facilitator assigns homework that includes guided meditations (Segal et al., 2013).

Case Example

Maria is a 42-year-old female who was successfully treated for major depressive disorder through individual psychotherapy. She is referred to a Mindfulness-Based Cognitive Therapy group. She meets with the group facilitator, who discusses Maria's experience with depression and helps her explore the thought and feeling patterns associated with her depressive episode. The counselor assesses that Maria is a good fit for the group and orients her to MBCT. Maria learns the basic premise of this intervention is to help her interrupt the negative patterns of thinking and feeling that can lead to a relapse of a depressive episode. Maria attends the MBCT group for eight weeks. In the group she is introduced to the tenets of mindfulness including detached awareness, nonjudgment, and self-compassion. Maria receives psychoeducation about recurrence of negative thought patterns and how these mindfulness practices help interrupt those patterns, decreasing the likelihood of depression relapse. Maria participates in mindfulness exercises in the group, including body scans and mindful breathing. She shares her experience with other group members. She is given homework assignments that include a CD to help her practice guided meditations outside of group sessions. After completing all eight group sessions, Maria attends a reunion session with her fellow group members.

Key Reference

Segal, Z. V., Williams, J. M. G., & Teasdale, J. D. (2013). *Mindfulness-based cognitive therapy for depression* (2nd ed.). New York, NY: Guilford Press.

Cognitive Behavioral Analysis System of Psychotherapy

Theory

Cognitive Behavioral Analysis System of Psychotherapy (CBASP) is another third wave approach. It was developed by McCullough (2000, 2015) for the treatment of chronic depression. CBASP is a form of Behavior Therapy that is based on a detailed situational analysis but also includes cognitive and interpersonal elements. The assumption behind this approach is that individuals with chronic depression function at relatively lows levels of social problem solving, emotional regulation, and interpersonal communication. Chronically depressed individuals tend to experience notable deficits in global thinking, communication, affect regulation, and capacity for empathy. They may also be more egocentric and are less likely to respond to corrective feedback (Arnow, 2005). McCullough's explanation for this is that many such individuals have regressed to the preoperational stage (the second stage of Piaget's cognitive-emotional development) and so are unable to engage in interventions that require formal operations (the fourth or mature stage of Piaget's cognitive-emotional development), such as cognitive disputation and restructuring (McCullough, 2000, 2003).

These deficits result in the decreased ability to understand their own role in their mood state as well as the relationship between thoughts, behaviors, and consequences. A primary goal of CBASP is to help individuals become aware of the connection between their interpersonal functioning and their depressed mood states (Negt et al., 2016). The primary focus of CBASP is situational analysis, in which the client learns to solve problems by identifying the consequences of his/her thoughts and behaviors and how these patterns can be modified to change the outcomes of situations (McCullough, 2000, 2003). This is accomplished in three phases: the elicitation phase, the remediation phase, and the generalization phase. In the elicitation phase, the client is helped to explore the description of a specific situation of concern. The counselor evokes the client's thoughts and behaviors during the event, asks the client to describe the event's actual outcome and the client's desired outcome, and asks the client if the desired outcome was attained. In the remediation phase, the client begins to understand the links between his/her behavior and environmental consequences as the counselor explores whether or not the client's thoughts and behaviors helped the client achieve the desired outcome. The counselor elicits new thoughts and behaviors that would help the client attain the desired outcome. Finally, in the generalization phase, the client explores how to apply this problem solving technique to other situations (Arnow, 2005).

Practice

Because the counseling process is guided by a series of stepped questions, this approach is relatively easy to learn and apply, particularly as it has been streamlined (Sperry, 2007, 2016b). The process begins with the counselor asking the client to identify a specific event to analyze and elicits a thorough description of the event (Step 1). Then the counselor elicits the client's thoughts that occurred during the event (Step 2). The counselor is careful to avoid interpretations made after the event and focus solely on thoughts that occurred during the event. Next, the counselor then elicits the client's behaviors during the event (Step 3). Between two and three thoughts and behaviors are elicited. The counselor then asks the client to identify the actual outcome of the situation (Step 4) and then the client's desired outcome (Step 5). The client is asked whether his/her expected or desired outcome was attained and why or why not (Step 6).

These first six steps complete the elicitation phase and the counselor moves to the remediation phase. The remediation phase begins with the counselor pointing out the link between the client's thoughts and behaviors and the environmental consequence, as well as the counselor asking permission to proceed with analysis so the client may explore how the situation may have turned out differently (Step 7). Then the counselor helps the client analyze each of the elicited thoughts (Step 8) as to whether they were helpful or hurtful in attaining the client's desired outcome. The client then is asked to generate alternative interpretations to "replace" the problematic ones. Similarly, the counselor helps the client analyze each of the elicited behaviors (Step 9) as to whether they were helpful or hurtful in attaining the client's desired outcome. The client then is asked to generate alternative behaviors to "replace" the problematic ones. Finally, in the generalization phase, clients are asked how working this process with the counselor will help them in other situations.

Case Example

Jeremy is a 44-year-old male suffering from chronic major depression. He reports he has felt depressed for several years and believes "it's probably not going to get better." Jeremy fails to see how he contributes to his depression and is merely waiting for it to get better. The counselor decides to use CBASP with Jeremy and begins by eliciting a situation that Jeremy found problematic. Jeremy describes a situation in which his coworkers did not invite him to a weekend outing. The counselor elicits Jeremy's thoughts during the situation. Jeremy identifies two thoughts: "They don't care about me" and "No one wants me around." Jeremy is then helped to identify two of his behaviors in the situation: "I heard them talking about the outing but I didn't approach them" and "I closed my office door." The counselor helps Jeremy identify that his desired outcome was to be invited to the outing but the actual outcome is that he was not invited. Because Jeremy realizes he did not get what he wanted out of the situation, he agrees to analyze what happened to see how it could turn out differently. When asked by the counselor, Jeremy states that neither of his thoughts helped him get his desired outcome. He generates two alternative thoughts that may have been more productive: "They are trying to plan something nice for everyone" and "They seem to like me." Jeremy is then able to identify two alternative behaviors, as he sees his behaviors did not help him attain his desired outcome: "I could have gone to talk to them about the plans" and "I could have been more friendly and approachable by not closing my door." Jeremy states he believes these thoughts and behaviors could have helped him achieve the outcome he desired and states he can try these alternatives in future situations.

Key References

McCullough, J. P. (2000). *Treatment for chronic depression: Cognitive behavioral analysis system of psychotherapy—CBASP*. New York, NY: Guilford Press.

McCullough, J. P., Schramm, E., & Penberthy, K. (2015). *CBASP as a distinctive treatment for persistent depressive disorder: Distinctive features.* New York, NY: Routledge.

Young, J. E., Klosko, J. S., & Weishaar, M. (2003). *Schema Therapy: A practitioner's guide.* New York, NY: Guilford Publications.

Motivational Interviewing

Theory

Motivational Interviewing (MI) is an intervention designed to enhance client readiness for change. MI helps clients explore their ambivalence and identify their own motivations to help them become more committed to change (Miller, 1983; Miller & Rollnick, 2012). Evolving from client-centered therapy, Motivational Interviewing is both collaborative and directive (Hettema, Steele, & Miller, 2005). MI allows clients to explore their own reasons for change. The counselor elicits the client's "change talk," which includes the client's wishes, need, ability, and motivations for change. As the client hears himself build a case for changing and hears the counselor's reflective response, the client's motivation is increased. The counselor helps bolster the client by affirming, summarizing, and reflecting the client's self-motivating speech (Miller & Rollnick, 2012).

Motivational Interviewing consists of two phases: increasing motivation and consolidating commitment. The client is encouraged to not only state reasons for change but also to make a verbal commitment to change. The fundamental components within MI are Collaboration: counselor and client work together; Evocation: change talk and solutions are elicited from the client; and Autonomy: the client is in charge of all decisions. This approach assumes the client's intrinsic motivation, the key change factor, will increase if the client leads the process (Miller & Rollnick, 2012).

Four general principles guide the Motivational Interviewing process. These include: express empathy, develop discrepancy, roll with resistance, and support self-efficacy. Expressing empathy involves seeing things through the client's eyes and expressing understanding. Empathy allows the client to feel accepted where they currently are and is more conducive to change than a punitive, non-accepting approach. Developing discrepancy is the principle that makes MI more directive than traditional client-centered therapy. Here, the counselor helps illustrate the discrepancy between where the client is and where the client would like to be. The apparent discrepancy highlights how the client's current behavior is not conducive to the outcome the client desires.

Rolling with resistance is the opposite of arguing with the client. Resistance can be reframed as the client's commitment to the current course of action. As opposed to challenging client resistance, the counselor uses it as an opportunity to explore the client's point of view. Self-efficacy refers to an individual's belief in his/her ability to carry out a course of action and succeed. The fourth principle of MI holds that counselors must support client self-efficacy by helping clients stay motivated and confident (Miller & Rollnick, 2012).

Motivational Interviewing is a brief intervention, usually completed in one to two sessions. It can be used as a stand-alone therapy, but is more commonly used in conjunction with other approaches. In short, MI is especially useful for clients who are less motivated for change or who are oppositional (Hettema et al., 2005).

Practice

The counselor first expresses empathy for the client's situation and conveys nonjudgmental understanding for the client's predicament. The counselor asks the client questions about the situation to elicit the client's desire for and need to change. The counselor helps the client explore his motivations for change while validating and affirming the client's statements. The counselor then summarizes and reflects the client's change talk, allowing the client to hear his own argument for change. If the client is resistant, the counselor does not engage in an argument with the client, but helps the client see the discrepancies between his current behavior and his desired state. Resistance may be framed as merely a commitment to the status quo (Hettema et al., 2005). The counselor is encouraging and reaffirms the client's feelings of efficacy and confidence.

Case Example

Patty is a 26-year-old female who seeks therapy because she feels fatigued and worries about her health. Patty reports that she smokes cigarettes and consumes about a pack per day. "I wish I didn't smoke," she tells the counselor listlessly. The counselor expresses understanding in that it must be difficult to be faced with the notion of quitting smoking. Patty states, "I don't know if I can ever quit." The counselor expresses empathy in how difficult the process must be but does not argue with Patty about the benefits of quitting smoking. Patty goes on to say that she wants to exercise and "fit into my beach clothes again." She states she feels tired all the time and gets winded when she climbs just one flight of stairs. The counselor gently points out the discrepancy in Patty's report. He illustrates that she would like to feel better physically but is continuing a behavior that counteracts that. The counselor asks Patty what the benefits of quitting smoking would be. She states she would be able to breathe easier, would not worry so much about her health, would save money, and would be able to start an exercise routine. The counselor validates and affirms what Patty says and summarizes her argument for quitting smoking. "That's a pretty good argument I came up with," Patty says, laughing. She states the outcomes of quitting smoking sound so good she feels more excited and motivated to do so. She says the pros of quitting now seem to outweigh the cons and she decides to commit to a course of action and begins by acquiring information on smoking cessation.

Key Reference

Miller, W. R., & Rollnick, S. (2012). *Motivational interviewing: Helping people change* (3rd ed.). New York, NY: Guilford Press.

Acceptance and Commitment Therapy

Theory

Acceptance and Commitment Therapy (ACT) is another third wave therapy. It was developed by Steven Hayes (Hayes, 2002) and derives from and extends the behavioral therapy tradition. It is rooted in the philosophy of functional contextualism, which focuses on identifying and changing the function and context of psychological events, rather than changing the events themselves. The underlying assumption is that avoidance of negative emotions leads to greater suffering. The goal is to foster psychological flexibility so the individual is not driven by stereotyped language and concepts of the self (Hayes, 2002). ACT helps individuals accept challenging experiences and emotions as well as increase their commitment to values and action. Individuals are helped to connect with their long-term goals and values as opposed to the immediate desires and responses that lead to psychological inflexibility (Hayes, Luoma, Bond, Masuda, & Lillis, 2006).

Six core processes are used to encourage psychological flexibility in Acceptance and Commitment Therapy. These include acceptance, cognitive defusion, being present, self as context, values, and committed action. Acceptance is seen as an alternative to avoidance. The client learns to accept unpleasant experiences without attempting to change them. Thoughts are allowed to pass without the client engaging with them.

Cognitive defusion is used to change the functions of thoughts rather than to change the thoughts themselves. Techniques are used to change the way the individual interacts with his thoughts by changing the context in which the thoughts function; that is, by watching a thought with detachment or repeating it aloud until it loses its meaning (Hayes & Strosahl, 2005).

Being present allows the client to experience life directly in the present moment with increased awareness and openness. Self as context allows further detachment from experiences. It involves seeing the self as the context from which observation occurs and is fostered through mindfulness exercises and metaphors. Values are qualities that the individual finds most important and are long-term goals to which the individual constantly strives.

Finally, committed action encourages the client to set goals and develop long-term patterns of action. Values are worked through, linked to shorter-term goals, and involve work both in session and through homework. These six ACT processes are interconnected and foster the overall goal of psychological flexibility (Hayes et al., 2016).

Practice

The counselor elicits the client's presenting problem and helps the client see how his avoidance of thoughts and feelings only serves to increase his suffering. The counselor illustrates that accepting these negative thoughts and feelings is the opposite of avoidance and helps decrease emotional suffering. The counselor helps the client begin to practice acceptance of unpleasant experiences and cognitive defusion. Through cognitive defusion, the client is able to allow thoughts to pass without judgment and without engaging in them. The client may use different techniques to remove himself from the thoughts. The counselor helps the client see himself as merely the context for these experiences. Metaphors and imagery may be used to illustrate this point. The counselor then helps the client identify his values and long-term goals. The client is helped to see how practice of acceptance and commitment leads to achievement of these values. The client commits to this course of action and to his values and, ultimately, through practice, becomes more psychologically flexible.

Case Example

Andrew is a 32-year-old male who presents to therapy with illness anxiety. Andrew states he frequently worries about falling ill and when he feels the slightest physical sensations and discomfort, he is filled with anxiety about being ill. The counselor helps Andrew understand that his attempts to avoid his anxious thoughts only increase his emotional suffering. The counselor helps Andrew begin to accept his anxious thoughts as something he experiences and not something he has to judge or actively try to change. Andrew practices cognitive defusion by allowing his thoughts to pass through his head without engaging with them. Sometimes, he says the anxiety-producing thought aloud until it is merely a sound. The counselor helps Andrew think of a metaphor to see himself as the context for his anxious thoughts. Andrew thinks of a parking lot. In a parking lot, cars come and go. Some stay longer than others, but eventually they all leave. Andrew uses this metaphor to practice cognitive defusion and seeing himself as the context. The counselor helps Andrew identify his long-term values. Andrew states one of his values is being a good family member. The counselor helps Andrew see that the less he engages with his anxious thoughts, the more he is able to focus on his family and others. Andrew commits to this course of action of pursuing his value goals.

Key References

Hayes, S., Strosahl, K., & Wilson, K. (2016). *Acceptance and commitment therapy: The process and practice of mindful change* (2nd ed.). New York, NY: Guilford Press.
Luoma, J., Hayes, S., & Walser, R. (2007). *Learning ACT: An acceptance and commitment therapy skills-training manual for therapists.* Oakland, CA: New Harbinger.

Pattern-Focused Therapy

Theory

Pattern-Focused Therapy is another third wave approach that was developed by Len Sperry (Sperry, 2016a, 2016c). It draws from Biopsychosocial Therapy (Sperry, 2006), Cognitive Behavioral Analysis System of Psychotherapy (McCullough, 2000), and Motivational Interviewing (Miller & Rollnick, 2012). The aim of this approach is to identify and replace maladaptive patterns with more adaptive ones. A pattern is defined as a stable, predictable style of thinking, feeling, behaving, and coping that is self-perpetuating and can be either adaptive or maladaptive (Sperry, 2010). Maladaptive patterns are rigid and ineffective and lead to increased symptoms and decreased interpersonal and intrapersonal functioning. Patterns range from maladaptive patterns that cause severe impairment and are diagnosed as personality disorders to highly adaptive patterns representing a high level of well-being (Sperry, 2016a and b). The goal of Pattern-Focused Therapy is to move the individual from a maladaptive pattern to a more functional, flexible, and appropriate adaptive pattern. Pattern change results in not only a decrease in symptoms and alleviation of the presenting problem, but also increased well-being (Sperry & Sperry, 2012).

Pattern-Focused Therapy is grounded in four basic premises. First, individuals unwittingly develop self-perpetuating, maladaptive patterns and these patterns are predictably reflected in a client's presenting problems. Second, changing maladaptive patterns is a critical component of evidence-based practice. Third, effective treatment is based on the client and counselor identifying, breaking, and replacing maladaptive patterns. This change results in the resolution of the presenting problem. Fourth, replacing maladaptive thought and behavioral patterns with adaptive, functional ones is likely to foster therapeutic change more effectively and quickly than with traditional cognitive restructuring or behavioral interventions (Sperry & Sperry, 2012; Sperry, 2016a).

Practice

Pattern-Focused Therapy is conducted through a collaborative relationship between the client and counselor, in which the client is first educated on the intervention's basic premises. Maladaptive patterns are identified through assessment and incorporated in the case conceptualization and treatment planning process such that treatment is focused on pattern change. Severity of symptoms, readiness for change, skill deficits, and strengths and protective factors should all be assessed and integrated into treatment planning (Sperry, 2016a).

Basic to the counseling process is a collaborative analysis of problematic situations viewed in terms of the maladaptive pattern. Clients are asked to describe the situation as well as their related thoughts and behaviors. They are encouraged to contrast their desired outcome in the situation to the one that actually occurred. As clients state they did not attain their desired outcome, they are encouraged to analyze their thoughts and behaviors in terms of whether they helped or hurt in achieving the desired outcome. Alternative thoughts and behaviors that may have been more helpful are generated. Finally, clients are asked how important it is to change their maladaptive pattern as well as how confident they are that they can do so.

Finally, because of the value placed on developing and maintaining a healthy and growing therapeutic relationship, near the end of each session the client rates—on an ultra-brief paper-and-pencil inventory—the therapeutic relationship. The results are shared and compared to previous session ratings, and the counselor and client discuss how their working together might be improved (Sperry, 2016a, 2016c).

This approach is relatively easy to learn and apply, particularly because of its questioning-processing sequence (Sperry, 2016b). The sequence begins with the counselor summarizing the client's maladaptive pattern and the more adaptive pattern to which the counseling is directed. Then the client is asked to identify a recent problematic situation (1). Next, the counselor elicits the client's thoughts that occurred during the event (2). The counselor then elicits the client's behaviors during the event (3). The client is asked to identify the actual outcome of the situation (4) and the expected or desired outcome (5). Then the client is asked whether the expected outcome was attained and why or why not (6). Because of the importance of respecting the client's prerogative, the MI approach called "permission seeking" is used to examine how the situation may have turned out differently (7). The counselor proceeds to help the client analyze each of the elicited thoughts (8) and behaviors (9) as to whether they were helpful or hurtful in attaining the client's desired outcome. The client then is asked to generate alternative interpretations and behaviors to "replace" the problematic ones. Finally, the MI questions, "How important is making changes in your maladaptive pattern?" and, "How confident are you in making these changes?' are asked (10) (Sperry, 2016a, 2016c).

Case Example

Casey is a 25-year-old female whose maladaptive pattern is identified as a paranoid style. Casey constantly suspects her friends and romantic partners of cheating or double-crossing her, resulting in hostile interactions and ruined relationships. After establishing the therapeutic relationship and informing Casey on the nature of pattern change, the counselor elicits a situation from Casey that they can analyze together. Casey reports an incident in which her boyfriend was looking at his phone many times in one evening. She states she thought he must be talking to another woman and may be even saying negative things about Casey. As a result, she grabbed his phone away and told him that no one but her could love him anyway. Casey states her desired outcome was to connect with and have a nice conversation with her boyfriend. Instead, she found he was only playing word games on his phone but he was so upset by her behavior that he stormed out, leaving no opportunity for resolution. Casey agrees she did not get what she wanted out of the situation and she and the counselor analyze her thoughts and behaviors. Since she decides that her thoughts and behaviors did not help her achieve her desired outcome, the counselor guides her through generating alternative thoughts and behaviors. Casey states that if she had thought her boyfriend could have been doing anything on his phone (e.g., reading the news, playing games), she would not have been so upset and had she just asked him what he was doing, she could have avoided the confrontation. On a scale of one to 10, Casey reports her level of importance for changing her pattern is a nine. She reports her level of confidence as a six and states she can increase her confidence if she practices noticing and redirecting her thoughts.

Key References

Sperry, L. (2016a). *Handbook of diagnosis and treatment of DSM-5 personality disorders: Assessment, case conceptualization, and treatment* (3rd ed.). New York, NY: Routledge.

Sperry, L. (2016b). Pattern-focused psychotherapy. In L. Sperry (Ed.), *Mental health and mental disorders: An encyclopedia of conditions, treatments, and well-being* (3 vols, pp. 816–818). Santa Barbara, CA: Greenwood.

References

Arnow, B. A. (2005). Cognitive behavioral analysis system of psychotherapy for chronic depression. *Cognitive and Behavioral Practice, 12*, 6–16.

Cockram, D. M., Drummond, P. D., & Lee, C. W. (2010). Role and treatment of early maladaptive schemas in Vietnam veterans with PTSD. *Clinical Psychology and Psychotherapy, 17*, 165–182.

Fassbinder, E., Schweiger, U., Martius, D., Brand-de Wilde, O., & Arntz, A. (2016, September). Emotion regulation in schema therapy and dialectical behavior therapy. *Frontiers in Psychology, 7*, 1–19.

Hayes, S. C. (2002). Buddhism and acceptance and commitment therapy. *Cognitive and Behavioral Practice, 9*, 58–66.

Hayes, S., Luoma, J., Bond, F., Masuda, A., & Lillis, J. (2006). Acceptance and commitment therapy: Model processes and outcomes. *Behaviour Research and Therapy, 44*, 1–25.

Hayes, S. C., & Strosahl, K. D. (2005). *A practical guide to acceptance and commitment therapy*. New York, NY: Springer-Verlag.

Hayes, S., Strosahl, K., & Wilson, K. (2016). *Acceptance and commitment therapy: The process and practice of mindful change* (2nd ed.). New York, NY: Guilford Press.

Hettema, J., Steele, J., & Miller, W. R. (2005). Motivational interviewing. *Annual Review of Clinical Psychology, 1*, 91–111.

Kuyken, W., Watkins, E., Holden, E., White, K., Taylor, R. S., Byford, S., Dalgleish, T. (2010). How does mindfulness-based cognitive therapy work? *Behaviour Research and Therapy, 48*, 1105–1112.

Linehan, M. M. (1993). *Skills training manual for treating borderline personality disorder*. New York, NY: Guilford Press.

Linehan, M. M., & Wilks, C. R. (2015). The course and evolution of dialectical behavior therapy. *American Journal of Psychotherapy, 69*, 97–110.

Malogiannis, I. A., Arntz, A., Spyropoulou, A., Tsartsara, E., Aggeli, A., Karveli, S., Vlavianou, M., Pehlivanidia, A., Papadimitriou, G. N., & Zervas, I. (2014). Schema therapy for patients with chronic depression: A single case series study. *Journal of Behavior Therapy and Experimental Psychiatry, 45*, 319–329.

McCullough, J. P. (2000). *Treatment for chronic depression: Cognitive behavioral analysis system of psychotherapy—CBASP*. New York, NY: Guilford Press.

McCullough, J. P. (2003). Treatment for chronic depression using Cognitive Behavioral Analysis System of Psychotherapy (CBASP). *Journal of Clinical Psychology, 59*, 833–846.

Miller, W. R. (1983). Motivational interviewing with problem drinkers. *Behavioral Psychotherapy, 11*, 147–172.

Miller, W., & Rollnick, S. (2012). *Motivational interviewing* (3rd ed.). New York, NY: Guilford Press.

Negt, P., Brakemeier, E., Michalak, J., Winter, L., Bleich, S., & Kahl, K. (2016). The treatment of chronic depression with cognitive behavioral analysis system of psychotherapy: A systematic review and meta-analysis of randomized-controlled clinical trials. *Brain and Behavior, 6*(8), 1–15.

Schroevers, M. J., Tovote, K. A., Snippe, E., & Fleer, J. (2016). Group and individual mindfulness-based cognitive therapy (MBCT) are both effective: A pilot randomized controlled trial in depressed people with a somatic disease. *Mindfulness, 7*, 1339–1346.

Segal, Z. V., Williams, J. M., & Teasdale, J. D. (2002). *Mindfulness-based cognitive therapy for depression: A new approach to preventing relapse.* New York, NY: Guilford Press.

Segal, Z. V., Williams, M. G., & Teasdale, J. D. (2013). *Mindfulness-based cognitive therapy for depression* (2nd ed.). New York, NY: Guilford Press.

Simpson, S. G., Morrow, E. V., & Reid, C. (2010). Group schema therapy for eating disorders: A pilot study. *Frontiers in Psychology, 1*(182).

Sperry, L. (2006). *Psychological treatment of chronic illness: The biopsychosocial therapy approach.* Washington, DC: American Psychological Association.

Sperry, L. (2007). Dealing with the spiritual issues of chronically ill clients in the context of couples counseling: A unique application of Cognitive Behavior Analysis System of Psychotherapy. *The Family Journal: Counseling and Therapy With Couples and Families, 15*, 183–187.

Sperry, L. (2010). *Core competencies in counseling and psychotherapy: Becoming a highly competent and effective therapist.* New York, NY: Routledge.

Sperry, L. (2016a). *Handbook of diagnosis and treatment of DSM-5 personality disorders: Assessment, case conceptualization, and treatment* (3rd ed.). New York, NY: Routledge.

Sperry, L. (2016b). Cognitive Behavioral Analysis System of Psychotherapy (CBASP). In L. Sperry (Ed.), *Mental health and mental disorders: An encyclopedia of conditions, treatments, and well-being* (3 vols, pp. 229–230). Santa Barbara, CA: Greenwood.

Sperry, L. (2016c). Pattern-focused psychotherapy. In L. Sperry (Ed.), *Mental health and mental disorders: An encyclopedia of conditions, treatments, and well-being* (3 vols, pp. 816–818). Santa Barbara, CA: Greenwood.

Sperry, L., & Sperry, J. (2012). *Case conceptualization: Mastering this competency with ease and confidence.* New York, NY: Routledge.

Thiel, N., Jacob, G. A., Tuschen-Caffier, B., Herbst, N., Kulz, A. K., Hertenstein, E., Nissen, C., & Voderholzer, U. (2016). Schema therapy augmented exposure and response prevention in patients with obsessive-compulsive disorder: feasibility and efficacy of a pilot study. *Journal of Behavior Therapy and Experimental Psychiatry, 52*, 59–67.

Young, J. (1990). *Cognitive therapy for personality disorders: A schema-focused approach.* Sarasota, FL: Professional Resource Exchange.

Young, J., Klosko, S., & Weishaar, M. (2003). *Schema therapy—a practitioner's guide.* New York, NY: Guilford Press.

Chapter 4

Processes

For many students, becoming proficient in CBT techniques is easier than mastering the fine points of CBT process. Learning CBT interventions comes easier than learning the nuances of CBT case conceptualization and change processes. Moreover, teaching and supervising counselors-in-training to apply these nuances with actual clients can be even more difficult.

This chapter reviews various CBT processes that counselors encounter with diverse clients. These include relationship building, the roles of counselor and client, and active engagement of the client in the counseling process. Then common obstacles in CBT practice such as relationship ruptures, interrupting the client, and working with clients with different levels of motivation for change are reviewed. Finally, Motivational Interviewing is highlighted in this discussion.

CBT Model of Psychopathology and Personality

Counseling theories articulate a theoretical framework "of personality, psychopathy, and therapeutic process" (Binder, 2004, p. 26). This framework provides a map that allows counselors to conceptualize and plan treatment interventions. Before planning treatment, counselors need a theoretical understanding of the development of personality dynamics (i.e., a theory of personality). Second, counselors need a theory of how suffering develops and when functioning becomes maladaptive (i.e., a theory of psychopathology). Counselors incorporate a developmental perspective of lifespan development that de-pathologizes many developmental issues such as bereavement or a client's adjustment to living away from their family for the first time in a dorm. Third, counselors need a theory of how maladaptive dynamics can be changed with therapeutic techniques and strategies (i.e., a theory of therapeutic processes) (Sperry, 2010).

Possessing such a theoretical map guides what and how a counselor collects client information, how they conceptualize presenting problems, and how the interventions are planned, implemented, and evaluated among different clients.

> Counselors must have a conscious cognitive map or working model of the immediate therapeutic situation, including just enough theory to comprehend the problem context and design intervention strategies, but not so much as to get in the way of attunement to the patient and spontaneous reactions to the changing context.
>
> (Binder, 2004, p. 27)

Counselors who understand this cognitive map will be better able to assist clients with complex issues and they will be able to provide clients with interventions that are targeted towards their specific strengths and deficiencies. Below we review the conceptual map for understanding CBT dynamics.

Personality

Personality is molded by inherent dispositions—particularly an individual's cognitive schemas and biological temperament—interacting with their environment and social context. These schemas develop early in life through various experiences and identification with significant others, and are reinforced by experience and further learning, which then influence the formation of specific beliefs, perceptions, values, and attitudes. In short, one's temperament and biological predispositions, personal meaning assigned to different life events, and personal learning determine how an individual's personality develops.

Psychopathology

There are multiple causes of suffering including neurobiological vulnerability, learning history, and schemas. Suffering is experienced when situations are perceived as threatening, and a set of cognitive, emotional, motivational, and behavioral schemas are activated. This suffering may be expressed as symptoms and functional impairment. Specifically, such distress leads to interpretations that are global, egocentric, and rigid, and that result in maladaptive cognitive processes such as distorted thinking, concentration, and recall (Sperry, 2010). Maladaptive or negative behaviors (deficits or excesses) further reinforce maladaptive cognitions, which in turn exacerbate symptoms.

Psychotherapeutic Process

CBT approaches are here-and-now approaches that attempt to modify maladaptive cognitions and behaviors using a variety of cognitive and behavioral methods. These techniques are tailored towards the client's thinking, mood, behavior, and personality dynamics. Because behavior is learned, maladaptive behavior can be unlearned while new behaviors and skills can be learned.

CBT Factors That Influence Psychological Suffering

Before reviewing primary change mechanisms from a CBT perspective, we will review some of the conceptual factors that are assumed to influence suffering from both behavioral and cognitive perspectives. These CBT constructs inform the case conceptualization process. The following list includes behaviors and cognitions to assess and treat among clients with various presenting issues (Anthony & Roemer, 2011).

Behaviors

Behavioral Deficits

Individuals who experience various behavioral skill deficits may not have been modeled or learned adaptive behaviors such as assertive communication or friendship skills. In such cases, deliberate skills training and practice can be introduced in sessions in individual and group settings.

Undercontrolled Behaviors

These particular behaviors are impulsive and often cause difficulty to the individual and, in some cases, to people around them. Examples of such behaviors are anger or rage, poor decision-making, addictive behaviors, or when an individual is overly spontaneous. CBT assists clients with these behaviors by helping them to respond and not impulsively react.

Overcontrolled Behaviors

These behaviors are common among individuals experiencing anxiety disorders, and are characterized by avoidance behaviors by which they avoid engaging in behaviors that they are capable of. Overcontrolled behaviors such as interpersonal or emotional avoidance are often dysfunctional when they lead to temporary relief (i.e., negative reinforcement) versus long-term benefits such as increased self-efficacy and learning from experience. Graded tasks, role-play, and exposure are commonly incorporated into CBT treatment to address these behavioral issues.

Overgeneralized Behaviors

This behavioral process becomes problematic when an individual has difficulty engaging in appropriate behaviors in interpersonal situations by struggling to identify discriminative cues. CBT can address these issues by assisting the client to learn to assess and effectively determine situational distinctions and learn new behavioral responses.

Difficult-to-Extinguish Behaviors

These behaviors are intermittently reinforced and are often through "one-trial learning," perhaps from a highly traumatic experience. An example includes avoiding certain locations or interpersonal engagement through avoidance to reduce the likelihood of future harm. Typical CBT interventions to address these behaviors include positive reinforcement for behaviors that clients utilize that are not associated with the problem behavior.

Cognitions

Levels of Cognition

Interventions at all three levels of thinking include cognitive testing, replacement, restructuring, reframing, disputation, and monitoring. See Chapter 5 for further explanation and examples of each of these levels of cognition. A cognitive conceptualization will include the client's (in "descending" order) automatic thoughts, intermediate beliefs, and core beliefs, also known as maladaptive "schemas," which are defined in the following sections.

Automatic Thoughts

These everyday thoughts, interpretations, meanings, beliefs, or visual images are a running commentary or reaction to what is happening to an individual in the moment. An example might be, "I am going to fail this test," which may influence an individual to stop studying for an exam since they have concluded that studying would not be beneficial.

Intermediate Beliefs

The next level of thought processes includes thoughts that are based on assumptions pertinent to an individual's view of themselves, others, the world, and the future. Such beliefs are in the "if-then" (also known as "conditional assumptions") manner of reasoning; an example could be an individual who concludes, "If I fail the test, I am not fit to be a college student and should drop out of school." In some cases, the client's automatic thoughts are objectively accurate, but their personal meaning or intermediate thoughts are distorted. For example, after failing a test, an individual thinks, "I failed the test after studying for 8 hours," but upon further investigation their intermediate belief is, "Many people studied for that exam for 3–4 hours and did much better than me; I am obviously an idiot and probably won't pass this class."

Core Beliefs or Schemas

At a deeper level of thought process, core beliefs or schemas are based on deeply held convictions about one's self, others, and the world (their cognitive triad). These beliefs are thematic and are at the foundation of the above thought processes. Common schema themes include: unloveability, abandonment, mistrust, entitlement, and defectiveness.

The behavioral and cognitive mechanisms that are addressed to effect change in the counseling process were discussed above. Understanding these dynamics provides insight into the mechanisms that CBT counselors must understand to conceptualize and treat the client's presenting issues. Next, counselors also incorporate a wellness model of mental health when considering client information to inform treatment decisions.

Psychological Wellness From a CBT Perspective

The mark of successful CBT is healthier and more effective ways of thinking and behaving. Counselors espouse a wellness model in their approach to helping clients, so listing the factors that influence suffering is only a part of the picture. Counselors seek to help clients by promoting wellness and incorporating strengths and client resources into the counseling process, rather than on curing illness or reducing pathology. The alternative model to this is a medical or illness model in which practitioners assess the problem, diagnose the illness, and treat the symptoms to eventually help return the client to their previous level of functioning. Although CBT conceptualization typically focuses more on deficits and disordered processes, Strengths-Based CBT (SB-CBT) incorporates a wellness perspective in the therapy process (Padesky & Mooney, 2012). As mentioned in Chapter 1, SB-CBT emphasizes clients' current wellness factors, examines recent coping attempts, seeks to explore when symptoms are not a problem, and elicits what is going well in an individual's life. Other CBT clinicians and researchers have identified psychological wellness from a cognitive-behavioral perspective (Newman, 2013):

From a CBT perspective, psychological wellness is comprised of a number of characteristics and capabilities, including a person's possessing: (1) a broad behavioral repertoire that can be used effectively to solve problems, to relate well to others, and to respond in differential ways that will be positively reinforced across many different situations; (2) cognitive flexibility, objectivity, astute observational skills, and hopefulness, along with a sense of self-efficacy; and (3) good emotional self-regulation, while still possessing an appropriate range of affect and a capacity for joy.

(p. 31)

Primary Change Mechanisms

CBT counselors work with clients to modify their maladaptive cognitions and behaviors using a variety of cognitive and behavioral methods while emphasizing the therapeutic relationship. We believe that good CBT practice that emphasizes the relationship is superior to CBT without a strong working alliance. Lambert's research (1992) identified that the therapeutic relationship accounts for a higher variance of change (30%) in the counseling process than the actual techniques that were used (15%). Newman's (2013) CBT definition of psychological wellness listed above also informs counselors about the factors that are built upon in the counseling process.

CBT counselors work with clients to increase adaptive behavioral approaches (such as coping skills, social skills, graded tasks) and to increase more adaptive cognitive processes through cognitive testing, replacement, restructuring, and Socratic questioning. Behavioral mechanisms of change include developing problem solving and emotional-regulation skills, acquiring healthy coping behaviors, and reducing behaviors that deflect from one's ability to live a meaningful life. Cognitive mechanisms of change include flexible and realistic thought processes, a sense of hope or optimism, and developing the capacity to learn from experience. CBT counselors help their clients to develop these skills through various techniques.

Stages of the Treatment Process

The process of change and the types of interventions required for effective treatment cannot be generic and unfocused. Additionally, treatment cannot simply just follow the client's lead towards improved functioning. Beitman (1991, 2003; Good & Beitman, 2006) articulated a change process design that is compatible with the process of CBT counseling. The Beitman model formulates four developmental stages of the counseling process that are quite compatible with CBT: engagement, pattern search, change, and termination. The stages are described below in detail.

Engagement

Engagement is a significant therapeutic process that occurs in the early phase of the counseling process, but it also continues through the termination process. Engagement requires the client to trust, respect, and accept the influence of the counselor. The building of trust and respect results in an interpersonal connection and ultimately a commitment to the counseling process. The counselor's empathic position towards the individual is essential in establishing a working therapeutic relationship. This is not to say that unmotivated and unengaged individuals will not attend sessions—they might—but there is little likelihood that meaningful change will occur. For example, a client might have an unrealistic expectation that they would like to reduce their anxiety without having to do any work in therapy. This might be the case when clients are prescribed medication (without talk therapy) to reduce their anxiety, as they assume a passive role in the management of their presenting issue. Counselors are charged with being aware not to reinforce the client's unrealistic expectations and lack of engagement in the change process. This is where CBT approaches are useful due to the nature of homework assignments that are part of between-session engagement and change. One early sign that engagement has been achieved is the individual's willingness to collaborate and take increasing responsibility for making necessary changes in their lives (Sperry, 2010).

Engagement also involves a socialization process that leads to a formal or informal treatment plan and includes important logistics such as fee, number of sessions, and psychoeducation about the CBT treatment process. Information about the therapeutic approach is typically discussed during the informed consent process and during the goal and task collaboration process. Lastly, the engagement process also includes the negotiation of treatment expectations, treatment goals, and role expectations and responsibilities for both the client and counselor.

Pattern Analysis

Pattern identification involves the identifying of the client's maladaptive pattern that reflects their manner of thinking, behaving, feeling, coping, and safeguarding. In the context of this book, pattern analysis refers to the individual's specific schemas or characterological traits, personality style temperament features, and level of functioning. Various assessment strategies can be used to assess an individual's pattern. These include a functional assessment interview (discussed in Chapter 2), personality assessment and therapeutic assessment, and the elicitation of early recollections. To the extent that the counselor understands and appreciates this pattern formulation, CBT interventions will tend to be more focused and efficacious (Sperry & Sperry, 2016).

Pattern Change

The purpose of determining underlying maladaptive patterns is to modify them so that the client is able to improve their functioning and eventually to become their own counselor. The process of pattern change involves: (a) the disordered or maladaptive pattern being assessed and relinquished; (b) a more adaptive pattern being adopted; and (c) the new pattern being generalized—thoughts, feelings, and actions are maintained. Specific strategies for pattern change target specific disordered styles and schemas, which include enduring, inflexible, and pervasive core beliefs about self and the world that greatly impact thoughts, beliefs, and behaviors. The goal of counseling is to effect change in these beliefs such that they are more flexible and functional. Treatment can either restructure, modify, or reinterpret schemas (Layden, Newman, Freeman, & Morse, 1993). Note that various versions of CBT approach pattern change from different angles; for example, REBT counselors will do this primarily through disputation, while ACT counselors will help the client reduce their unworkable behaviors, engage in mindfulness practice, and work with the client in engaging in behaviors that are in accordance with their values.

Pattern Maintenance

As healthier patterns become a sustained dynamic in the individual's life, the issue of relapse prevention needs to be addressed. As formal treatment sessions become less necessary, the issue of termination becomes the therapeutic focus. Counseling in this stage emphasizes helping a client to maintain change through active coping and self-care, and also creating a relapse prevention plan. New symptoms or old ones may appear after counseling is terminated, which may prompt additional sessions. Pattern-Focused Therapy will be discussed in detail in Chapter 8.

Phases of CBT Counseling

Judith Beck (2011) articulated a concrete process for conducting a typical CBT session. CBT counselors typically structure the session to provide a focus and a concrete format to assist individuals who are seeking counseling services. Clients often come in for counseling services because they feel overwhelmed and have tried various solutions that have either exacerbated their problems or have created only minor improvement.

The structuring process provides direction towards focused treatment as opposed to the client being expected to speak about their issues in a monologue fashion.

Agenda Setting

The structuring process includes the following steps: (a) brief mood check; (b) bridge from the previous counseling session; (c) agenda setting; (d) discussion of the agenda items and reviewing previous homework; (e) setting new homework; and (f) final summary and feedback (Beck, 2011). It should be noted that the session structure need not be rigid in nature; counselors can adjust this process based on the needs of their clients. For example, some clients may arrive to session extremely anxious and uncomfortable; in these cases the session may start with some breathing or mindfulness techniques before discussing the agenda. Setting the agenda in the first few sessions helps socialize the client with the CBT model and also maintains the idea that the session is tailored towards specific treatment goals. During the agenda-setting process, the counselor elicits the names of the problems/goals that the client would like to focus on in the session so they can be put on the agenda.

Beginning counselors often benefit from using agenda setting during their sessions to provide focus and direction for each session. Judith Beck (2011) provided the following session format for CBT agenda setting:

Initial Part of Session

1. Set the agenda (include a rationale for doing this)
2. Do a mood check
3. Obtain an update (since the last appointment)
4. Review homework
5. Prioritize the agenda

Middle Part of Session

6. Work on a specific goal and teach CBT skills in that context
7. Follow-up discussion with homework assignment and relevant issues
8. Working portion of session and second goal

End of Session

9. Provide a summary or elicit one from the client
10. Review new homework tasks
11. Elicit feedback about the counselor's approach and overall process

Mood Check

There are various methods to implement the mood-check process. However, counselors can ask qualitative mood-check questions such as, "how is your mood today?" or they can ask a more quantitative question such as, "On a scale from 0 to 10, where 0 as the worst and 10 as the best you have ever felt, what rating would you give your mood today?" If any major changes in their mood have occurred, the counselor will ask what factors accounted for this change; if improvements have occurred it is useful to examine what actions they had taken to account for this improvement.

Obtaining an Update

This is done to examine how the client's week has been in regard to their presenting problem and level of distress. Additionally, counselors will seek to find out about how the client's week has gone overall, including improvements, active coping steps, acute stressors, and other issues that are added to the agenda based on level of importance. This update can be obtained by asking, "How has your past week gone in regard to your progress with your goals of _____?" Another wellness-focused approach of obtaining an update includes asking, "What has gone well over the past week for you?" or, "Can you think of any times over the past week where the problem was not a problem?"

Review Homework

This is done to determine if the client completed the homework from the previous session. It is crucial to review the homework each time that it is given or the client will likely stop doing it. Spend time reviewing what they learned from the homework and if any challenges were encountered. As a result of the outcome of the homework, discuss what assignments will be helpful for the following session.

Prioritizing the Agenda

After the counselor has done a mood check, obtained an update, and reviewed the homework, the next step includes collaborating with the client to determine which agenda items should be covered in the session and also to determine if there are too many agenda items. After this step occurs, the working portion of the session begins and various interventions can be utilized during this process.

End-of-Session Summary and Feedback

The goal of the end-of-session summary is to focus the client's attention on the most significant points and insights from the session. In some cases, the counselor will summarize what was reviewed in the session; in other cases the counselor will ask the client to summarize what was discussed and to identify which points they will take with them. After the summary the counselor will ask the client for feedback about the session. This can include questions such as, "What was your experience of the session today?" or, "Was there anything that we did today that was particularly helpful, and anything that was less helpful?" See Chapter 7 for a discussion of several measures that examine the therapeutic process and provide a format for receiving end-of-session feedback from clients.

The Therapeutic Relationship in CBT Practice

Increasingly, CBT, particularly Cognitive Therapy, considers that "a sound therapeutic alliance" (Beck, 1995) is essential for effective counseling outcomes. We believe that a counselor who is a strong CBT technician and who does not establish a strong therapeutic relationship will struggle to help clients achieve optimal treatment outcomes. The counseling process is considered a collaborative endeavor with specific expectations for the client and counselor.

Hardy, Cahill, and Barkham identified three stages of the counseling relationship in CBT practice: establishing a relationship, developing the bond and relationship, and then maintaining it (2007). In the first stage—building positive expectations of counseling—regarding both the outcome and what is expected of both client and counselor is necessary. Hardy, Cahill, and Barkham (2007) cite research indicating that higher expectations predict positive outcomes of CBT. Once clients have hope that therapy will help and are motivated to change, the counselor turns to the second stage—developing the relationship—which involves promoting trust in the counselor, client openness to the counseling process, and commitment to working with the counselor towards mutually agreed-upon goals. In the third stage—maintaining the relationship—the goal is "continued satisfaction with the relationship; a productive and positive working relationship; increased ability for clients to express their emotions and to experience a changing view of self with others" (Hardy, Cahill, & Barkham, 2007, p. 31).

Wright and Davis (1994) stated that the "therapeutic relationship is an essential, interactive component of cognitive behavioral therapy" (p. 42). These researchers investigated clients' expectations of their counselor. They compiled responses from interviews and videotapes and constructed a hypothetical letter that a client might address to a counselor based on the findings of their interviews:

- First, provide a safe and professional setting for our meeting.
- Second, treat me with respect as a person.
- Third, take my concerns seriously.
- Fourth, I want to think you have my best interests in mind.
- Fifth, I want to know what you are doing.
- Sixth, give me practical information.
- Seventh, allow me to make choices with your information and suggestions.
- Eighth, stay flexible in your thinking about me.
- Ninth, follow up on your recommendations.
- Tenth, pace yourself; if you are overworked, unhappy, or tense, I may think you aren't being a very good example (pp. 24–30).

Clinical experience holds that counselors who embody the core conditions articulated by Carl Rogers will typically facilitate the development of an effective relationship. The active practice and embodiment of empathy, respect, and acceptance is demonstrated through active listening and empathic responding (Rogers, 1961). When a strong therapeutic relationship is established, clients will feel accepted, supported, and valued, and believe that their counselor cares about them. When a client believes that their counselor wants them to authentically succeed, they become hopeful and confident that treatment will be successful.

Research has validated that a therapeutic relationship is a significant factor in the change process in counseling; however, it does not support Rogers's claim that the three core conditions are the necessary and sufficient conditions for therapeutic change (Norcross, 2002). These relationship dynamics in the counseling process are positively related to effective therapeutic outcomes (Orlinsky et al., 2004). Counselors in an effective counseling relationship present in a warm and friendly manner and are confident, empathic, affirming, interested, and respectful towards the client, and they relate with honesty, openness, and trustworthiness. During treatment they remain flexible and alert while also providing a safe environment in which clients can discuss their concerns and inner experiences. In addition, they attend to the client's concerns and facilitate the expression of affect to enable a meaningful discussion. Finally, effective counselors are active in the treatment process, they provide accurate interpretations of the client's behavior, and they draw attention to past therapeutic successes and improvements (Orlinsky, Grawe, & Parks, 1994; Orlinsky et al., 2004; Ackerman & Hillensroth, 2003).

Roles in the Counseling Process

The Role of Counselor

The counselor is expected to set the agenda, develop a plan for treatment, implement it, and maintain a treatment focus (Ledley, Marx, & Heimberg, 2005). The counselor's role is to educate the client about the link between thoughts and feelings and serve as a guide in the change process (Gilbert & Leahy, 2005). This is a very active role that is collaborative and encouraging, as well as one in which the counselor emphasizes client wellness, strengths, resources, and abilities. The counselor is responsible for cultivating the therapeutic relationship and managing relationship ruptures.

Role of Client

The client is expected to engage in the counseling process by reporting their thoughts, feelings, and behaviors that occur in various situations pertaining to their presenting problems. Clients are also expected to collaborate with the counselor on setting the agenda for the session, provide feedback to the counselor, and complete between-session homework (Ledley et al., 2005). Since CBT is an action-oriented approach, clients are responsible for between-session work and self-monitoring when appropriate. Additionally, clients are expected to take notes in session to document new ideas, insights, and homework assignments.

Client Versus Patient

Does is matter if we use the term "client" or "patient" when referring to the individuals who seek help from us? We believe that there are some philosophical distinctions to consider. Using either term comes from the counselor's views of themselves and the individuals they are working with. The counseling profession views the individuals who we serve as individuals who are collaborators in the change process and are, in large part, the experts; therefore, it seems that the most appropriate term is "client."

The term "client" implies that the individual is seeking a service in which they hold significant responsibility. This term is more collaborative, humanistic, and egalitarian. This is a philosophical view that is consistent with the values of the counseling profession. The term "patient" assumes that the helper is an expert and the patient will follow directives from them. The word "patient" implies that the individual is ill, impaired, or deficient. Clearly different organizations such as medically focused settings will typically refer to all individuals as "patients" since services are being delivered in a medical setting. In summary, counselors avoid over-pathologizing and want to encourage active coping and collaborate with their clients.

Obstacles in Implementing CBT

Here we will look at four common obstacles that counselors may face when implementing CBT interventions with their clients.

Early Bereavement

Traditional CBT is not a treatment of choice to utilize with clients who are seeking counseling for bereavement-related issues. Clients will often benefit from supportive bereavement counseling while standard CBT approaches might not be needed, as the client can benefit from empathic listening and responding, as well as from a less structured approach. In cases of complex or extended bereavement issues, CBT strategies are indicated. For additional information about what constitutes typical bereavement among diverse client populations, the reader is referred to Irish, Lundquist, and Nelson (1993) and to Shapiro (1994).

Inaccurate Case Conceptualization

Clients come to counseling with their own conceptualization of the cause of their problems, while their counselor may have a very different conceptualization of the client's presenting issues. In some cases, the counselor may have developed a conceptualization that the client disagrees with or understands very differently. This could be due to a lack of training in the competency of case conceptualization, premature use of interpretations, cultural differences, countertransference, and many other factors.

Inaccurate case conceptualizations will likely lead to incorrect treatment protocols and poor therapy outcomes. It is often important for the counselor to check some of their initial hypotheses with the client in a tentative fashion by allowing the client to correct the initial conceptualization. This process is where the counselor and client hopefully will have a "meeting of the minds" and a "meeting of the hearts" (Sperry, 2010). They collaboratively examine the conceptualization and discuss mutually agreed-upon treatment goals. Beck offered the following questions to consider when problems arise in the conceptualization process (2011, p. 335):

Have I checked out my hypotheses with the patient?

If a patient has difficulty understanding what I am trying to express, is it due to a mistake I have made? To my lack of concreteness? To my Vocabulary? To the amount of material I am presenting in one chuck or in one session?

Is a difficulty in understanding due to the patient's level of emotional distress in the therapy session? To distraction? To automatic thoughts the patient is having at the moment?

Interrupting the Client

Interrupting clients while they are speaking in session is often very difficult for counselors-in-training; however, this can often assist clients to refocus their energy towards achieving treatment goals. Therapy is most efficient when a treatment focus has been clearly established and agreed upon by both the client and counselor. In some cases, clients will spend a great deal of time discussing topics that are preventing work from occurring in session. Our experience of asking clients to reflect about their feelings after engaging in long monologues during individual or group counseling has consistently shown that clients don't typically feel better by "getting a load off of their chest." Counselors can respectfully interrupt the client by asking if this dialogue will be helpful in working towards their stated therapy goals. Below is an example of how interrupting the client could be done in a therapeutic manner.

Client: I get so mad at my neighbor; he doesn't care about anyone. He stays up all night listening to extremely loud music, doing drugs, and having people visit his dorm to buy drugs. It's like he doesn't care about anyone but himself. I could just explode with anxiety when I think about him. I've never gotten along with him and he doesn't even try to consider my feelings . . .

Counselor: May I interrupt you for a moment? I wanted to make sure we are on the same page. You were originally discussing your homework, which was to engage in active self-care during the weekends, and then you discussed problems with your neighbor. Which do you think would be more important to work on? Your active self-care goals, or your conflict with your neighbor?

This interruption allowed the client to decide if they want to engage in the originally discussed goals or to refocus the session on a new goal. This process can be particularly useful for clients who frequently complain about difficulties and often do not look for methods to effectively cope with their problems at hand. Reviewing the client's feelings after talking about their experience of speaking about a problem in session also reinforces the notion of the thought-feeling connection.

Relationship Ruptures

Clinicians, particularly those in training, question the validity of the concept of relationship strains and ruptures, considering it to be resistance. Alliance ruptures are defined as a conflict or breakdown in the therapeutic relationship between the client and counselor (Samstag, Muran, & Safran, 2003).

> The interpersonal nature of alliance ruptures distinguishes the term from other definitions of impasses that emphasize either patient characteristics (e.g., resistance, negative transferences) or counselor characteristics (e.g., empathic failure, countertransference reaction). In other words, a rupture is not a phenomenon that is located exclusively within the patient or caused exclusively by the counselor. Instead, a rupture is an interactive process that includes these kinds of defensive experiences as they play out within the context of each particular therapeutic relationship.
>
> (Samstag et al., 2003, p. 188)

Traditionally, problems in the therapeutic relationship, including strains and ruptures, are presumed to occur in CBT as a result of the client's cognitive distortions (Ochoa & Muran, 2008). However, Beck (2005) acknowledges that counselors may also have a role in relationship ruptures. She notes that these relationship difficulties "may have a practical basis (the counselor is interrupting too much or too abruptly), a psychological basis (the patient has interfering beliefs such as: 'If my counselor doesn't give me 100%, it means she doesn't care.'), or both" (2005, p. 64). That being said, a Cognitive Therapy approach towards relationship strains and ruptures is primarily focused on cognitive distortions: eliciting cognitive distortions about the rupture; helping the client test the validity of the distorted cognitions; identifying and modifying faulty beliefs and assumptions; and, evaluating these assumptions in the contexts of other relationships (Beck, 2005).

Non-Motivated Clients

Since most CBT approaches are designed to be used with clients who are in the action stage of change, counselors are expected to augment their treatment with interventions designed to help non-motivated clients. One such approach, Motivational Interviewing, is an approach that is used to assist clients in the process of considering change (e.g., to leave an abusive relationship). This approach makes an assumption that clients presenting for therapy are not necessarily motivated to commit to the therapeutic process. Individuals often present in therapy with a desire for their symptoms to be reduced, but they are not always prepared to do the heavy lifting that therapy often requires.

Stages of Change and Motivation

Prochaska and DiClementi (1992) found that individuals who change their behaviors, on their own or with a counselor's help, typically proceed through five stages of change. The stages are: precontemplation, contemplation, preparation, action, and maintenance. Movement through these stages is not necessarily a linear process; rather clients may vacillate between various stages throughout treatment. Relapse is common among various psychological conditions. This model is quite useful in understanding and predicting client change across a wide array of client concerns in counseling.

A preliminary assessment of readiness for change can be extremely valuable and useful in treatment planning. Since most clients cycle in and out of these stages several times before achieving their goals, it is helpful to gauge the current stage during the initial session and to monitor movement of these stages. Ideally, the client enters therapy at the preparation or action stage, which means that treatment outcomes will be predictably positive. When the client enters at the precontemplative or contemplative stage, the counselor's primary task is to tailor treatment in order to move the client towards the action stage while still finding the balance between the client's own self determination and their overall well-being.

Readiness is typically assessed through observation or ongoing assessment. Asking a client, "On a scale of 1-to-10, how motivated are you feeling about working towards this particular goal?" can be a simple scaling question used to examine the client's readiness and motivation to engage in the counseling process. Markers, by stage, to elicit or observe when assessing readiness include:

Precontemplation: The client does not consider his or her behavior to be a problem and does not currently consider making any change.

Contemplation: The client considers that his or her behavior may be a problem but they do not commit to any change.

Preparation: The client has made a commitment to change a behavior and has plans to make the change in the near future. The client may have identified steps towards change in this stage.

Action: The client is actively making changes and is not returning to pre-treatment behavior/thought patterns.

Maintenance: The client has maintained change for over six months (Prochaska & DiClementi, 1992).

Motivational Interviewing Interventions to Optimize Readiness for Change

The treatment implications regarding the concept of readiness for change are immense. Counseling students and trainees who are unaware of the readiness for change model often attempt to implement action-oriented interventions such as cognitive restructuring with clients whom are at the contemplation stage of change. The implications of this error can be great since clients may feel misunderstood or might deduce that the counselor is incompetent. Several strategies for fostering readiness have been proposed, implemented, and researched. The following outline indicates some of the targets for Motivational Interviewing (MI) in regards to clients in each stage of change as well as suggests possible MI interventions that are tailored to clients in each stage (Duncan, Hubble, & Miller, 1997; Miller & Rollnick, 2002).

Stage	Interventions
Precontemplation	1. Explore the client's view of the problem and solution 2. Suggest the client think about the situation from another perspective 3. Provide education and information 4. Discuss the idea of possible change without judgment
Contemplation	1. Encourage the client to think about making changes 2. Suggest an observational task (i.e., what happens to make the situation better or worse) 3. Join with the client's ambivalence to action with a go-slow directive 4. Utilize a decisional balance technique to consider the good and less good implications of changing and not changing (e.g., "What are the good things and less good things about your daily drinking?")
Preparation	1. Offer several viable treatment options 2. Invite client to choose from among these options
Action	1. Elicit details of the client's successful efforts 2. Reinforce those efforts and encourage other efforts 3. Provide direct support to the client in regard to relapse prevention and obtaining relevant skills
Maintenance	1. Support the client's successful efforts 2. Predict relapse and setbacks 3. Help the client create contingency plans

As mentioned before, the majority of therapeutic approaches assume that the client is in the action stage of change. This is simply not the case based on Prochaska and DiClementi's 40/40/20 rule. Their research indicates that among client's receiving counseling and psychiatric services, 40% are in the precontemplation stage of change, 40% are in contemplation, and 20% are in determination or action stages of change (Prochaska & Velicer, 1997). Based on these findings, counselors need to be familiar with strategies to effectively work with clients who are in the precontemplation and contemplation stages of change.

Concluding Note

The therapeutic relationship can and does have a profound effect on treatment process and outcomes. This chapter described an expanded view of the therapeutic relationship, reviewed change processes from a CBT perspective, discussed obstacles in the counseling process, and emphasized the importance of considering the client's readiness for change as well as the value of Motivational Interviewing. In the next chapter, CBT interventions will be described with extensive case examples.

References

Ackerman, S., & Hillensroth, M. (2003). A review of therapist characteristics and techniques positively impacting the therapeutic alliance. *Clinical Psychology Review, 23*, 1–33.

Anthony, M. M., & Roemer, L. (2011). *Behavior therapy*. Washington, DC: American Psychological Association.

Beck, J. (1995). *Cognitive therapy: Basics and beyond*. New York, NY: Guilford Press.

Beck, J. (2005). *Cognitive therapy for challenging problems: What to do when the basics don't work*. New York, NY: Guilford Press.

Beck, J. (2011). *Cognitive behavior therapy: Basics and beyond* (2nd ed.). New York, NY: Guilford Press.

Beitman, B. (1991). Medication during psychotherapy: Case studies of the reciprocal relationship between psychotherapy process and medication use. In B. Beitman & G. Klerman (Eds.), *Integrating pharmacotherapy and psychotherapy* (pp. 21–44). Washington, DC: American Psychiatric Press.

Beitman, B. (2003). Introduction. In B. Beitman, B. Blinder, M. Thase, M. Riba, & D. Safer (Eds.), *Integrating psychotherapy and pharmacotherapy: Dissolving the mind-brain barrier* (pp. xv–xix). New York, NY: Norton.

Binder, J. (2004). *Key competencies in brief dynamic psychotherapy: Clinical practice beyond the manual*. New York, NY: Guilford Press.

Duncan, B., Hubble, M., & Miller, S. (1997). *Psychotherapy with "impossible" cases: Efficient treatment of therapy veterans*. New York, NY: Norton.

Gilbert, P., & Leahy, R. (2005). Introduction and overview: Basic issues in the therapeutic relationship. In P. Gilbert & R. Leahy (Eds.). *The therapeutic relationship in the cognitive behavioral psychotherapies*. (pp. 2–23). London: Routledge.

Good, G., & Beitman, B. (2006). *Counseling and psychotherapy essentials: Integrating theories, skills, and practices*. New York, NY: Norton.

Hardy, G., Cahill, J., & Barkham, M. (2007). Active ingredients of the therapeutic relationship that promote client change: a research perspective. In P. Gilbert & R. Leahy (Eds.), *The therapeutic relationship in the cognitive behavioral psychotherapies* (pp. 24–42). New York, NY: Routledge.

Irish, D. P., Lundquist, K. F., & Nelson, V. J. (Eds.). (1993). *Ethnic variations in dying, death, and grief: diversity in universality*. Washington, DC: Taylor & Francis.

Lambert, M. J. (1992). Psychotherapy outcome research: Implications for integrative and eclectic therapists. In J. C. Norcross & M. R. Goldfried (Eds.), *Handbook of psychotherapy integration* (pp. 94–129). New York, NY: Basic Books.

Layden, M., Newman, C., Freeman, A., & Morse, S. (1993). *Cognitive therapy of border- line personality disorder*. Boston, MA: Allyn & Bacon.

Ledley, D., Marx, B., & Heimberg, R. (2005). *Making cognitive-behavioral therapy work*. New York, NY: Guilford Press.

Miller, W., & Rollnick, S. (2002). *Motivational interviewing: Preparing people for change* (2nd ed.). New York, NY: Guilford Press.

Newman, C. F. (2013). *Core competencies in cognitive-behavioral therapy: Becoming a highly effective and competent cognitive-behavioral therapist*. New York, NY: Routledge.

Norcross, J. C. (Ed.). (2002). *Psychotherapy relationships that work: Therapist contributions and responsiveness to patient needs*. New York: Oxford University Press.

Ochoa, E., & Muran, J. (2008). A relational take on termination in cognitive-behavioral therapy. In W. O'Donhoue & M. Cucciare (Eds.), *Terminating psychotherapy: A clinician's guide* (pp. 183–204). New York, NY: Routledge.

Orlinsky, D., Grawe, K., & Parks, B. (1994). Process and outcome in psychotherapy. In A. Bergin & S. Garfield (Eds.), *Handbook of psychotherapy and behavior change* (4th ed., pp. 270–376). New York, NY: Wiley-Blackwell.

Orlinsky, D., Ronnestad, M. & Willutzi, U. (2004). Fifty years of psychotherapy process-outcome research: Continuity and change. In M. Lambert (Ed.). *Bergin and Garfield's handbook of psychotherapy and behavior change* (5th ed., pp. 307–389). New York, NY: Wiley.

Padesky, C. A., & Mooney, K. A. (2012). Strengths-based cognitive behavioural therapy: A four step model to build resilience. *Clinical Psychology & Psychotherapy*, 19(4), 283–290.

Prochaska, J. O., & DiClemente, C. (1992). *The transtheoretical approach*. New York, NY: Basic Books.

Prochaska, J. O., & Velicer, W. F. (1997). The transtheoretical model of health and behavior change. *American Journal for Health Promotion*, 12, 38–48.

Rogers, C. (1961). *On becoming a person*. Boston: Houghton Mifflin.

Samstag, C., Muran, J., & Safran, J. (2003). Defining and identifying alliance ruptures. In D. Chairman (Ed.), *Core processes in brief dynamic psychotherapy: Advancing effective practice* (pp. 182–214). New York, NY: Erlbaum.

Shapiro, E. R. (1994). *Grief as a family process*. New York, NY: Guilford.

Sperry, L. (2010). *Core competencies in counseling and psychotherapy: Becoming a highly competent and effective therapist.* New York, NY: Routledge.

Sperry, L. & Sperry, J. (2016). Cognitive behavioral therapy of DSM-5 personality *disorders: Assessment, case conceptualization, and treatment* (3rd ed.). New York, NY: Routledge.

Wright, J. H., & Davis, D. (1994). The therapeutic relationship in Cognitive-Behavioral Therapy: Patient perceptions and therapist responses. *Cognitive and Behavioral Practice, 1,* 25–45. doi: 10.1016/S1077-7229(05)80085-9

Chapter 5

Cognitive-Behavioral Interventions

Previous chapters have introduced the reader to the broad therapeutic landscape called Cognitive Behavior Therapy (CBT). The Introduction described the importance and value of this broad approach to counseling. The first chapter discussed the history and evolution of CBT, while the second chapter focused on its theoretical premises and core competencies. The third chapter described and illustrated the contemporary versions of CBT, while the fourth chapter described its basic processes. This fifth chapter may be the most useful chapter so far, as it describes the common treatment interventions that a counselor can incorporate in their counseling practice, irrespective of their practice setting or their theoretical orientation.

This chapter focuses on 13 common cognitive-behavioral interventions that are useful—and even essential—in everyday counseling practice. These interventions are described and illustrated. Hopefully, they will be usefull to counselors in school, rehabilitation, mental health, or integrated healthcare settings. Arguably, they can be incorporated in a counselor's practice irrespective of the counselor's preferred theoretical orientation.

These interventions are: behavioral activation, cognitive disputation and restructuring, emotional regulation training, empathy training, exposure, habit reversal, impulse control training, interpersonal skills training, mindfulness, problem solving training, relapse prevention, social skills training, and thought stopping.

The same format is followed for each of these interventions: The entry begins with a definition of the intervention. Next, the intervention is described in terms of its origins and mechanism of change. Then the common uses or indications are specified, along with any contraindications or conditions for which the intervention is unlikely to be successful. Following this is a step-by-step treatment protocol that identifies the specific counseling process that a counselor would follow in applying the intervention. Then a case example illustrates the use of this protocol. Finally, a resource section provides key references that more fully describe the intervention and its application.

Behavioral Activation

Definition

Behavioral activation is a behavioral intervention to help individuals break cycles of inactivity and avoidance. While primarily utilized with depressed individuals, it is also used with other conditions involving avoidance.

Description

Behavioral psychology focuses primarily on environmental and contextual factors instead of internal factors (i.e., psychodynamics and unconscious processes). Accordingly, depression is viewed contextually as a cycle that feeds upon itself. As individuals become depressed, they begin to limit activities and experiences as a method of avoiding thoughts and feelings. Consequently, the more they limit their movement and experience fewer pleasurable activities, the less positive reinforcement they receive, and the more they become depressed. For example, they increasingly avoid answering the phone, which limits the positive reinforcement from social interaction. They also will avoid necessary tasks, which leads to feelings of defeat. The result is that the depression cycle increases.

Breaking the cycle of inactivity through behavioral activation and pleasant activity scheduling is more beneficial than cognitive restructuring or disputation. Behavioral activation includes pleasant activity scheduling and an analysis of the function of the client's behaviors. Pleasant activity scheduling helps clients begin to add pleasurable and rewarding activities back into their lives despite their cognitions and lack of motivation. Both pleasurable and necessary activities should be scheduled, striking a balance between the two.

Indications and Contraindications

Behavioral activation and pleasant activity scheduling was initially used with clients with mild to moderate depression, particularly in clients who struggle with analyzing their cognitions or engaging in cognitive disputation or restructuring. This intervention can also be used with other symptom disorders, such as anxiety disorders in which the individual has lost interest in activities with others, or with certain personality disorders when clients withdraw from others.

Treatment Protocol

1. First, the counselor explains the rationale of the intervention to the client. The counselor helps the client understand how their pattern of inactivity reinforces their symptoms.

2. Second, the counselor and client make a list of activities the client currently engages in, a list of tasks the client must perform but has been avoiding, and a list of pleasurable activities the client would enjoy. The counselor should assess how the client's current behavior is reinforcing their symptoms.

3. Third, the counselor shows the client how to structure activities into a weekly schedule, starting with the easiest activities first. Larger tasks should be broken down into smaller steps. The client should aim for one to two activities in the first week. The client can use a planner that breaks days into hourly increments.

4. The client keeps a log of activities and moods and brings it to subsequent sessions. The client continues to plan activities that serve as approaching rather than avoiding behaviors and that increase their goals.

Illustration

Donald is a 51-year-old Caucasian male diagnosed with major depressive disorder. Donald reports low mood, fatigue, and loss of pleasure. The counselor evaluates Donald's current repertoire of behaviors and finds he avoids daily tasks and limits his engagement in pleasurable activities. Donald reports he has been avoiding cleaning out his garage and car, and both serve as a daily reminder of his fatigue and lack of motivation. Donald feels guilty and defeated by his inability to complete these tasks. He reports he watches television and falls asleep on the couch every night.

The counselor explains that Donald's pattern of inactivity serves to reinforce his depression. The counselor illustrates how the client's feelings of defeat and thoughts of helplessness are related to his avoidance of cleaning out the garage, fueling his cycle of depression. Donald agrees to try behavior activation and pleasant activity scheduling despite his fatigue and low motivation.

The counselor helps Donald write a list of his current behaviors, which include watching television, avoiding phone calls, and falling asleep on the couch. Additionally, they write a list of tasks Donald needs to complete but has been avoiding. Finally, they write a list of pleasurable activities Donald would like to engage in, which include spending time with friends, running, and kayaking. The counselor teaches Donald to schedule events on a weekly calendar. The counselor stresses the importance of not setting goals that are too lofty and balancing tasks that are enjoyable with ones that give Donald a sense of achievement.

For the first week, Donald completes two scheduled tasks—cleaning out his car's trunk and running around the block twice. Donald brings his journal of activities and moods to the next session. He reports that he found little pleasure in the activities but continues to schedule activities for the next week. In the following weeks, Donald reports he has cleaned up most of his garage, increased his running time, and gone kayaking with friends. He states he finds more pleasure in these activities than he did initially and finds his mood generally improved.

Resources

Martell, C. R., Addis, M. E., & Jacobson, N. S. (2001). *Depression in context: Strategies for guided action.* New York, NY: Norton.

Veale, D. (2008). Behavioral activation for depression. *Advances in Psychiatric Treatment, 14*, 29–36. Retrieved from http://dx.doi.org/10.1192/apt.bp.107.004051

Veale, D., & Wilson, R. (2007). *Manage your mood: A self-help guide using behavioral activation.* London: Robinson.

Cognitive Disputation and Restructuring

Definition

Cognitive disputation is a component of cognitive restructuring that uses logic to help individuals understand the irrationality of their maladaptive thoughts. Cognitive restructuring is an intervention for identifying and modifying self-defeating beliefs or cognitive distortions.

Description

A basic premise of cognitive therapies is that individuals are affected more by what they think and believe about their experiences than by the experiences themselves. Cognitive restructuring aims to correct these maladaptive thoughts by replacing them with more logical ones, and the first step in this process is cognitive disputation. Cognitive disputation allows the counselor to challenge irrational thoughts and illustrate their fallacy to the client by using logic. The ultimate goal is to teach the skill of disputation so that clients can eventually challenge their own thoughts without the use of a counselor.

Thoughts can be disputed by the counselor guiding the client through Socratic questioning, or by the counselor directly disputing the thoughts. The former approach is based on Beck's Cognitive Therapy and focuses on logical errors or cognitive distortions (i.e. catastrophizing, all-or-nothing thinking). The latter approach is based in Albert Ellis's Rational Emotive Behavior Therapy and focuses on an individual's beliefs that things "should" be a certain way and that consequences are unbearable. Both approaches encourage the client to test their thoughts against reality, with Beck's method encouraging clients to view their thoughts as testable hypotheses rather than facts. Cognitive disputation requires clients to become aware of their thoughts, often through recording them as a homework assignment, as well as chronicling events that may later serve as disputations for irrational thoughts. Both thoughts about specific situations and general beliefs may be disputed.

Indications and Contraindications

Cognitive disputation is useful for treating depression, anxiety, eating disorders, substance abuse, and marital distress. Cognitive disputation is contraindicated for individuals who have limited cognitive capacity, including those with intellectual disability, borderline intellectual functioning, dementia, and psychosis. Behavioral interventions, particularly behavioral activation and exposure therapy, are indicated for individuals with a limited ability to conceptualize their own thinking. Cognitive disputation may not be as effective as exposure therapy for obsessive-compulsive disorder, as these individuals are typically aware of the irrationality of their thoughts but experience anxiety symptoms nevertheless. For some individuals, skills training may be necessary before cognitive disputation; particularly if a client lacks social skills, social skills training would be more beneficial than disputing his beliefs about his lack of social skills. Finally, clients must be sufficiently motivated to participate in Cognitive Therapy before the counselor utilizes disputation.

Treatment Protocol

1. First, the counselor helps the client identify maladaptive thoughts. The client may examine thoughts about a specific situation and/ or complete homework to list thoughts that arise during daily situations.
2. Then the counselor explains the rationale for cognitive disputation and illustrates how cognitions are related to feelings and behaviors.
3. Next, the counselor disputes the client's maladaptive thoughts and illustrates how they are irrational. These thoughts may be disputed through Socratic questioning or by directly trying to convince the client of the irrationality of their thoughts. The counselor invites the client to view the thought as a hypothesis and test it against reality.
4. The client is given homework to continue to identify maladaptive thoughts as they arise. The counselor may also ask the client to journal about daily activities and occurrences to provide a basis for disputing other beliefs.
5. Finally, the client practices disputing his or her own thoughts both in and out of session.

Illustration

Jordan is an 18-year-old Caucasian male in his first year of college. He reports feelings of loneliness and intermittent depression and expresses a desire to make friends. "I just don't feel like I belong here or like anyone here wants to hang out with me," he states during the intake session with the counselor. His male counselor asks for an example of Jordan's predicament, and Jordan describes attending a party he was invited to, at which he didn't speak to anyone and spent the entire time by himself before leaving early.

The counselor helps Jordan identify what he was thinking during the party. Jordan identified two thoughts: "No one wants me here anyway" and "No one wants to talk to me." He illustrates to Jordan how these thoughts are maladaptive and are linked to his feelings and behavior. Jordan begins to understand how his thoughts contribute to his loneliness and keep him from actually trying to interact with others, ensuring he does not make friends.

The counselor invites Jordan to view his identified thoughts as hypotheses and ask himself if they are rational. He points out the logical errors in his thinking (all-or-nothing thinking and selective abstraction). Then he probes Jordan for more details about the event that might help him test his thoughts against reality. Jordan states a classmate invited him to the party, proving that his first thought, "No one wants me here," is irrational. Jordan then realizes that several people attempted to interact with him at the party but he did not engage with them because of his feelings of inadequacy. Jordan understands that his second thought, "No one wants to talk to me," is irrational as well and his own belief prevented him from engaging with others.

The counselor then gives Jordan homework to keep track of his thoughts and daily activities. In the following session, Jordan reports one of his thoughts was, "I'm not likeable." When reading through his list of activities from the previous week, Jordan mentions he was invited to work on a group project in his romance literature class. He uses this occurrence as evidence to dispute Jordan's global belief, "I'm not likeable." Jordan is encouraged to practice cognitive disputation outside of sessions.

Resources

Beck, A. T. (1979). *Cognitive therapy of depression.* New York, NY: Guilford Press.

Ellis, A., & MacLaren, C. (1998). *Rational emotive behavior therapy: A therapist's guide.* San Luis Obispo, CA: Impact.

Emotional Regulation Training

Definition

Emotional regulation training is an intervention that helps individuals identify, accept, and manage their emotions. It is particularly effective for those with emotional dysregulation—that is, emotional responses that quickly change (labile) and are difficult to control.

Description

Emotional regulation training can be beneficial for individuals with labile moods and difficulty controlling their emotions. Individuals who can benefit from emotional regulation training often experience a worsening of their emotional states when they try to avoid them and when they feel guilt or anxiety over the mood states. Emotional regulation training is an essential intervention in Dialectical Behavior Therapy. It is also used in other therapeutic approaches such as Acceptance and Commitment Therapy, Emotion-Focused Therapy, and various Mindfulness-Based Therapies. It helps individuals first identify and describe their emotions by being mindful of these emotional responses.

Exposure to emotional experiences without negative consequences typically decreases the individual's negative response to their moods. Individuals then learn to understand their emotional needs and the primary thoughts and feelings that underlie certain emotions. Primary emotions can be adaptive contextually but often result in shame, anxiety, or anger, leading to a maladaptive spiral of distressing emotions. Emotional regulation training helps individuals accept their emotional experiences and reduce avoidance behavior, leading to more adaptive self-management.

Indications and Contraindications

Emotional regulation training can be used for children, adolescents, and adults. While children may have more difficulty doing the cognitive work associated with emotional regulation, it is particularly important for them to decrease shame and guilt related to emotions before they develop more deeply ingrained maladaptive patterns. Emotional regulation training can be applied in an individual or group setting.

Treatment Protocol

1. First, the counselor assesses the client's current level of skill in identifying, describing, attending to, and regulating mood states. The counselor uses this baseline information to develop a treatment plan for ameliorating skill deficits.

2. Second, the counselor helps the client learn to identify, label, and describe emotions. The client is encouraged to observe emotions and describe the context in which they occur and all related sensations, including physical ones.

3. Third, the counselor encourages the client to avoid escape mechanisms and be mindful of emotional experiences. The client should come to understand that they do not need to feel guilt, shame, or other negative secondary emotions in response to their primary emotions. The client practices increasing acceptance of their emotions without judgment. Role-play may be used to assist the client in this process.

4. The counselor then helps the client understand the function of their emotions and learn to connect emotions to their context. The client learns that emotions are part of a normal phenomenological experience and can be adaptively regulated rather than feared.

5. The client is encouraged to implement healthy lifestyle changes and increase positive experiences while reducing stressors. The client practices tolerating and regulating emotions and learns to use emotional information to understand their needs, modulate interpersonal relationships, and make more effective decisions.

Illustration

Jessica is a 28-year-old female diagnosed with borderline personality disorder. She seeks treatment because of conflict in her relationship with her boyfriend. During a recent altercation, Jessica threw dishes on the floor and berated her boyfriend after he asked if he could go away on a weekend fishing trip.

Her counselor assesses Jessica's level of skill in emotional regulation and finds she has difficulty identifying, describing, and regulating her moods, particularly her propensity to blame others and respond impulsively. The counselor teaches Jessica to identify, label, and describe her emotions. Jessica then practices tuning in to and labeling her emotions and physical sensations. When her boyfriend cancels dinner plans, she observes how she feels lonely and scared and feels pain in her stomach. Jessica also observes she feels guilty and flawed because of her emotions. The counselor helps her practice accepting her emotions without judgment and staying in the present until her negative emotions subside.

The counselor helps Jessica to learn the meaning beneath her emotions and she finds she needs to feel more socially connected and soothe herself more. She starts spending more time with friends and doing things that make her feel good such as eating healthily, exercising, and reading while taking bubble baths. Jessica increases her positive experiences through these lifestyle changes and continues practicing her emotional-regulation skills.

Resources

Linehan, M. (2015). *Skill training manual for treating borderline personality disorder* (2nd ed.). New York, NY: Guilford Press.

Mennin, D. S., & Fresco, D. M. (2014). Emotion regulation therapy. In J. J. Gross (Ed.), *Handbook of emotion regulation* (2nd ed., pp. 469–490). New York, NY: Guilford Press.

Empathy Training

Definition

Empathy training is a therapeutic intervention useful for increasing an individual's capacity and skills for empathy.

Description

Empathy training can help individuals improve their abilities to listen, understand, and respond empathically. While often applied on its own, empathy training is a central component of Relationship Enhancement Therapy. Empathy training, along with other skills, is used to help individuals cultivate understanding of themselves and others, fostering healthier relationships and deeper connections. Empathy training is designed to improve an individual's negotiation and problem solving skills and reduce reflexive responses. It can also help with emotional regulation as individuals learn to connect the meanings they attribute to others' behaviors with the emotions they experience. Individuals practicing empathy often find they feel more supported, increase their compassion, and experience less emotional reactivity.

Indications and Contraindications

Empathy training can be implemented with individuals, couples, and families. It is especially indicated for personality-disordered individuals. While it can be used in an individual setting, it is best applied with couples so the other person can reflect if an individual's understanding is accurate.

Treatment Protocol

1. First, the counselor assesses the client's ability to listen empathically, accurately understand interpersonal cues, and respond empathically.
2. Second, the counselor models the empathic skills until the client begins to develop and incorporate these skills.

3. Third, the counselor coaches the client in the empathic skills and encourages the client to explore underlying needs and vulnerabilities.
4. If the client is participating with a partner, the client is asked to articulate their interpretation of the other person's feelings and attitudes. The other person reflects if the client's understanding is accurate or not. As the client learns to listen empathically, their reflexive reactions begin to diminish.
5. Finally, the client monitors their emotional reactivity and practices empathic skills.

Illustration

Jack is a 46-year-old male hedge fund manager who agrees to go to couples counseling with his wife. His wife, Julia, complains that Jack is insensitive, self-centered, and self-aggrandizing. She expresses being upset that Jack seems to ignore her and take no interest in her unless they attend social functions with important people when Jack says Julia's job is to be "arm candy." Julia says she loves Jack's charming personality but wishes they could connect on an emotional level.

The counselor evaluates Jack's current ability to relate empathically and assesses Jack's deficits in empathic listening, understanding, and responding. The counselor instructs Jack on listening empathically, accurately understanding interpersonal cues, and responding empathically. The counselor models these skills and urges Jack to explore the needs and vulnerabilities underlying his behaviors.

The counselor then asks Jack's wife to tell him how she feels about something and she states she was upset at the last party they went to. The counselor asks Jack how he understands his wife's feelings and Jack states he believes his wife is not interested in anything that is important to him. His wife states this interpretation is incorrect and, in fact, she was upset because Jack spent the whole time talking to other people, leaving her alone. Jack then understands his wife wants to spend time together and practices communicating this understanding to her. Jack continues practicing empathic listening, understanding, and responding. Monitoring his emotional reactivity, Jack finds he feels happier and more connected to and supported by his wife as he practices empathy.

Resources

Guerney, B. (1988). *Relationship enhancement manual*. State College, PA: IDEALS.

Scuka, R. (2005). *Relationship enhancement therapy: Healing through deep empathy and intimate dialogue*. New York, NY: Routledge.

Exposure

Definition

Exposure is a behavioral intervention useful in treating various anxiety conditions, including phobias and panic. It works by exposing individuals to their feared objects, situations, or sensations.

Description

Rooted in behavioral psychology, exposure therapy aims to decrease anxiety by exposing an individual to feared stimuli. Individuals with phobias often learn to fear a neutral stimulus after a particularly frightening experience in which their fight-flight system was activated. This results in the tendency to avoid that stimulus while continuing to overestimate its danger. Avoidance acts as a negative reinforcement, and individuals remain hypervigilant and overreact in the face of largely benign stimuli. An individual exposed to a feared stimulus will experience a flood of anxiety that will eventually peak and then subside. As the anxiety subsides, the individual learns they overestimated the danger; new reactions are formed based on non-negative information and the individual begins to habituate to the stimulus. Exposure as a therapeutic intervention operates on the neuropsychological principle that anxiety is self-limiting and cannot last at its peak level for more than two hours.

Methods of exposure can vary. *In vivo* exposure is typically preferred but may not be feasible or ethical in certain circumstances (e.g., death or illness). Using *in vivo* exposure, the individual encounters the feared object in real life. An alternative to *in vivo* exposure is *imaginal* exposure, in which the counselor guides the client to visualize an encounter with the feared stimulus. *Virtual reality* exposure uses technology to simulate *in vivo* exposure. Finally, *interoceptive* exposure is often used to habituate clients to the panic sensations they fear by inducing them in session (e.g., through heavy breathing). Additionally, the pace in which an individual is exposed can vary. *Flooding* exposes the individual directly to the feared object and induces peak anxiety. *Gradual* exposure, on the other hand, allows the counselor and client to create a hierarchy of the feared stimulus. Individuals are then exposed to the stimuli at the bottom of the hierarchy and slowly work their way up, habituating a little at a time (e.g., a person with a phobia of snakes may at first be exposed to a picture of a snake). *Gradual* exposure works on the principal of successful approximations. *Systematic desensitization* allows for the use of relaxation techniques (e.g., deep breathing) to assist in the habituation process along the hierarchy.

Indications and Contraindications

Exposure therapy is useful in treating specific phobias, panic, agoraphobia, social anxiety, obsessive-compulsive disorder, generalized anxiety, and post-traumatic stress. Some disorders such as body dysmorphic disorder have also been shown to respond to exposure therapy. Additionally, *imaginal* exposure is useful for intrusive thoughts in clients with obsessive-compulsive disorder. *In vivo* exposure is contraindicated in situations where it may be unfeasible or unethical—that is, where the feared stimulus is in fact harmful, dangerous, or traumatic (death, illness, violence). In such cases, *imaginal* exposure should be utilized. Most clients with phobias, panic, obsessive-compulsive disorder, etc. possess some insight into the irrationality of their fears. For clients who do not have this level of insight, exposure is contraindicated. Special care must be taken with individuals with personality disorders and clinical depression, as both may interfere with the treatment and habituation process.

Treatment Protocol

1. First, the counselor decides if the exposure will be *gradual* or through *flooding*, and if *systematic desensitization* relaxation techniques will be used. If *gradual* exposure is the selected method, the counselor helps the client construct a hierarchy of fears, ranging from least to most anxiety provoking. The counselor and client then complete the following steps according to the pace they select.
2. Next, the counselor decides if the exposure will be *in vivo* or *imaginal*. *Interoceptive* exposure may be used for clients with panic and *virtual reality* exposure may be used in instances where it is feasible and preferred.
3. Third the counselor assists the client in exposure to the feared stimulus, using the agreed-upon method and pace. During the exposure, the counselor encourages the client to remain exposed to the feared stimulus as long as is needed for the anxiety response to peak and subside. The counselor uses *response prevention* to keep the client from avoiding the stimulus, either through physical escape, shifting thoughts elsewhere, or dissociation. When possible, *in vivo* exposure is preferred as clients are more likely to avoid their thoughts in *imaginal* exposure. Relaxation techniques may be used along the way if *systematic desensitization* is the chosen method.
4. Prolonged exposure is repeated until the client has fully *habituated* and the irrational fear response is *extinguished*.

Illustration

Dahlia is a 42-year-old Caucasian female with a specific phobia of escalators, which developed after an incident in which the bottom of her long skirt became caught in between the gap in the escalator stairs. Dahlia reports having to grab the bottom of her skirt and fiercely yank it out of the escalator, tearing it at the hem. During the experience, Dahlia reports symptoms of panic and an overwhelming fear that she would be dragged to her death or caught and strangled in her own clothing somehow. Since this experience, Dahlia cannot approach an escalator without experiencing panic symptoms and even averts her gaze when walking past an escalator. Dahlia acknowledges this was a freak occurrence as her skirt was made of a fine, gauzy material that trailed behind her and the same thing would likely not happen with any of her other articles of clothing. She also admits she had previously ridden escalators in this skirt, even the very day of the incident, without instance. She also realizes that she was in no real danger of serious injury since it was her skirt that was caught and, while embarrassing, she could have removed it if the situation progressed. Still, Dahlia cannot seem to convince herself that she is safe to ride escalators again.

Together, the counselor and Dahlia decide to use *gradual, in vivo* exposure with *systematic desensitization* techniques. The counselor helps Dahlia create a *hierarchy* of her fear and she writes the following: 1. looking at an escalator (least feared); 2. standing near an escalator; 3. riding an escalator (most feared). The counselor teaches Dahlia some deep breathing techniques and she practices these in session.

Dahlia and the counselor agree to meet at the local mall on a weekday morning when not many people are around. They stand at the bottom of an escalator and Dahlia does not avert her eyes. As she gazes at the escalator, Dahlia's breathing and heart rate increase and she looks visibly uncomfortable. The counselor encourages her not to look away and reminds her to engage in the deep breathing technique. Dahlia continues for 20 minutes until her anxiety subsides. They then approach the escalator and stand near it where Dahlia can touch the railing. Again, Dahlia's anxiety surges and she takes several steps back. The counselor presses her to move closer to the escalator again and utilize deep breathing. This time Dahlia's anxiety lasts about 35 minutes.

Finally, the counselor encourages Dahlia to board the escalator. With great resistance, she does so and experiences a flood of anxiety. Dahlia begins to tremble and cry. She breathes heavily and says she feels her heart is pounding out of her chest. When she reaches the top of the escalator, Dahlia decides she is done for the day and will leave. The counselor encourages her to get on the descending escalator and stay in the present moment. She does so and, with the counselor's help, spends the next

80 minutes going up and down the escalator while practicing deep breathing. She states she doesn't feel she can take any more but, eventually, her anxiety subsides and she learns she overestimated the danger. "This is a lot easier than I thought. I feel okay," she states.

Dahlia and the counselor meet at the escalator for several more sessions. This time she gets directly on the escalator. Each time she experiences less anxiety but remains on the escalator until it subsides. Dahlia now reports she can use the escalator without fear and feels she can return to a normal life.

Resources

Abramowitz, J. S., Deacon, B. J., & Whiteside, S. P. H. (2011). *Exposure therapy for anxiety: Principles and practice* (1st ed.). New York, NY: Guilford Press.

Boettcher, H., Brake, C. A., & Barlow, D. H. (2015). Origins and outlook of interoceptive exposure. *Journal of Behavior Therapy and Experimental Psychiatry*, 53, 41–51. doi:10.1016/j.jbtep.2015.10.009

Wiederhold, B. K., & Wiederhold, M. D. (2005). *Virtual reality therapy for anxiety disorders: Advances in evaluation and treatment* (1st ed.). Washington, DC: American Psychological Association.

Habit Reversal

Definition

Habit reversal is a behavioral intervention used to reduce verbal and motor tics, stuttering, and impulse control disorders such as hair pulling and skin picking.

Description

Habit reversal is intended to reduce the occurrence of tics and impulsive behaviors by replacing these behaviors with inconspicuous, opposing behaviors. Habit reversal includes four stages: awareness training, developing a competing response, increasing motivation, and generalization of skills. In the awareness stage, the client increases awareness of the behavior by describing it or performing it in a mirror, as well as identifying situations in which the behavior frequently occurs. In the competing response stage, the client learns a behavior that is incompatible with the unwanted behavior. The competing response should be opposite of the unwanted behavior, inconspicuous in social situations, be performed for several minutes, induce isometric tension of the muscles involved in the unwanted behavior, and strengthen the opposing muscles. In the motivation stage, the client explores reasons to discontinue the unwanted behavior, including times when the behavior has proved embarrassing or bothersome (habit inconvenience review). Additionally, in this stage the client's friends and family are implored to encourage the client's reduction of the unwanted behavior (social support procedure), and the client publicly controls the unwanted behavior in front of trusted people (public display). Finally, in the generalization phase, the client symbolically rehearses the competing behavior in other situations.

Indications and Contraindications

Habit reversal is useful in treating tic disorders, hair-pulling disorder, skin-picking disorder, stuttering, and other habits such as nail biting, teeth grinding, scratching, and oral-digital habits. It can be used with children, adolescents, and adults. Habit reversal is contraindicated for clients with borderline intellectual functioning or intellectual disability.

Treatment Protocol

1. The counselor helps the client become aware of the unwanted behaviors. The client describes the behavior in detail while performing the behavior looking in a mirror. The counselor points out when the behavior occurs in session until the client notices the behavior. The client identifies warning signs such as urges, physical sensations, or thoughts, as well as all the situations in which the behavior most frequently occurs.
2. The counselor helps the client identify a competing behavior that is opposite of the unwanted behavior and is inconspicuous in public. The competing behavior should induce isometric tension of the muscles involved in the unwanted behavior, as well as strengthen the opposing muscles. The client practices the competing behavior for several minutes at a time.
3. The counselor encourages the client to make a list of problems, inconveniences, and embarrassments caused by the unwanted behavior. The client demonstrates suppression of the unwanted behavior in front of friends and family, and loved ones praise the person for control of the behavior.
4. The client practices the competing behavior in a variety of settings. The counselor helps the client symbolically rehearse performing the competing behavior in different areas of the client's life.

Illustration

Maria is a 34-year-old Hispanic female who presents for counseling with Trichotillomania (hair-pulling disorder). Maria reports pulling her hair out, particularly when experiencing stress, since she was 19 years old. She arrives at intake wearing a hat but when she removes it, it is evident she has bald spots at the crown of her head and right temple. Her eyebrows also appear sparse. Maria attempts to cover the bald spots by wearing hats, pulling her remaining hair over the areas, and using makeup. She states she feels intense urges to pull her hair associated with stress and anxiety. Although she is embarrassed by her areas of missing hair, she feels she cannot control pulling her hair. Maria's embarrassment has led her to spend most of her time at home with her family, where she can spend up to three hours at a time pulling her hair. She says she would like to control this behavior and move on with her life, stating her goals are to obtain a job and to date.

The counselor helps her become aware of when she pulls her hair and the situations that trigger her hair pulling. Maria identifies that anxiety about her future and about social interactions trigger her hair pulling. The counselor also points out instances in session, while talking about stressful subjects, when Maria's hand drifts up to her eyebrows. Maria identifies strong physical urges to pull her hair. Next, the counselor helps Maria decide on a competing behavior that she can do without being noticed in public. Maria decides she will put her hands in her pockets or sit on her hands when she feels the urge to pull her hair. She practices this competing behavior in and out of session, for at least three minutes at a time.

In a following session, the counselor helps Maria write a list of times she has been inconvenienced or embarrassed by her hair pulling. Maria identifies being embarrassed by being seen with bald spots, and a time a friend noticed the hair missing on her temple and eyebrows. Maria's parents praise her effort to reduce hair pulling and notice she hasn't pulled her hair for the last week. Maria spends an entire evening watching a movie with her family and does not pull her hair.

Finally, the counselor helps her symbolically rehearse not pulling her hair when she is alone in her room, when she is with her family, and when she sees her friends. Maria slowly starts resisting the urge to pull her hair when she is alone and with others, putting her hands in her pockets until the urge passes.

Resources

Azrin, N. H., & Peterson, A. L. (1988). Habit reversal for the treatment of Tourette syndrome. *Behaviour Research and Therapy, 26*(4), 347–351. doi:10.1016/0005-7967(88)90089-7

Woods, D. W., & Miltenberger, R. G. (1995). Habit reversal: A review of applications and variations. *Journal of Behavior Therapy and Experimental Psychiatry, 26*(2), 123–131. doi:10.1016/0005-7916(95)00009-O

Impulse Control Training

Definition

Impulse control training is a therapeutic intervention that aims to decrease involuntary urges towards a behavior.

Description

Impulse control problems may be manifested as individual behaviors (e.g., gambling), as psychological disorders (e.g., Kleptomania), or as a component of a psychiatric disorder (e.g., ADHD). Individuals with impulse control issues have difficulty resisting involuntary, maladaptive urges that are typically destructive to the self or others. After a thorough assessment of the behaviors and their preceding thoughts and feelings, the counselor trains the client to control the impulses using cognitive and behavioral strategies.

Indications and Contraindications

Impulse control training can be used for Intermittent Explosive Disorder, Kleptomania and other impulse control disorders, gambling, substance abuse, Attention Deficit Hyperactivity Disorder, Trichotillomania, skin-picking disorder, nail biting, compulsive spending, and personality disorders.

Treatment Protocol

1. First the counselor assesses the client's impulsive behaviors as well as the thoughts and feelings that frequently tend to lead to these impulses.
2. Next, the counselor helps the client become aware of his/her patterns of thoughts and feelings and how they lead to maladaptive behaviors. The counselor enlists the client to keep a journal of thoughts and feelings associated with these behaviors.
3. Third, the counselor teaches the client a competing response to the impulse. The counselor then has the client activate an impulse and use the competing response to neutralize the impulse.
4. The client is encouraged to repeat this process until impulses are controlled for increasingly longer periods. The counselor may give the client feedback as the client practices controlling impulses.

Illustration

Janice is a 28-year-old female diagnosed with Intermittent Explosive Disorder. She presents to therapy after an incident in which she threw her plate against the wall at a restaurant. Janice reports she was angered by something the waiter said and reacted the way she did because she had "no time to think." Janice admits this is a recurring problem.

The counselor assesses the thoughts and feelings that lead to Janice's aggressive impulses and finds they are most often connected to Janice perceiving someone is disrespecting her. The counselor helps her understand the pattern of her thoughts and their relation to her behavior. Janice begins keeping a journal of her thoughts and impulses and the counselor uses this to further illustrate the connection between the two.

The counselor teaches Janice how to use soothing self-talk and environmental changes as competing responses to her impulses. The counselor has her activate an aggressive impulse in session, by thinking about her interaction with the waiter, and then neutralize the impulse by taking ten deep breaths and telling herself, "I don't have to get angry." Janice practices this until she can control her impulses for increasingly longer periods of time. One evening while having dinner at her parents' home, her mother criticizes her clothing. Janice identifies her thoughts and feelings and controls her aggressive impulse using calming self-talk and going outside for a 15-minute walk.

Resource

Grant, J. E., Donahue, C. B., & Odlaug, B. L. (2011). *Treating impulse control disorders: A cognitive-behavioral therapy program*. New York, NY: Oxford University Press.

Interpersonal Skills Training

Definition

Interpersonal skills training is a behavioral intervention that encompasses a range of skills that promote interpersonal effectiveness.

Description

Interpersonal skills training refers to a range of proficiencies that include assertiveness, conflict resolution, and communication skills. The training also aims to minimize maladaptive and aversive behaviors that may inhibit social interaction. Development of adaptive interpersonal skills typically facilitates improved social support that acts as a protective factor against a host of psychological and physiological symptoms.

Skills training is individualized and based on the client's level of functioning and focuses heavily on cognitive flexibility and production of novel responses to promote interpersonal effectiveness. Interpersonal effectiveness is defined as the ability to coordinate and apply a complex combination of social skills to facilitate interaction, maintain relationships, cope with interpersonal conflicts, and manage social goals in a variety of cultural contexts. Adaptive interpersonal skills should help the individual achieve goals that are compatible with their values and allow the individual to maintain self-respect.

Indications and Contraindications

Interpersonal skills training can be implemented with a variety of individuals with interpersonal skill deficits. Skills, however, should be evaluated within the context of cultural norms and adaptive skills should be compatible with the individual's values and allow for the maintenance of self-respect.

Treatment Protocol

1. First, the counselor evaluates the client's current level of skills and interpersonal functioning across the different contexts, including assertiveness, communication, etc. Role-play and simulation can facilitate assessment. The counselor assesses the client's skills within a cultural context and identifies potential behavioral alternatives.
2. Second, the counselor helps the client with acquisition of adaptive skills through psychoeducation, instruction, modeling, and shaping.
3. Third, the client practices the behaviors in session through rehearsal and role-play and the counselor provides constructive feedback and coaching.
4. Fourth, the client practices the new skills in different situations and can continue the coaching with the counselor. The client uses the news skills to build positive social relationships and minimizes situations and consequences that reinforce maladaptive behaviors.

Illustration

Daphne is a 31-year-old female graduate student who self-refers to counseling because of being "frazzled and run down." She reports she spends so much time taking care of her mother that her grades have started suffering. She reports that in one week she had to drive an hour each way to her mother's house to help with grocery shopping and chores, pick her friend up at the airport, and cover her coworker's shift, leaving her no time to do her homework. Daphne says she is angry but doesn't know how to say "no." She reports that once in a while she "blows up" at her mother but still does what is asked of her.

The counselor evaluates Daphne's current level of skills and interpersonal functioning and finds she has difficulty communicating her needs and emotions. The counselor teaches her that by not communicating her feelings, she deprives others the opportunity to understand her. This results in Daphne bottling up her feelings, only to explode later on. The counselor engages Daphne in behavioral rehearsal where she role-plays assertiveness and communication skills, starting with role-plays regarding her mother. The counselor models the skills and provides her with constructive feedback during the role-play.

Daphne continues practicing these interpersonal skills and tells her mother she cannot complete all the chores she asks her to do every week. She communicates her feelings to her mother assertively and finds she feels less angry and does not blow up if she allows herself to get in touch with her feelings. She now uses her new skills to set boundaries and communicate her needs and feelings effectively.

Resource

Linehan, M., & Ebrary, I. (2015). *DBT skills training manual* (2nd ed.). New York, NY: Guilford Press.

Mindfulness

Definition

Mindfulness is awareness of one's internal states and surroundings without judgment.

It can be used as a therapeutic intervention to reduce stress, anxiety, mood symptoms, and mindless action.

Description

Mindfulness originated in Buddhist and Christian meditative practices and has since been used to relieve symptoms of cognitive distress, improve self-management, reduce automatic behavior and improve purposeful behavior, and allow individuals to recognize impending relapse or mood symptoms and then utilize coping skills to manage these occurrences. Today, mindfulness is commonly employed as a meditative technique, as a skills training intervention, or as a component of other interventions. It can be taught in a group or individual setting, and is a core intervention in both Dialectical Behavior Therapy and Mindfulness-Based Cognitive Therapy.

Mindfulness encourages awareness and observation of thoughts, sensations, and mood states without active engagement with or judgment of them. The individual brings awareness to current bodily sensations, emotional responses, states of mind, thoughts, and mental images, as well as remains fully present in the moment without trying to escape these sensations, observing and describing them as objective facts. For example, one might observe physical symptoms of anxiety and describe, "My throat feels tight right now."

Indications and Contraindications

Mindfulness can be used for chronic pain, cancer and other illnesses, anxiety disorders, mood disorders, eating disorders, substance abuse, and personality disorders.

Treatment Protocol

1. First, the counselor instructs the client to observe thoughts without labeling or describing them. The client may complete homework that allows them to observe thoughts, feelings, and sensations. For example, the client can complete a daily activity such as eating. The client should focus on the smells, texture, temperature, physical sensations, etc. during the experience.
2. Second, the client is encouraged to describe thoughts and sensations as they arise (e.g., "The cucumber is cold on my tongue") without making judgments (e.g., "I don't like it"). The counselor instructs the client to make a running commentary on events and experiences without judgment.
3. Third, the counselor instructs the client to give full attention to every experience, focusing 100% of their attention to that experience.
4. Finally, the client is expected to practice mindfulness techniques daily, either as a continuous meditation or during everyday activities.

Illustration

Jamie is a 23-year-old graduate student who reports stress and anxiety related to pressure from school and a separation from her boyfriend. She reports frequent headaches, insomnia, and tension in her neck and shoulders, also stating that her increased stress makes it difficult for her to concentrate on her schoolwork. Jamie states she would like some practical tools for managing her stress during her busy schedule.

The counselor explains the concepts of mindfulness to Jamie and has her practice the technique of observing without judgment. The counselor gives Jamie homework to observe her feelings and sensations without judgment. As part of the homework, she practices mindfully eating a slice of apple, noticing the cool sensation, the crunching texture and sound, and the subtle sweetness without attributing meaning to the observations.

During the second week, the counselor has Jamie recount an incident at work by specifying only facts and not making judgments. Jamie reports her coworker "told a story" instead of saying she "tried to waste everyone's time." Jamie practices these observations daily for the next two weeks.

Finally, the counselor instructs Jamie to practice remaining in the present and giving her complete attention to any current task. Jamie continues to practice daily and eventually notices she is now slower to react and feels less stressed.

Resources

Crane, R. (2009). *Mindfulness-based cognitive therapy: Distinctive features.* New York, NY: Routledge.

Forsyth, J. P., & Eifert, G. H. (2007). *The mindfulness and acceptance workbook for anxiety.* Oakland, CA: New Harbinger Publications, Inc.

Problem Solving Training

Definition

Problem solving training is a behavioral intervention that helps individuals build skills to cope with distressing situations.

Description

Problem solving training is based on the premise that increasing levels of social skill will lead to a decrease in emotional and behavioral symptoms and that adaptive problem solving strategies can be learned. This intervention teaches individuals to identify and systematically solve problems with skills they can continue to apply in the future. Individuals are trained to systematically find ways to either alter a problem or their distressing responses to a problem, or both.

Effective problem solving is the adaptive method of understanding a problem and systematically searching for and applying solutions as opposed to acting out the maladaptive impulsive or avoidant styles. Problem solving training involves identification of problematic situations, generation of alternatives, decision-making, and implementation phases. During the problem-identification phase, the counselor helps the individual describe and define the problem, identify causative factors, and set realistic goals. When defining the problem, the individual should be thorough, use clear language, delineate between facts and assumptions, and identify feeling cues associated with the problem. The individual is encouraged to view the problem from a different perspective so that they can generate alternatives.

Indications and Contraindications

Problem solving training can be used with children, adolescents, and adults for a variety of concerns, though it is believed the intervention is less effective as a preventative therapy. Problem solving training can be applied in individual, couple, or group contexts. This technique is useful for externalizing disorders that include impulsivity, aggression, relational problems, anger, and antisocial behaviors. It is also useful for internalizing disorders including depression, anxiety, and social anxiety. When generating alternative behaviors, the counselor should take care not to be judgmental of ineffective proposed alternatives, as the point of this exercise is to improve flexibility. Caution should be taken, however, if the client proposes alternatives that are harmful or destructive.

Treatment Protocol

1. First, the counselor assesses the client's current problem solving skills related to problem identification, goal setting, generating alternatives, decision-making, and implementation.
2. Second, the counselor processes a specific problem with the client. The client is encouraged to describe the problem in detail and put the ambiguous aspects into words. The counselor asks focused questions to help the client identify emotions and feeling cues associated with the problem. The client is then encouraged to view the problem from different perspectives.
3. Third, the counselor guides the client through generating alternatives. The client and counselor develop a list of alternatives. The counselor takes a nonjudgmental stance and encourages the client to brainstorm a number of possible solutions.
4. Fourth, the client evaluates each of the alternatives and their potential consequences and decides on a course of action. If the proposed solution requires a level of skill (e.g., communication) the client does not possess, skills training may be utilized. The counselor and client can role-play the solution to be implemented and the counselor can provide feedback and model behavior.
5. Finally, the client implements the chosen solution. If results are not satisfactory, the client can choose another alternative from the list.

Illustration

Indira is a 31-year-old sales associate who sought counseling for being overwhelmed with professional and personal demands. As a result her job performance has suffered and she fears that she might be fired. She also reports having hurriedly made some investment decisions that her boyfriend suggested three months ago. She indicates that she lost a considerable sum of money and now regrets that decision. Her boss wants her to consider taking a new position with her company that is on the other side of town. The upside is that there is a raise and the downside is that it would double her commute time.

The counselor assesses Indira's current problem solving skills related to problem identification, goal setting, generating alternatives, decision-making, and implementation. The counselor finds that Indira is able to identify her problems but has difficulty setting goals, generating alternatives, and deciding on them. The counselor then has Indira describe her concern about the job offer. The counselor has her expand on the details and describe her feelings of being fearful and overwhelmed.

Indira then generates four alternatives for her problem and weighs the potential consequences of each. She decides to implement the alternative of telling her boss that she has decided to turn down the job offer. She and the counselor engage in behavioral rehearsal in which she role-plays how she will tell her boss. Indira implemented the alternative and found her boss to be understanding and supportive, while she feels more confident and comfortable with her decision.

Resources

D'Zurilla, T. J., & Nezu, A. M. (2007). *Problem-solving therapy: A positive approach to clinical intervention* (3rd ed.). New York, NY: Springer.
Haley, J. (1987). *Problem-solving therapy* (2nd ed.). San Francisco, CA: Jossey-Bass.

Relapse Prevention

Definition

Relapse prevention is a therapeutic intervention used to assist an individual in maintaining treatment gains, including sobriety, and reducing relapse in the face of everyday stressors and high-risk situations.

Description

According to relapse prevention theory, the quality of an individual's coping skills largely determines whether an individual will relapse (lapse from healthy to unhealthy behavior) or maintain their treatment gains. When faced with a distressing life event, such as the loss of a job or a loved one's illness, employing effective coping strategies will lead to an increase in perceived self-efficacy and a decrease in the likelihood of relapse. Relapse prevention aims to increase coping skills and client self-efficacy. On the other hand, an individual who employs ineffective coping mechanisms in response to similar events will experience a decrease in perceived self-efficacy and be more likely to relapse. In short, relapse prevention aims to increase coping skills and client self-efficacy.

Relapse prevention typically involves relapse education, identification of warning signs and high-risk situations, learning effective coping skills, challenging irrational beliefs, adjusting expectations, and creating a toolkit that includes social support, self-care, and avoidance of relapse triggers. Ultimately, relapse prevention constitutes a change in lifestyle that promotes a positive and healthy way of being.

Indications and Contraindications

While relapse prevention was initially used with individuals in recovery for substance abuse, it is now used for many other presenting problems ranging from eating disorders, anxiety disorders, smoking, and self-harm. Relapse prevention plans should be tailored to each individual and should start by focusing on basics (e.g., "not using today") for individuals who just completed detox and are still cognitively affected by their substance use.

Treatment Protocol

1. First, the counselor assesses the client's patterns of use, coping skills, self-efficacy, expectations, and readiness for change. The client and counselor make a list of the client's high-risk situations, such as potentially stressful events the client finds intolerable and people and places known to trigger use.
2. Next, the counselor educates the client on relapse and relapse prevention. The client and counselor evaluate the high-risk situations and how they result in relapse. The counselor helps the client identify and challenge irrational beliefs about use and dispel myths that use will provide emotional relief.
3. The client and counselor make an inventory of warning signs of relapse, including major stressors as well as cumulative small stressors. Clients are encouraged to address initial small stressors instead of waiting for the final stressor that results in their breaking point.
4. The client and counselor make a relapse prevention plan and toolkit that includes maintenance through continued therapy, 12-step meetings,

social support and a list of people to call, a list of people and places to avoid, the use of a sponsor, and improved self-care.

5. The client implements a lifestyle change that includes taking care of one's health, exercise, engaging in pleasurable hobbies, partaking in stress-relieving activities such as mediation and yoga, participating in positive social interactions and maintaining a social network, and avoiding places and people associated with use. The client is also encouraged to take inventory of warning signs daily and follow up with the counselor as needed.

Illustration

Jackson is a 31-year-old Caucasian male currently completing inpatient treatment for moderate Alcohol Use Disorder. Jackson reported he had maintained two years of sobriety but relapsed when his coworker was fired and Jackson was forced to do more work. He stated that using alcohol is the only thing that helps him "really calm down and take my mind off work." Jackson's recent relapse led to him drinking so heavily after work that he began coming to work late, hung over, or still under the influence. After arriving to work under the influence, Jackson was reprimanded by his boss and referred to treatment. Jackson stated his weekly schedule consists of work and then drinking until he passes out. He does not exercise, spend time with friends, or engage in any other hobbies.

The counselor assesses Jackson's patterns of use, coping skills, self-efficacy, expectations, and readiness. The counselor finds Jackson uses alcohol as his primary coping mechanism and his use is triggered by stress. He appears highly motivated to stop using, as he is concerned about his job, but expresses uncertainty about his ability to maintain sobriety and expects he will probably fail. The counselor and Jackson make a list of high-risk situations and Jackson identifies stress at work, loneliness, and financial stress as his high-risk stressors.

The counselor educates Jackson on relapse prevention and together they trace back his recent relapse as a culmination of spending more time at work, feeling he could not speak up to his boss, and cutting positive lifestyle choices such as exercise from his life. The counselor helps Jackson recognize the irrationality of his belief that alcohol is the only way to find emotional relief. He also helps Jackson identify how he previously maintained sobriety through yoga, time with friends, and attending 12-step meetings.

With the counselor, Jackson makes a plan to attend 12-step meetings, participate in yoga, avoid his favorite bars and drinking buddies, and surround himself with positive social support. Jackson makes a list of phone numbers of people he can call when he is feeling low. Upon completing treatment, he follows through with his plan and takes an inventory of warning signs every morning and evening. At a follow-up session in a month, he reports he is taking a photography class and has joined a group of photographers who meet weekly at a local community center. Jackson reports he feels more effective at maintaining his sobriety.

Resources

Gorski, T., & Miller, M. (1986). *Staying sober: A guide for relapse prevention.* Aspen, CO: Independence Press.

Marlatt, G. A., Donovan, D. (2005). *Relapse prevention, second edition: Maintenance strategies in the treatment of addictive behaviors.* New York, NY: Guilford Press.

Social Skills Training

Definition

Social skills training is a behavioral intervention with a cognitive component that helps individuals develop or increase their social skills to facilitate healthier social interaction.

Description

Social skills training is a useful intervention for reducing social impairment and improving social skills in children, adolescents, and adults. It can be provided through either individual or group counseling, or both. Treatment includes minimizing undesirable behavior while increasing prosocial behavior. Social skills vary by culture and context but most frequently include approaching others (smiling, shaking hands), making conversation, sharing, taking turns, making eye contact, using the appropriate speech volume and tone, and displaying appropriate emotional responses.

Indications and Contraindications

This intervention is appropriate for children, adolescents, and adults and useful for Social Phobia, Autism, Attention Deficit Hyperactivity Disorder (ADHD), Schizophrenia Spectrum Disorders, and non-clinical individuals seeking to improve their social skills. It can be administered in individual or group therapy settings. It is not a stand-alone therapy but an adjunct to other treatments. Counselors must be careful to pace social skills training correctly and not to begin instruction without sufficient client assessment. Care should also be used in evaluating normative behaviors in context and counselors should pay attention to cultural differences and discrimination. Competing behaviors that interfere with optimal skills should be addressed. Children with ADHD comorbid with Oppositional Defiant Disorder have been shown not to respond as well to social skills training. Additionally, children with problem behaviors placed in SST groups with other behaviorally disordered children may show worsening in behavior because of peer contagion effects.

Treatment Protocol

1. First, the counselor evaluates the client and assesses current level of social skills, identifies targeted behaviors within a social and cultural context, and the disparity between current and targeted skills. The counselor may assess the client through observation, role-play, and one-way mirrors.
2. Next, the client and counselor set goals for desired behaviors and the counselor decides on intervention methods based on the assessment. Training should be a progression towards increasingly challenging goals.
3. Third, the counselor provides instruction for the target behavior either verbally or in written, video, or audio format. The counselor then models the behavior, bringing attention to specific details (e.g., tone of voice and nonverbal behaviors). Modeling may also be conducted in person or through written, video, or audio format.
4. Next, the client rehearses the behavior through role-play. The counselor coaches the client through rehearsal, providing corrective feedback as well as praise. Praise is extended for approximations of the desired behavior.
5. The client may also need relaxation training and cognitive restructuring for self-defeating thoughts, and is encouraged to deliver self-praise.
6. Next, the client is assigned homework that includes practicing the behavior, using positive self-statements, and keeping a log of behaviors to monitor progress.
7. Finally, generalization and maintenance of the behavior is encouraged through self-monitoring and self-reinforcement.

Illustration

Zack is an 18-year-old Caucasian male diagnosed with Autism Spectrum Disorder, Level 1, who self-referred to counseling, stating he feels depressed because he has no friends. He also states he would like to date but has no opportunities to talk to girls. The counselor assesses Zack's interaction during the clinical interview and through a role-play. The counselor observes that Zack fails to make eye contact, has limited speech duration (displayed through one-word answers), voice volume (raising his voice to give answers), and failure to display appropriate emotional response (not smiling when meeting someone). The counselor discussed treatment goals with Zack and decided on a course of social skills training.

The counselor gives instructions for appropriate behaviors to bridge the gap between Zack's displayed and targeted behaviors. The counselor then models the appropriate behavior in person (e.g., simulates approaching someone and introducing himself). The counselor brings attention to his posture, eye contact, relaxed demeanor, and speech tone and volume. Zack then rehearses the behavior and the counselor provides corrective feedback on Zack's eye contact and limited speech duration. Zack then holds eye contact for several seconds before averting his eyes and the counselor praises him for the increased eye contact.

After practicing 10 scenarios that involve the appropriate behaviors, Zack demonstrates improved ability to approach and make conversation with someone. Zack states he feels nervous speaking to strangers and thinks he is being judged. The counselor provides relaxation training (deep breathing) and cognitive restructuring. Zack practices the behaviors with people in his classes and keeps a log of his interactions. He reports being able to approach someone at his school's recreation center and asking to partake in a game of pool. As instructed by the counselor, Zack praises himself for his accomplishment and engages in positive self-statements such as, "you can do it" when he feels doubtful.

In the sixth session, Zack is encouraged to role-play asking a girl out on a date. He is coached in smiling and sustained eye contact. He also practices exchanging phone numbers and setting a date and time to meet. The counselor encourages Zack to continue to generalize his new behaviors to other contexts and consistently monitor and praise himself.

Resources

Bellack, A. S. (2004). *Social skills training for schizophrenia: A step-by-step guide* (2nd ed.). New York, NY: Guilford Press.

Kelly, J. A. (1982). *Social-skills training: A practical guide for interventions.* New York, NY: Springer.

LeCroy, C. W. (1983). *Social skills training for children and youth.* New York, NY: Haworth Press.

Liberman, R. P., DeRisi, W. J., & Mueser, K. T. (1989). *Social skills training for psychiatric patients.* New York, NY: Pergamon Press.

Thought Stopping

Definition

Thought stopping is a therapeutic intervention used to interrupt and replace distressing, ruminative thoughts.

Description

Thought stopping is an intervention that aims to interrupt, remove, and replace distressing thoughts. Originally designed for use with obsessive thoughts, thought stopping assumes that interruption of obsessive thoughts will decrease their frequency and, in turn, the anxiety associated with them. While numerous case studies detail client reports of relief from unwanted thoughts using this technique, more research is needed to establish the extent of its efficacy.

Indications and Contraindications

Thought stopping can be used for obsessive thoughts associated with obsessive-compulsive disorder, psychotic symptoms, depression, panic, generalized anxiety, tobacco use, drug and alcohol use, and body dysmorphic disorder. It can be used as either a stand-alone or auxiliary treatment. Little empirical evidence exists to support thought stopping as an efficacious technique. Suppression of obsessions in clients with obsessive-compulsive disorder has been shown to increase the frequency and intensity of these thoughts. Additionally, development of obsessions has been linked to suppression of unwanted thoughts. Therefore, thought suppression may be an ineffective, or even detrimental, technique for individuals with obsessive-compulsive disorder.

Treatment Protocol

1. First, the counselor assesses the client's symptoms and behaviors. The client and counselor generate a list of the client's common distressing thoughts. Thoughts are ranked in a hierarchy from least to most distressing. Thought stopping practice will progress from the least to the most distressing thought. The distressing thoughts are discussed as well as the reason for suppressing them.
2. The client is asked to close his eyes and focus on the distressing thought. The client is instructed to raise a finger when he is focused on the thought. When the client raises his finger, the counselor yells, "Stop!" The command is meant to startle the client. The counselor and client repeat this for either about 10 minutes or 20 repetitions.
3. The client then practices the technique by saying "Stop!" aloud or in his head when a disturbing thought manifests. The client may modify the procedure by replacing the "Stop!" command with a word other than "stop," snapping a rubber band on the wrist, or picturing a stop sign. The counselor can help the client generate a more pleasant thought to replace the suppressed thought.

Illustration

Jasmine is a 48-year-old African-American woman who self-refers to counseling because of anxiety. She reports having distressing thoughts that seem to spiral out of control and leave her feeling immobilized with overwhelming anxiety. She expresses worry that there is something wrong with her because of the disturbing nature of her thoughts.

The counselor assesses Jasmine and assures her that disturbing thoughts are common and most people experience them at some point in their lives. Jasmine is relieved and states she would like to rid herself of the upsetting thoughts. The counselor helps Jasmine write a hierarchy of her disturbing thoughts from least to most distressing. She lists (1) she will be fired from her job; (2) she will become ill, leaving no one to care for her children; and (3) her children will die in a house fire.

The counselor instructs Jasmine to close her eyes and focus on her first distressing thought: she will be fired from her job. As instructed, Jasmine raises a finger when she is focused on the thought. The counselor yells, "Stop!" The command startles Jasmine and the counselor explains that she cannot focus on two thoughts at once—both the distressing thought and the "Stop" command. Then the procedure is repeated 19 more times until she reports feeling more comfortable with the technique. The counselor helps her think of a more pleasant thought to focus on each time she suppresses the unwanted thought.

Jasmine then practices the "Stop" command outside of sessions when she experiences the distressing thought. She imagines herself hugging her children during a happy memory every time she suppresses her disturbing thought. She and the counselor eventually repeat the same procedure for each of her targeted disturbing thoughts.

Resources

McKay, M., Davis, M., & Fanning, P. (2012). *Thoughts and feelings: Taking control of your moods and your life* (4th ed.). Oakland, CA: New Harbinger Publications.

Wolpe, J., & Lazarus, A. A. (1966). *Behavior therapy techniques: A guide to the treatment of neuroses*. New York, NY: Pergamon Press.

Yamagami, T. (1971). The treatment of an obsession by thought-stopping. *Journal of Behavior Therapy and Experimental Psychiatry*, 2(2), 133–135. doi:10.1016/0005–7916(71)90028–0

Concluding Note

You have now been introduced to 13 common interventions that many counselors find useful in their everyday counseling practices. Whether they are counseling interns or experienced counselors, they find that they routinely utilize these interventions. We invite you to learn more about them. If you are an intern in a clinic or agency setting, consider how a particular intervention may be a good "fit" for a client. Seek out the advice and support of a supervisor, apply it to that case, and then evaluate the results. If you are an experienced counselor, you might attend a workshop or watch a video about one or more interventions that might be a good "fit" for a client. You might also want to seek consultation with a colleague with expertise in the interventions. Then apply it and evaluate it.

Chapter 6

Diversity and CBT Practice

Multicultural awareness and sensitivity are significant values in the counseling profession today. Cultural sensitivity is just as important in Cognitive Behavior Therapy (CBT) practice. Because counselors are expected to demonstrate sensitivity to diversity and cultural issues, the effective implementation of CBT interventions not only expects such sensitivity, but requires it.

This chapter begins with a case vignette, which will be referenced throughout the chapter to illustrate various concepts about diversity issues in CBT practice. Then Culturally Responsive CBT (CR-CBT) will be highlighted and diversity in CBT practice will be discussed, followed by a review of CBT implications among several minority populations. And finally, assessment of cultural factors and cultural case conceptualization are emphasized through an extensive case example, as well as culturally responsive cognitive and behavioral interventions.

Case of Julia

Julia is a 17-year-old first-generation Mexican-American female who was referred for counseling because of a three-month episode of depressed mood and several binge drinking episodes. She is conflicted about her decision to relocate for college next year instead of staying home and taking care of her terminally ill mother. Her family expects her to stay home, while she feels torn about wanting to move to college to pursue her dream job of becoming a nurse. She is angry at her older sister who left home at 17 after her parents insisted that she take care of them when they get old or become ill. Her Anglo friends encourage her to go to college and pursue her dreams.

Culturally Responsive CBT

Culturally Responsive CBT (CR-CBT) was developed by Pamela Hays to help practitioners provide counseling in a manner that is more responsive to clients from minority groups and various cultures. Actually, CBT is uniquely suited to multicultural counseling practice in five ways.

> First, CBT emphasizes the need to conduct case conceptualization and tailor interventions to each client's unique situation, and this position counters stereotypical thinking regarding members of minority identities. Second, CBT emphasizes clients' expertise regarding themselves and their ability to learn and apply skills in the future without the need for a therapist. The emphasis communicates respect, and respect is a key value held by members of many minority cultures. Third, CBT emphasizes conscious processes that can be described and taught. This approach is primarily important with clients who are less verbal or who have limited language proficiency and with individuals who come from cultures where the unconscious is not a commonly understood concept. Fourth, CBT focuses on a holistic understanding of clients including cultural strengths and supports that can be used to reinforce desired change. This recognition of culturally based resilience factors is also empowering and shows respect. Fifth, CBT is firmly rooted in behaviorism, which focuses on the influence of environments on behavior. Culture is a foundational part of social and physical environments and as such can be incorporated into CBT.
>
> (Wenzel, Dobson, & Hays, 2016, p. 147)

This approach utilizes CBT strategies while modifying them to fit the client's cultural identity, cultural context, and overall treatment expectations and preferences. Some key components of CR-CBT include emphasizing culturally bound strengths and social supports, acceptance of core cultural beliefs, and the use of validation to support clients who have experienced oppression (Hays, 2016). Thought modification is approached differently than traditional Cognitive Therapy in which counselors help clients to consider the helpfulness of their thoughts versus examining the rationality or validity of such thoughts. CR-CBT concepts will be incorporated into the intervention portion of this chapter to emphasize how CBT counselors can effectively work with diverse clients in various contexts.

Counseling and Diversity: In General and in CBT

Today CBT counselors are charged with working with very diverse client populations. They are expected to provide high-quality counseling services with individuals from diverse nationalities, sexual orientations, gender identities, disabilities, religions, ethnic cultures, socioeconomic classes, and ages. To provide evidence of this, the 2010 Census reported that over one-third of the U.S. population included individuals of ethnic minority cultures such as African and African-American, Pacific Islander, Middle Eastern, Asian, and South Asian (U.S. Census, 2011). Given the widespread use of CBT approaches today, counselors need to be aware of cultural considerations when using CBT among various client populations. This is consistent with the shifting values of the various mental health disciplines over the past four decades. For example, in 1973 the American Psychological Association's board of trustees voted to eliminate homosexuality as a diagnosis in the Diagnostic and Statistical Manual of Mental Disorders (DSM, Greenberg, 1997). As the counseling profession becomes more inclusive of various cultural groups, the CBT models are well suited for multicultural use due to their flexible and eclectic nature.

Diversity and cultural awareness have been increasingly embraced within counseling training programs in the past decade. This is particularly evident in required graduate-level course work in which cultural awareness is the primary focus. While cultural awareness is a necessary condition, it is by no means the sufficient condition for effective treatment. Sufficient conditions include cultural sensitivity, cultural awareness, cultural competence, and awareness of personal biases.

Cultural competence is demonstrated by the capacity to achieve culturally sensitive therapeutic relationships, cultural formulations and culturally informed treatment plans, as well as positive treatment outcomes with diverse individuals. How culturally sensitive and competent are counseling trainees and professional counselors? Available data that answers this question is somewhat sobering. A study of practicing therapists found that the overwhelming majority believed that it was most important to develop cultural formulations and also important to use these culturally sensitive case conceptualizations to guide their clinical practice. In other words, there is a high level of cultural awareness. However, very few clinicians—about 14%—reported that they actually developed or used these formulations to guide their clinical practice (Hansen, Randazzo, Schwartz et al., 2006), suggesting that cultural sensitivity and competence among those practitioners was low. Trainees seem to share a similar fate (Neufield et al., 2006). Because cultural sensitivity and cultural competence increasingly will be expected of counselors, the need for additional training in this core competency is becoming more pressing. This chapter addresses this need.

In terms of cultural competence in counseling practice, D'Andrea and Daniels (2001) articulated a multicultural framework that includes a list of cultural factors in their RESPECTFUL model:

RESPECTFUL

R Religious values
E Economic/class issues
S Sexual identity issues
P Psychological developmental issues
E Ethnic/racial identity issues
C Chronological
T Trauma and threats to well-being
F Family issues
U Unique physical issues
L Language and location of residence issues

Likewise, Hays (1996, pp. 332–334) established a model that outlines a similar cultural framework in her ADDRESSING model:

ADDRESSING

A Age/generational
D Disability (developmental)
D Disability (acquired)
R Religion
E Ethnicity/race
S Social status
S Sexual orientation
I Indigenous heritage
N National origin
G Gender

Both of the models provide a framework that counselors can use to guide the assessment process and a system for counselors to complete their own self-assessment to assess their own biases, power, and privilege, as well as to examine how these dynamics can and do influence the counseling process. These cultural factors were highlighted by the American Counseling Association (Arrendondo & Perez, 2006) and the American Psychological Association (2003) because of their historical neglect.

A competent CBT counselor will seek to maximize their rapport with clients from diverse backgrounds by seeking familiarity and education about customs, rituals, and cultural information that are very important to their non-majority clients. Newman (2013) offered examples of incorporating this cultural understanding in CBT practice by encouraging a non-Jewish practitioner to inquire about the shiva that recently took place in the home of a Jewish client who is receiving counseling for bereavement; or when a non-Hispanic counselor is working with a Latina client, they can display an understanding and appreciation of a client's preoccupation with organizing her daughter's quinceañera. This awareness and sensitivity shows the interest and effort that should be practiced when working with client from a culture from which the counselor does not belong. The next section will discuss assessing cultural dynamics in CBT counseling practice.

Assessing Cultural Dynamics

How should counselors go about understanding a client and the influence of their culture? Some counselors believe that their clients should educate them about their culture from their perspective. Wenzel, Dobson, and Hays noted, "it is unfair to expect clients to educate therapists about their culture. In addition, reliance on the clients alone for cultural information is risky because such descriptions are likely to hold biases" (2016, p. 150). Although receiving information from the client about their culture is very useful, counselors are responsible for educating themselves about various cultures and cultural histories. Hays (2009) noted that counselors should not assume that they know an individual's race or ethnicity based on the client's appearance, but that it is important to ask the client to self-identify. Counselors are charged with being aware of common cultural values, cultural views of mental health issues, and common perceptions about how various populations perceive being a consumer of counseling services. For example, European-American individuals often value independence, while individuals from Asian cultures often place high value on cooperation and interdependence.

Becoming a culturally competent CBT counselor requires the knowledge, skills, and attitudes to perform an accurate cultural assessment (Sperry, 2010). Such an assessment will examine the following areas: cultural identity; age; gender and sexual orientation; ethnicity and race; migration and country of origin; religion; socioeconomic status; language; explanatory model and illness perceptions; level of acculturation; dietary influences; and education (GAP Committee on Cultural Psychiatry, 2002). Typically, practitioners assess and report only three of these 12 factors: age, gender, and ethnicity. For example, the first sentence in the "Identifying Information and Chief Complaint" section of a clinical report usually begins with a statement of age, ethnicity, and gender: "This is a 17-year-old Mexican-American female." Although gender may be specified, sexual orientation is infrequently indicated. Three other dynamics are either assumed or specified somewhere else in a clinical report. These are: language, SES, and education. This means that the remaining five of the 12 dynamics of culture are not assessed or addressed at all by most counselors. Eliciting information regarding the listed cultural factors can be accomplished in approximately seven to eight minutes. This information can be valuable in understanding the clients coping and cultural and social resources as well as in treatment planning and treatment implementation (Ridley & Kelly, 2007).

CBT With Diverse Populations

This section provides suggestions for working with clients from various populations; it will review some of the recent empirical support examining the use of CBT among various cultures. We are in no way suggesting that individuals from each culture discussed below are homogenous; rather, we are merely providing a starting point to consider some common dynamics that may arise when working with clients from several cultural groups. Each cultural group shares various traditions, language, values, moral and religious values, and social norms. Several examples of different cultural groups are listed below with some clinical insights that counselors should consider when working with these groups.

The Asian-American Culture and CBT

It is important to note that each culture clearly has different subgroups with their own norms and traditions. Different Asian nationalities include Chinese, Japanese, Pacific Islanders, Taiwanese, Haiwaiians, Vietnamese, and Filipinos (Iwamasa, Hsia, & Hinton, 2006). Sue and Sue (2008) identified that Asian-American clients respond positively to concrete strategies and clear goals in counseling. They also identified that Solution-Focused Brief Therapy and CBT are often well-received by these individuals. Hwang (2006) offers a framework for utilizing CBT with clients from various cultures, including Chinese-Americans. For example, Hwang and Wood discussed that CBT typically assists individuals with modifying negative self-talk, while such negative self-talk may be viewed as a motivating factor to achieve goals in Chinese cultures (2007).

The Latino Culture and CBT

Latino clients are either born in the United States or are born in countries such as Cuba, Mexico, and other Southern and Central American countries (Organitsa, 2006). Some common values to consider when working with Latino and Latina clients are *personalismo* and *familismo*. The value on personal relationships, or *personalismo*, is a significant dynamic for counselors to consider before moving towards the task-oriented process of CBT. This can be fostered by emphasizing relationship building and offering personalized attention before transitioning to the working phase of each session (Organista & Muñoz, 1996).

The value of family and collectivist orientation, or *familismo*, are very important in the Latino culture. A white European-American counselor may unintentionally impose their own values on a Latino client to follow their own culture norms, such as individualism and independence. In regard to the case of Julia, she holds the belief "I must be there for my family because I can't let them down," which is a cultural belief and not an irrational belief. A counselor should refrain from encouraging a client to "take care of yourself first" and should consider saying, "You can take better care of your family by taking better care of yourself" (Organista, 2006, p. 81).

Organitsa identified that counselors attempting to increase assertiveness skills with a Latino client should be aware of the cultural norms around conflict and communication (2006). For example, respect (*respeto*) and obedience to authority are significant values among many Latino individuals. Further, Comas-Díaz and Duncan (1985) noted that Latino individuals value smooth and non-confrontational interactions (*sympatía*) when communicating with individuals of different status, such as counselors or employers. When engaging in assertiveness training and role-play enactments with Julia, the counselor should consider her cultural preference to engage in non-confrontational interactions. This might include working with her to communicate with her parents about her preference to attend college in a context where she feels safe and is not experiencing a strong emotional reaction.

LGBTQ and CBT

Counselors who work with LGBTQ individuals are strongly encouraged to assess their personal beliefs, biases, and attitudes about working with this population (Safren & Rogers, 2001). Beyond their own beliefs, they need to be aware of the societal experience of LGBTQ individuals. LGBTQ issues may not be the presenting difficulty that individuals initially demonstrate, but counselors will benefit from being prepared to examine the role that the individual's sexual orientation has in their life.

Balsam, Martel, and Safren (2006) identified some of the following benefits of using CBT with LGBTQ individuals:

- CBT conceptualizations do not view LGBTQ individuals as having any inherent forms of pathology.
- CBT is collaborative in nature, and may give the client a voice that they may not experience in a heterosexist society.
- CBT provides individuals with a range of skills-training approaches to cope with various presenting issues and life stressors.
- CBT can be used to assist LGBTQ individuals to restructure or dispute homophobic beliefs.

Hays (2016) offered the following multicultural adaptations for clinicians to provide culturally sensitive CBT interventions when working with clients from minority groups:

1. Engage in deliberate ongoing cultural self-assessment throughout your training and throughout your career.
2. Identify culturally related strengths and support your clients to identify helpful interpretations and helpful behavioral responses to their presenting difficulties.
3. Validate the client's experience of oppression and other cultural difficulties before implementing thought-changing strategies.
4. Utilize and emphasize collaboration over confrontation, and be mindful of the client-counselor power differential.
5. When implementing cognitive restructuring, examine the helpfulness of beliefs versus the validity of thoughts or beliefs.
6. Don't challenge core cultural beliefs.
7. Develop homework assignments that consider the client's expectations of therapy and also emphasize cultural congruence. Consider referring to homework as "practice."

DSM-5 Assessment of Cultural Factors

The DSM-5 provided culturally focused questions to assist counselors in completing a culturally sensitive formulation. We've incorporated several of the culturally focused DSM-5 assessment questions in a brief transcript with Julia (American Psychiatric Association, 2013):

Counselor: I hear you describing some significant discouragement and confusion about what to do about going off to college with your friends or to stay home and take care of your mother. I am wondering if there are any kinds of support that make your problems better, such as support from family, friends, or others?

Julia: Yeah, I'd say that talking to my aunt who lives in New York really helps me feel better. I feel like she really understands how I feel and she knows how to encourage me. I also feel better when I am praying at home or at church. I've always been a very spiritual person.

Counselor: Those sound like very helpful resources that you have available to you. Have you had the chance to pray lately or speak with your aunt?

Julia: Well I've been so upset lately that I haven't had the chance to, but I will talk to my aunt next week because it's her birthday.

Counselor: That sounds like a good idea. Those seem like helpful steps you could take if you are feeling depressed over the next week. To shift gears a bit, what are the most important aspects of your background or cultural identity?

Julia: Besides loving Mexican food (laughs), I'd say family and close relationships are really important to me. I just get so annoyed that I have put my life on hold to be the caretaker for my mother since she was recently diagnosed with cancer and my dad needs to work full-time to support all of the medical bills.

Counselor: I hear how difficult it must be to feel pulled in two opposing directions.

Julia: Yeah, it doesn't seem like there is an easy solution.

Counselor: I agree that there may not be an easy solution, but hopefully our work together might help relieve some of your concerns (pauses). Some people explain that their problems are caused as the result of having bad luck, problems with other people, biological explanations, or other reasons. What do others in your family, friends or community think is causing your problem?

Julia: I'm not sure, I would guess that my parents think that I am struggling because I haven't been to church in several weeks, they always attribute problems to the devil being involved. They are sort of church freaks. Most of my friends know that I am depressed because I probably won't be able to start college with them this coming fall. I think that I've been feeling depressed because I don't know what will be the best decision for me.

Note how the above questions allowed the counselor to gather a cultural formulation in which they are able to identify how cultural variables cause, influence, or perpetuate the presenting issues. The DSM-5 questions also allowed the counselor to probe for cultural strengths and resources. These questions are a significant improvement from the nonexisting cultural assessments from previous editions of the DSM.

Cultural Formulation

Given the significant role that cultural traditions, practices, beliefs, values, and attitudes can play in the lives of various clients, competent and effective counselors routinely seek to learn various cultural information about their clients during the initial phases of counseling. Such information helps counselors better understand their clients' various cultural issues that contribute to client suffering as well as potential resources and protective factors (Ridley & Kelly, 2007).

At a time when cultural sensitivity and competence are becoming the norm in counseling practice, developing these essential competencies is no longer optional for trainees and practitioners. This section defines cultural formulations and describes four elements useful in specifying such formulations that inform CBT counseling practice (Sperry & Sperry, 2012). Then the case of Julia is used to illustrate the four elements of a cultural formulation.

Definition of Cultural Formulation

A cultural formulation answers the "what role does culture play?" question in a clinical case report or comprehensive case conceptualization. A cultural formulation informs the case conceptualization and also informs the treatment interventions that are utilized. This formulation is a structured summary of cultural factors and dynamics that are typically explained in the "Social History and Cultural Factors" section of a clinical case report (Sperry, 2010). Further, the cultural formulation explains an individual's ethnic or cultural identity, their current level of acculturation, and their cultural explanation (Sperry, 2010). It provides a personal or cultural explanation of the client's condition as well as the influence of cultural factors on the client's personality and overall functioning. Likewise, it forms the basis for anticipating if cultural dynamics may impact the counselor-client relationship, and if culturally sensitive treatment is appropriate (GAP Committee on Cultural Psychiatry, 2002).

Elements of a Cultural Formulation

The cultural formulation consists of four key cultural dynamics: cultural identity, acculturation level and acculturative stress, cultural explanatory model, and the impact of cultural dynamics versus personality dynamics (Sperry & Sperry, 2012).

1. Cultural Identity

The cultural formulation takes shape during the assessment process. As part the "Social and Cultural History" of that assessment, the counselor presumably probes for information on the client's cultural identity (i.e., sense of identification with a cultural or ethnic group). This self-identification is an indicator of their sense of belonging to a particular ethnic group, whether it is their original ethnic group or the mainstream culture. Such attitudes influence an individual's stated ethnic or cultural identity.

For example, a light-skinned, Haitian-American client identifies herself as a "Caucasian-American" to distance herself from what she perceives as negative stereotypes of Haitians and African-Americans. Similarly, in the case of Julia discussed throughout this chapter, she identifies some ties to her Mexican-American culture and identifies having more in common with her Anglo friends. Her Mexican-American identity is limited only to her parents speaking Spanish, Mexican cuisine, and various family traditions.

2. Acculturation and Acculturative Stress

Acculturation is a known stressor and risk factor that can affect the mental health and behavior of individuals adapting to a culture that is different from their culture of origin. This is in contrast with enculturation, which is the process of learning one's own culture of origin including its rituals, traditions, language, and values (Berry, 1997). Adapting to a new and different culture can be stressful and is called acculturative stress. Acculturative stress differs from everyday stress because it involves acculturation-specific dynamics and difficulties such as ethnic identity, cultural values, discrimination, and second-language competence, which can result in psychological distress (Berry & Annis, 1974; Wu & Mak, 2012). Such distress is not uncommon in the acculturation process. It can be as direct as racial remarks about skin color or subtler discrimination resulting from stares over an accent or awkward stares from others when a gay couple is holding hands in new neighborhood that is covertly anti-gay.

Research suggests that psychological adjustment issues are associated with acculturation challenges and that sociocultural adjustment or competence serves to modulate the effects of acculturative stress (Wu & Mak, 2012). Such sociocultural competence can be increased by language proficiency, effective social interaction and support, and communication competence, which includes knowledge and skills in intercultural communication styles, rules, and social norms (Sperry & Sperry, 2012).

Level of acculturation can be estimated with a practitioner or self-rating measures. A commonly used acculturation assessment tool is the *Brief Acculturation Scale* (Burnam, Hough, Karno, Escobar, & Telles, 1987). This scale consists of three items rated on a 5-point scale: client's language (native versus English), generation (first to fifth), and social activities (preference for native friends from their culture of origin versus new friends). It simply identifies three levels of acculturation: low, medium, and high; it is also counselor-rated based on the client's subjective responses during the interview. Julia's acculturation level is in the low to moderate range while her parents' level of acculturation is in the low range. Julie struggles with the clash between her familial and culturally bound expectations to stay home and take care of her ill mother, while her parents present with a low level of acculturation due to their limited English-speaking skills and having only a few close family friends who are also from Mexico.

3. Cultural Explanation

A client's beliefs about the cause of their problem or concern is very clinically useful, as are the words or idioms they use to express their distress (Bhui & Bhugra, 2004). Counselors should routinely assess clients' culture explanation, also known as explanatory model; that is, clients' beliefs regarding the cause of their symptoms, condition, or impairment such as "a chemical imbalance," being possessed by spirits, bad luck, being punished by God, etc. (Sperry, 2010). In addition, eliciting clients' preferences and expectations for treatment and, if indicated, past experiences of healing in their culture provides useful information in the treatment planning process (Sperry, 2010). Eliciting a client's cultural explanation is compatible with an REBT or Cognitive Therapy perspective because it is used to assess their automatic thoughts and assumptions about their problems and potential solutions. Julia reported that her parents would attribute her current problems to her not attending church for the past three months, which is a belief indicative of a lower level of acculturation. Julia identified that she believes that her problems are a result of feeling stuck about the decision to go to college or to stay home and help her mother.

4. Culture versus Personality

Another dynamic to consider when developing a cultural formulation is identifying the impact of cultural dynamics and personality dynamics on the client's current level of functioning (Sperry, 2010). Personality dynamics include the client's personality style, such as characterological patterns. The counselor's task is to assess and determine the influence of cultural dynamics and personality dynamics.

When a client's acculturation level is high, cultural dynamics may have somewhat little influence on their functioning while their personality features may have a substantial impact. When a client's acculturation level is low, cultural dynamics may have a significant impact. In some cases, both personality and cultural dynamics have a significant impact. This is particularly common in patriarchal cultures, which expect women to be dependent and subordinate to men, and in which female clients also exhibit a marked dependent personality style. The value in determining the mix of cultural and personality dynamics is critical in decisions about the extent to which culturally sensitive treatment or referrals may be indicated. In the case of Julia, it appears that both her personality and cultural dynamics are clinically operative. Specifically, she presents with significant dependent personality traits that also are consistent with her collectivistic cultural expectations to care for parents as they are aging.

Culturally Focused CBT Interventions

Awareness of environmental and culturally related stressors is crucial when working with an individual who has experienced direct or indirect discrimination. Jumping immediately to interventions that assume that the client needs to change their behaviors or interpretations could be perceived as blaming or dismissive. Disputation or restructuring may actually have iatrogenic effects if the counselor ignores or is unaware of the reality of the negative social attitudes that an individual from a minority group experiences in public.

Behavioral Interventions

Hays identified various methods to adapt behavioral interventions among individuals from various cultures through her CLASS acronym, which stands for Creating a healthy environment; Learning something new; Assertiveness, conflict resolution, and other communication skills; Social support; and Self-care activities (Hays, 2014, 2016). These are defined below:

Creating a healthy environment includes making changes in the client's social and physical environment to influence desired behavior. This could be done by working with the client who is experiencing workplace bullying to file a grievance, talk with a supervisor, or take some type of action. *Learning something new* can include assisting the client to learn a new skill or behavior that is consistent with their culture. *Assertiveness, conflict resolution, and other communication skills* can include assisting the client to develop these skills while respecting their cultural norms concerning speaking to authority figures such as parents or elders. Note that assertiveness in some cultures and situations could cause significant problems; for example a transgendered individual might experience a hostile situation or workplace if they speak up (Wenzel et al., 2016). *Social support* is encouraged in the counseling process to achieve therapy goals; for example, encouraging a client to connect to family, friends, support groups, religious organizations, and communities. Lastly, *self-care activities* can include such behaviors as daily exercise, journaling, calling a friend, or mindfulness practice.

Cognitive Interventions

Replacement

Examining the validity of thoughts and beliefs of a client from a minority group can present significant changes, particularly if the counselor is not familiar with or from that cultural group. The counselor needs to be well acquainted with the client's cultural background before examining the validity of beliefs. An alternative to cognitive restructuring and Socratic questioning is to examine whether the client's specific interpretations are helpful or harmful. This technique is from Cognitive Behavioral Analysis System of Psychotherapy (CBASP) developed by McCullough (2000; McCullough, Schramm, & Penberthy, 2015) for the treatment of chronic depression (Driscoll, Cukrowicz, Reardon, & Joiner, 2004). Replacement allows the client to evaluate how their interpretations can divert them from achieving a specific desired outcome. Replacement puts the client in the position of being the expert and is a collaborative method of modifying maladaptive thoughts while being sensitive to cultural beliefs. Further discussion and case examples of this technique are provided in Chapter 5.

Recognizing and Using Cultural Strengths

Cognitive restructuring emphasizes realistic and positive self-talk. Unfortunately this can be considered boastful or arrogant by clients from cultures that value modesty (e.g., Asian and Native cultures). An alternative method is to ask clients what the important people in their lives would identify as their best qualities (Hays, 2016). In addition to individually focused strengths, counselors can examine the client's culture concerning strengths. Some examples include spirituality, religious faith, musical abilities, alternative healing methods, and a commitment to supporting one's own group.

Stories and Metaphors

In Native cultures, stories and metaphors are a method for individuals to offer each other solutions without explicitly offering suggestions for solving a particular problem. This manner of offering new perspectives or solutions respects the listener's autonomy to use the information however they see useful. Counselors can use stories and metaphors to illustrate therapy concepts or to offer new alternatives. Acceptance and Commitment Therapy, Adlerian Psychology, and Narrative Therapy are all approaches that emphasize the use of metaphors in therapy for various reasons.

Art and Music Therapies

Drawing and music playing can be very powerful interventions to incorporate into the counseling process, especially when clients are in three to five hours of inpatient group therapy sessions per day. Both drawing and music can be useful in engaging clients' speech disorders, or for clients who have difficulty speaking the dominant language, and for less talkative clients. In a group-counseling format, clients can draw a picture that represents their goals for therapy, then the group discussion can transition to cognitions and behaviors that will support movement towards their therapy goal. In a group drumming format, members can play a rhythm that reflects how they are feeling and then a discussion of coping skills and helpful attitudes can follow. It is of particular note that art and music interventions should be implemented by counselors with appropriate training in those modalities. See Gladding (2016) for a comprehensive discussion of the use of creative arts such as play and music in the counseling process.

Most Generous Interpretation Technique

This reframing technique was developed by Hays (2016) and is used to assist clients who are experiencing conflict with others. The process encourages the client to consider alternative interpretations of others' behaviors during times of conflict or when others are exhibiting behaviors that are upsetting to them. Here is how Hays explains this approach to clients:

> When we say something hurtful to someone, we often give ourselves the benefit of the doubt, explaining our behavior with "Well, I was really tired, and I hadn't eaten, and I still had all this work to do, so I snapped at her, but I didn't really mean it." In contrast, if someone says the same thing to us, we may say, "What a jerk." So with the most generous interpretation technique, you just tell yourself the most generous explanation of the other person's behavior that helps you feel more compassionate, or at least less irritated by them, for example, "Maybe her dog died today. Or maybe she just tested positive for cancer. Or maybe her spouse just told her that she doesn't love her."
>
> (pp. 244–245)

Homework

CBT is an action-oriented therapy approach in which homework directly influences the change process. Various cultural expectations will influence the client's view of using homework during the counseling process.

For example, Chinese immigrants living in Australia hold values of hard work, self-improvement, and respect for education; often have a strong desire to protect their families' reputation; and display a high level of adherence to homework assignments (Foo & Kazantzis, 2007). On the other hand, some clients may have a distaste for counseling homework because it may feel like school or they may view it as being too formal (e.g., older Native clients). Hays (2016) recommends using alternative words such as *practice, activity, or mission* rather than the term homework.

Case Vignette

The case below includes a full-scale case conceptualization of the case of Julia which has been mentioned throughout this chapter. It starts with a CBT assessment statement and a full-scale case conceptualization, and is followed by a case transcript in which CR-CBT is implemented. This case was adopted from *Case Conceptualization: Mastering This Competency With Ease and Confidence* (Sperry & Sperry, 2012).

Cognitive-Behavioral Assessment

Julia reported that her parents, her boyfriend, and her friends regularly tell her what she should be doing with her life. She also believes that she is misunderstood by most people in her life, she assumes that others will only accept her if she makes the "right" decision, and lastly she fears that she will end up being a failure if she stays home to care for her ill mother. An assessment of maladaptive behaviors and cognitions identified the following: She considers herself to be shy, passive, and "someone who always puts others first." She identified a pattern of conflict avoidance and she has recently felt "stuck" and started drinking alcohol with friends to relax and forget about everything that is bothering her. Some of her automatic thoughts include: "If I go to college my parents will give up on me," "Nobody understands me," and "I don't know what to do, I hate always trying to make everyone else happy."

Case Conceptualization Statement

Clinical Formulation

Julia's depressive symptoms, confusion, and recent binge drinking episodes seem to be her reaction to the pressures coming from her parents, her friends, and herself to make a decision to either go away to college with her friends next fall or to stay home and to help care for her ill mother. Julia has made ongoing efforts to be a good daughter and friend but recently has become increasingly "stuck" in responding to the needs of others at the expense of her own. Her reaction is understandable given her upbringing in a traditional Mexican-American family, in which family is highly valued and there is a significant collectivistic societal influence. Cognitively, her self-view involves core beliefs about being defective, inadequate, and responsible for others' needs. Her worldview involves core beliefs about the world and others as demanding, but also insensitive to her needs. She strongly believes that she will be viewed as being a bad daughter if she leaves her family for college or that she will let herself down if she stays home to care for her ill mother. Her beliefs are consistent with a dependent personality pattern in which she tends to perceive situations as difficult and unfair; this includes a pattern of putting others' needs first and herself last. Her maladaptive schemas include defectiveness, self-sacrifice, and approval seeking. Behaviorally, this pattern of pleasing others manifests itself in shyness, passive communication, and neglecting her needs, which resulted in skill deficits with assertive communication, negotiation, and conflict resolution. Her difficulty with assertiveness and her unwillingness to disappoint her parents serves to maintain this pattern.

Cultural Formulation

Julia identifies herself as a lower-middle class Mexican-American with a moderate level of involvement with her heritage. Her level of acculturation is in the low to moderate range while her parents' level is in the low range. Since her older sister refused to follow the cultural expectation that the oldest daughter would support her parents should they require care-taking, that responsibility is now on Julia since her sister abandoned the family to avoid the familial expectations. Julia's ambivalence about whether to follow cultural norms and expectations and her own career goals is very distressing for her. She attributes her presenting problems to a "lack of faith in God." Although she and her family experienced some initial relocation adjustment challenges and even some discrimination upon arrival in America, both issues were resolved by them moving to a "safer" Mexican-American neighborhood. It appears that both personality and cultural factors are operative in Julia's presentation. Specifically, cultural dynamics that foster dependency (e.g., good daughters care for their parents when help is needed) serve to support her dependent personality dynamics.

Treatment Formulation

The challenge for Julia to function more effectively is to find a balance in meeting both her own needs and the needs of others. Goals for treatment include helping her increase her sense of self-efficacy and helping her build assertiveness skills while also considering her cultural values. Another goal is to decrease her depressive symptoms, which may well be situational and resolve as she can communicate her needs more assertively. After forming a strong therapeutic relationship, CR-CBT will be used to analyze troublesome situations precipitated or exacerbated by maladaptive beliefs and/or behaviors while also remaining sensitive to her unique experience of her cultural dynamics. Assertiveness skills will be addressed in group therapy and role-play in her individual sessions. Her beliefs will be processed with guided discovery and will be addressed with cognitive replacement. Role-play will be used to help her improve her assertiveness skills while the counselor can also work with her on examining the helpfulness of beliefs that she must take care of others. Other interventions will include Socratic questioning, thought stopping, and exposure. The counselor will assess and incorporate any noted cultural strengths in the therapy process (e.g., her family and culture value caring and compassion towards others). The counselor can assist Julia to turn some of that care and compassion towards herself.

Case Transcript With Julia Utilizing Cognitive Replacement

Counselor: When you tell yourself "If I go to college my parents will not love me anymore," does this help or hurt you in regard to your recently identified goal of making decisions that will be best for you and your family?

Julia: I guess it doesn't help, it makes me feel discouraged and like I don't have any good options other than staying home with my family.

Counselor: What idea or thought might be more helpful when you start to get discouraged about your dilemma of deciding to move away go to college with your friends or stay back at home and help take care of your mother?

Julia: Maybe I could remind myself that they will love me no matter what I choose—and that if I stay home to help take care of my mom, I could still attend a local college and eventually transfer to where my friends are after a few semesters if my mom's health improves.

Counselor: That sounds like an encouraging type of belief. How might that thought be helpful to you if you replaced your old belief with this new one?

Julia: It would make me calm down and realize that it isn't the end of the world if I can't start college at the same time that my other friends will start.

Counselor: I can see that this is a pretty reasonable interpretation. How likely is it that you would be able to pull this thought out next time you start feeling discouraged about your college situation?

Julia: I'd say it's very likely, I'll write it down in my notebook because it helps me remember what we've spoken about in our meetings.

Note how the counselor worked with the client to modify her beliefs while also respecting her Mexican-American values to put family first. The counselor utilized replacement and asked the client about the usefulness of her thought. The replacement process allowed the client to find a belief that would be less discouraging. This empowering approach places the client in the position to modify thoughts while the counselor can avoid challenging or evaluating thoughts based on cultural expectations. This process can also prevent the counselor from imposing their bias, which might be from a more individualistic society.

Social Justice

Besides delivering quality therapeutic interventions, do you believe that counselors have a responsibility to address social and systemic injustices that impact their clients? Given that clients may be struggling with mental health issues such as anxiety or depression, the systems and injustices that occur in the society that clients live in must be considered—ultimately this is understanding the person in their environment. Social justice involves "promoting access and equality to ensure full participation in the life of a society, particularly for those who have been systemically excluded" (Lee, 2012, p. 110). For counselors, social justice is one of five core professional values stated in the ACA *Code of Ethics*. The ACA *Code of Ethics* identifies social justice as "the promotion of equity for all people and groups for the purpose of ending oppression and injustice affecting clients, students, counselors, families, communities, schools, workplaces, governments, and other social and institutional systems" (2014, p. 21). This definition casts a wide net that may be somewhat daunting for counselors who want to work at a micro-level context where the primary intervention level is face-to-face talk therapy. Often, novice counselors in the field learn quickly about policies and disparities that exist in society when working in a broken mental healthcare system that leaves many clients without appropriate access to care.

Social justice implies that counselors are expected to ensure that their clients have access to services, resources, information, and equal opportunities. Further, social justice counseling refers to a counseling process that considers that racism, discrimination, oppression, and privilege have an impact on clients and therefore the goal is to approach clients with an equal distribution of power and to advocate for resources through various efforts (Chang & Gnilka, 2010). Typically, social justice is associated with macro-level interventions in which counselors work to address policy issues such as poverty, discrimination, and social reform. We believe that CBT counselors are responsible for stepping outside of their comfort zone of direct therapeutic interventions and are charged with advocating for their clients through multicultural competence, eliminating barriers to care, speaking with local political officials about mental health services, and being aware of their own privilege and the impact that it may have on their clients.

Concluding Note

This chapter examined the multicultural considerations of utilizing CBT in counseling practice. It provided cultural assessment guidelines and also a review of Culturally Responsive CBT interventions. Lastly, a case conceptualization of the case of Julia was provided in which cultural formulation content was highlighted.

References

American Counseling Association. (2014). *ACA code of ethics*. Alexandria, VA: Author.

American Psychiatric Association. (2013). *Diagnostic and statistical manual of mental disorders* (5th ed.). Alexandria, VA: Author.

American Psychological Association. (2003). Guidelines on multicultural education, training, research, practice, and organizational change for psychologists. *American Psychologist, 58*, 377–402.

Arrendondo, P., & Perez, P. (2006). Historical perspectives on multicultural guidelines and contemporary applications. *Professional Psychology: Research and Practice, 37*, 1–5. Retrieved from http://dx.doi.org/10.1037/07355-7028.37.1.1

Balsam, K. F., Martel, C. R., & Safren, S. S. (2006). Affirmative cognitive-behavioral therapy. In P. A. Hays & G. Y. Iwamsa (Eds.), *Culturally responsive cognitive- behavioral therapy: Assessment, practice, and supervision* (pp. 223–244). Washington, DC: American Psychological Association.

Berry, J. (1997). Immigration, acculturation, and adaptation. *Applied Psychology: An International Review, 46*(1), 5–34.

Berry, J., & Annis, R. (1974). Acculturative stress. *Journal of Cross-Cultural Psychology, 5*(4), 382–405.

Bhui, K., & Bhugra, D. (2004). Communication with patients from other cultures: The place of explanatory models. *Advances in Psychiatric Treatment, 10*, 474–478.

Burnam, M., Hough, R., Karno, M., Escobar, J., & Telles, C. (1987). Acculturation and lifetime prevalence of psychiatric disorders among Mexican Americans in Los Angeles. *Journal of Health and Social Behavior, 28*, 89–102.

Chang, C. Y., & Gnilka, P. (2010). Social advocacy: The fifth force in counseling. In D. G. Hays & B. T. Erford (Eds.), *Developing multicultural counseling competency: A systems approach* (pp. 53–71). Columbus, OH: Pearson Merrill Prentice Hall.

Comas-Díaz, L., & Duncan, J. W. (1985). The cultural context: A factor in assertiveness training with mainland Puerto Rican women. *Psychology of Women Quarterly, 9*, 463–476. Retrieved from http://dx.doi.org/10.1111/j.1471-6402.1985.tb00896.x

D'Andrea, M., & Daniels, J. (2001). RESPECTFUL Counseling: An integrative model for counselors. In D. Pope-Davis, & H. Coleman (Eds.), *The Interface of Class, Culture and Gender in Counseling* (pp. 417–466). Thousand Oaks, CA: Sage.

Driscoll, K., Cukrowicz, K., Reardon, M., & Joiner, T. (2004). *Simple treatments for complex problems: A flexible cognitive behavior analysis system approach to psychotherapy.* Mahwah, NJ: Lawrence Erlbaum Associates.

Foo, K. H., & Kazantzis, N. (2007). Integrating homework assignments based on culture: Working with Chinese patients. *Cognitive and Behavioral Practice, 17*, 157–166.

GAP Committee on Cultural Psychiatry (2002). *Cultural assessment in clinical psychiatry.* Washington, DC: American Psychiatric Press.

Gladding, S. T. (2016). *The creative arts in counseling* (5th ed.). Alexandria, VA: American Counseling Association.

Greenberg, G. (1997). Right answers, wrong reasons: Revisiting the deletion of homosexuality from the DSM. *Review of General Psychology, 1*(3), 256–270. doi:10.1037/1089–2680.1.3.256

Hansen, N., Randazzo, K., Schwartz, A., Marshall, M., Kalis, D., Fraziers, R., Norvig, G. (2006). Do we practice what we preach? An exploratory survey of multicultural psychotherapy competencies. *Professional Psychology: Research and Practice, 337*, 66–74.

Hays, P.A. (1996). Addressing the complexities of culture and gender in counseling. *Journal of Counseling and Development, 74*, 332–338.

Hays, P. A. (2009). Integrating evidence-based practice, CBT, and multicultural therapy: 10 steps to culturally competent practice. *Professional Psychology: Research and Practice, 40*, 354–360.

Hays, P. A. (2016). *Addressing cultural complexities in practice: Assessment, diagnosis, and therapy* (2nd ed.). Washington, DC: American Psychological Association.

Hwang, W. (2006). The psychotherapy adaption and modification framework: Application to Asian Americans. *American Psychologist, 61*, 702–715.

Hwang, W., & Wood, J. (2007). Being culturally sensitive is not the same as being culturally competent. *Pragmatic Case Studies in Psychotherapy, 3*, 44–50.

Iwamasa, G. Y., Hsia, C., & Hinton, D. (2006). Cognitive-behavioral therapy with Asian Americans. In P. A. Hays & G. Y. Iwamasa (Eds.), *Culturally responsive cognitive-behavioral therapy: Assessment, practice, and supervision* (pp. 117–140). Washington, DC: American Psychological Association.

Lee, C. C. (2012). Social justice as a fifth force in counseling. In C. Y. Chang, C. A. Barrio Minton, A. Dixon, J. E. Myers, & T. J. Sweeney (Eds.), *Professional counseling excellence through leadership and advocacy* (pp. 109–120). New York, NY: Routledge.

McCullough, J. (2000). *Treatment for chronic depression: Cognitive behavioral analysis system of psychotherapy.* New York, NY: Guilford Press.

McCullough, J. P., Schramm, E., & Penberthy, K. (2015). *CBASP as a distinctive treatment for persistent depressive disorder: Distinctive features.* New York, NY: Routledge.

Neufield, S., Pinterits, E., Moleiro, C., Lee, T., Yang, P., & Brodie, R. (2006). How do graduate student therapists incorporate diversity factors in case conceptualizations? *Psychotherapy: Theory, Research, Practice, Training, 43,* 464–479.

Newman, C. (2013). *Core competencies in cognitive-behavioral therapy: Becoming a highly effective and competent cognitive-behavioral therapist.* New York, NY: Routledge.

Organitsa, K. C. (2006). Cognitive-behavioral therapy with Latinos and Latinas. In P. A. Hays & G. Y. Iwamasa (Eds.), *Culturally responsive cognitive-behavioral therapy: Assessment, practice, and supervision* (pp. 73–96). Washington, DC: American Psychological Association. Retrieved from http://dx.doi.org/10.1037/11433-003

Organista, K. C. (2006). *Cognitive-behavioral therapy with Latinos and Latinas: Culturally response cognitive-behavioral therapy.* Washington, DC: American Psychological Association.

Organista, K. C., & Muñoz, R. F. (1996). Cognitive behavior therapy with Latinos. *Cognitive and Behavioral Practice, 3,* 255–270.

Ridley, C., & Kelly, S. (2007). Multicultural considerations in case formation. In T. Eells (Ed.), *Handbook of psychotherapy case formulation* (2nd ed., pp. 33–64). New York, NY: Guilford Press.

Safren, A., & Rogers, T. (2001). Cognitive-behavioral therapy with gay, lesbian, and bisexual clients. *Psychotherapy in Practice, 57*(5), 629–643.

Sperry, L. (2010). *Core competencies in counseling and psychotherapy: Becoming a highly competent and effective therapist.* New York, NY: Routledge.

Sperry, L., & Sperry, J. (2012). *Case conceptualization: Mastering this competency with ease and confidence.* New York, NY: Routledge.

Sue, D. W., & Sue, D. (2008). *Counseling the culturally diverse: Theory and practice* (5th ed.). Hoboken, NJ: Wiley-Blackwell.

U.S. Census Bureau. (2011). *2010 census shows America's diversity (American Community Survey).* Retrieved from www.census.gov/newsroom/releases/archives/2010_census/cb11-cn125.html

Wenzel, A., Dobson, K., & Hays, P. (2016). *Cognitive behavioral therapy techniques and strategies.* Washington, DC: American Psychological Association.

Wu, E., & Mak, W. (2012). Acculturation process and distress: Mediating roles of sociocultural adaptation and acculturative stress. *Counseling Psychologist, 40,* 66–92.

Chapter 7

Evaluation

Evaluation is used throughout the counseling process to measure various outcomes such as symptoms, counseling goals, irrational beliefs, and overall psychosocial functioning. Evaluation helps counselors better understand the challenges and strengths that each client possesses. Similar terms include assessment and appraisal. This chapter starts by highlighting research supporting the efficacy of CBT among various psychological and medical conditions. CBT has been noted for being one of the most evidenced forms of psychotherapy in the world, and also the most-utilized counseling approach. In the era of evidence-based practice and now with the "pay-for-performance" paradigm approaching, CBT is well positioned as a treatment of choice accepted by most insurance companies and third-party payers. Next, monitoring treatment outcomes and a discussion of several outcomes measures will be reviewed. Finally, culturally competent CBT assessment and CBT supervision will be covered.

Over 500 outcome studies have supported the efficacy of Cognitive Behavior Therapy among various psychological and medical problems, making it the gold standard of talk therapy approaches. Studies have demonstrated the efficacy of CBT in community settings (Shadish, Matt, Navarro, & Philips, 2000) and even computer-assisted therapy (Khanna & Kendall, 2010; Wright et al., 2002). Ample evidence supports that CBT is an effective treatment for a wide range of psychological conditions (see Hollon & Beck, 1994).

Beck (2011) identified a list of psychiatric, psychological, and medical problems (with psychological components) that have been successfully treated with CBT. The psychiatric disorders and similar behavioral issues include: major depressive disorder, generalized anxiety disorder, geriatric depression, panic disorder, agoraphobia, social phobia, obsessive-compulsive disorder, post-traumatic stress disorder, substance use disorders, conduct disorder, Attention Deficit Hyperactivity Disorder, body dysmorphic disorder, eating disorders, health anxiety, personality disorders, sexual disorders, habit disorders, bipolar disorder (with medication), and schizophrenia (with medication). Psychological problems include: couple problems, family problems, complicated grief, caregiver distress, anger and hostility, smoking cessation, and suicide attempts. Medical problems with psychological components include: chronic back pain, sickle cell disease pain, sleep disorders, migraine headaches, cancer pain, somatoform disorders, tinnitus, irritable bowel syndrome, chronic fatigue syndrome, rheumatic disease pain, erectile dysfunction, vulvodynia, hypertension, insomnia, gulf war syndrome, and dental phobia.

Readers should note that empirically supported treatments (ESTs) and randomized controlled studies (RCTs) are designed to be replicated to show evidence of their effectiveness, but they have considerable weaknesses with generalizability among diverse clinical treatment populations (Hays, 2016). Therefore, implementation of CBT among diverse client populations may often require modification. However, with the push for evidence-based interventions for reimbursement, the current process for validating talk therapy interventions will have to suffice. Outcome assessment is a process that is commonly used by counselors for reimbursement, research purposes, and as a clinical tool in the counseling process. This next section will review the outcome assessment process and it will discuss several outcomes measures.

Outcome Assessment

Counselors provide ongoing assessment of client functioning and overall outcomes throughout the counseling process. There are actually two types of assessment: ongoing assessment and final outcome assessment. Ongoing assessment (also referred to as formative evaluation) involves the monitoring of specific treatment indicators over the course the counseling process, such as a suicidal ideation or depressive symptoms. Ongoing assessment is usually incorporated in each session or at various intervals such as every third session. The purpose of this type of assessment is to provide the counselor with information to monitor specific indicators such as symptoms, the therapeutic relationship, levels of functioning, and other indicators of improvements or lack of improvements that allow the counselor to collaborate with the client to make an appropriate shift in treatment with regard to the focus of treatment, the therapeutic relationship, or specific interventions (Sperry, Carlson, & Kjos, 2003). The second type of assessment, final outcome assessment, is the overall evaluation (also referred to as summative evaluation) of what improved after the counseling process has ended. This evaluation may involve standardized measures utilized in a pre–post test manner. For example, in a case where anxiety was the presenting problem, Beck Anxiety Inventory (BAI) scores at the end of treatment are compared with scores on that same inventory at the onset of treatment. Or, this might involve a review of counseling outcomes in terms of the original treatment plan's goals and whether or not particular objectives were completed. The next section of this chapter focuses primarily on various types of ongoing assessment, including a scale that is used to measure the therapeutic relationship.

From Premature Termination to Positive Therapeutic Relationships and Treatment Outcomes

It is a surprise to many counseling trainees that clients leave treatment early and that often their departure is typically unplanned and often against the counselor's advice. Estimated dropout rates range from 30% to 60% of clients in some studies (Reis & Brown, 1999). A meta-analysis on premature termination from counseling identified dropout rates averaging about 47% (Wierzbicki & Pekarik, 1993). Another review of several studies found that 65% to 80% of clients leave treatment before the 10th session. An even higher percentage is indicated for adolescents and clients from minority populations (Garfield, 1994). Besides potentially harmful effects on clients who are suffering, premature termination also limits opportunities for counseling trainees to develop competencies involved in the working stage of counseling and also in the planned and progressive termination stage of treatment.

So why do clients leave counseling prematurely? Studies on treatment dropout acknowledged several reasons, including cognitive dysfunction, abuse history, personality disorders, interpersonal difficulty, legal issues, and problems with counselors or the treatment itself (Aubuchon-Endsley & Callahan, 2009). Of these various reasons, counselors have some influence over the last one. It is well known that clients drop out of therapy either because the treatment is not helping them or because they are not sufficiently engaged in the treatment process because of a therapeutic relationship issue (Miller, Duncan, Sorrell, & Brown, 2005). Therefore, it is essential to identify if the client's expectations and goals for treatment are being met and also to actively engage them in the treatment process. Further, many CBT counselors will ask their clients, "What would you like my help in working on today?" in each session. This collaborative approach allows clients to help focus the direction of each session, which can help with treatment retention. Monitoring the treatment process and outcomes is a strategy for actively engaging clients in the treatment process.

Some counselors informally monitor client progress and may make course corrections based on their clinical observations of the client's response to treatment. Yet, therapists' ability to make accurate assessments and clinical judgments, even late in therapy, has been questioned, especially with clients who are not experiencing benefits in the counseling process (Lambert & Ogles, 2004). Monitoring treatment for some counselors remains largely based on clinical experience and intuition, even though research suggests that clinical experience makes little or no difference in counselors' clinical judgment. Nevertheless,

> mental health experts often justify predictive judgments on the basis of their years of experience. This situation is particularly troubling when coupled with research evidence that therapists are reluctant to recognize deterioration, tend to overestimate improvement rates . . . and are inclined to devalue actuarial/statistical data.
>
> (Hannan et al., 2005, p. 156)

In short, counselors who monitor client improvements but do not use standardized counseling outcomes measures are likely to underestimate negative outcomes and overestimate treatment improvements, usually to the detriment of their clients.

Counselors can better help their clients by utilizing standardized outcome and process measures. CBT counselors who rigidly and vigorously attempt to restructure a client's self-doubting belief may actually cause more harm than good. Counselors need feedback from their clients to provide effective treatment. Incorporating feedback about a client's desire to discuss other issues besides their automatic thoughts about themselves could actually be the discussion that prevents them from abandoning treatment early. Research consistently shows that when counselors receive feedback from clients, their treatment effectiveness and therapeutic relationship increase significantly. One study showed that when counselors had access to therapeutic relationship and outcome information, their clients were less likely to abandon treatment prematurely, were less likely to decline, and were more likely to achieve clinically significant improvements (Whipple et al., 2003). Another study found that therapists who received direct feedback from their clients were 65% more likely to achieve positive treatment outcomes than therapists who did not receive such feedback (Lambert et al., 2001). A third study that included over 6000 clients found that therapists who utilized ongoing feedback measures had noticeably higher retention rates and a doubling of overall client improvements compared to therapists who did not elicit such feedback (Miller, Duncan, Brown, Sorrell, & Chalk, 2006). In sum, when both the counselor and client know how the client rates the therapeutic relationship and treatment outcomes, three things can be predicted: (1) an effective therapeutic relationship is more likely to be developed and nurtured, (2) the client will remain in treatment, and (3) positive treatment outcomes are more likely. Thus, ongoing monitoring of the treatment process and outcome appears to be essential to effective CBT practice.

Training and Use of Outcomes Measures

The obvious question is: Why don't more counselors use formal outcomes measures in daily counseling practice? Did their graduate studies not train them in the use of such measures? If they were trained to use such measures, do they use them in their post-graduate training practice? Although not specifically among counselors, research addressing such questions is quite sobering. Recent survey results show that only about 47% of accredited American Psychological Association Postdoctoral Internship Center (APPIC) internship sites use outcomes measures in their clinical work. Even more puzzling is that there is considerable incongruity between the percentage of interns who are trained in the use of outcome assessment measures and those who actually use outcome assessment measures in their post-graduate training practice. Research indicates that only 29–37% of these practitioners report using outcome assessment measures in their clinical practice (Mours, Campbell, Gathercoal, & Peterson, 2009)!

In the era of accountability, these results are especially disheartening. It is even more discouraging that so few clinicians trained in outcomes assessment decide not to utilize this very important competency. Next, several outcomes measures and process assessments are discussed.

Treatment Outcomes and Process Assessment Scales

A number of commercially available outcome and process measures are available in the public domain and for purchase from various publishers. Following is a brief description of some of the most well-known and frequently used measures in clinical practice today. These measures are particularly compatible with various CBT approaches.

OQ-45

The OQ-45 (Lambert et al., 2004) is perhaps the most commonly used treatment outcomes measure used around the world today. It is a 45-item self-report outcomes measure that is designed for ongoing measurement of client progress, and is used from the onset of counseling through termination. The OQ-45 measures client functioning in three domains: symptoms (e.g., anxiety and depression); interpersonal functioning (e.g., conflict in relationships and loneliness); and social role (e.g., difficulties in home, workplace, or school duties). Functional level and change over the course of treatment can thus be assessed, allowing treatment to be modified based on changes noted by the counselor. The OQ-45 also assesses substance abuse and potential violence at work, and even includes risk assessment items for suicide potential. Counselors will find this measure useful because it efficiently monitors information that often needs to be assessed consistently among certain clients, such as suicidality. It has been translated into more than 10 languages and is based on normative data and has adequate validity and reliability. It is reasonably priced and can be administered and scored in either electronic or paper format.

Session Rating Scale

The Session Rating Scale (SRS) (Duncan et al., 2003) is a brief and easy-to-administer therapeutic relationship measure that consists of four items. The client is given a sheet of paper on which four horizontal lines 10 cm long are printed, with scores ranging from 0 to 40. On the first line the client rates how well understood and respected they felt over the course of their counseling session. On the second line the client rates how much the client and counselor worked on what they wanted to talk about. On the third line, the client rates how good a "fit" the therapy approach was for them. On the fourth line the client rates how satisfied they felt about the session. The scale is completed by the client immediately after the session has ended.

Based on the fact that over 1000 studies (Orlinsky, Ronnestad, & Willutzki, 2004) identified that a positive therapeutic relationship or alliance is one of the best predictors of therapeutic outcomes, this measure may be one of the most important outcomes measures discussed in this book. Ongoing use of the SRS will lead to improved counseling outcomes and will help counselors reduce dropout rates. Use of the SRS is free of charge to individual mental health practitioners by license agreement found at www.talkingcure.com. This measure has significant clinical utility for CBT counselors. An example of the SRS process is presented below.

SRS Case Transcript

Counselor: [in the last minutes of the session] Jake, I see that we are running down to our last ten minutes of our time together this morning. I like to take a metaphorical temperature in the room with each person that I meet with to see if there is any feedback that they can provide me with about how our work together is going. Would you mind completing this form called the Session Rating Scale? It only takes a few moments, but it can be really useful in helping us to best work together.

Client: Sure, I'll fill it out if you think this will be helpful [client completes form and hands it back to the counselor].

Counselor: Thank you for filling this out. I am going to take a quick look at it to see if I have any questions for you [counselor reads the form]. I see that you seemed to think that my overall approach is a good fit you, what do you like in particular about my approach in working with you?

Client: I like the fact that you have concrete things to talk about and that you usually give me some type of homework or experiment to try in helping me manage my social anxiousness. My past counselor would just stare at me and ask about my feelings.

Counselor: Thanks, that's useful for me to know. Changing gears to one of the other responses, I see that you rated the item, "There was something missing in the session today" at about a 60%, can you tell me more about that response?

Client: Sure, I noticed that we spent a great deal of time talking about my homework and then reviewing my strengths and weaknesses about how I dealt with my most recent social experiment, but I felt like I didn't have enough time to talk to you about my concerns about my upcoming date.

Counselor: I'm really glad that you told me that, how about we put that first on the agenda for our meeting next week?

Client: Yeah, that would be good.

Counselor: Great, are you okay with us including this feedback process at the end of our next few sessions?

Client: Yeah, I think it was helpful. I like that it includes me in the process.

Note how the SRS process provided a structure in which the counselor could review the client's overall experience of the session. This feedback process allows the client to be more active in the therapeutic process because they provide direct feedback about their view of the relationship, goals and topics discussed, and the counseling approach/method. Counselors can greatly improve their counseling outcomes by incorporating this process into their work with clients.

Outcomes Rating Scale

The Outcomes Rating Scale (ORS) (Miller & Duncan, 2000) is a short and easy-to-administer outcomes measure consisting of four items. The scale measures a client's individual sense of personal being as well as how they feel about close relationships, and their social and work life. Typically done at the beginning of a session, a client is given the ORS scale to complete with a pen or pencil and they are asked to mark a line somewhere on all four horizontal lines to indicate how things went in the past week. On the first line, the client indicates how they had felt over the past week. The second line indicates their close relationships. The third line indicates their social and work life. Lastly, the fourth line indicates their overall sense of well-being. Use of the ORS is free of charge to individual mental health counselors and can be found at www.talkingcure.com and www.heartand soulofchange.com. The ORS has modified versions that can be used with young children and adolescents, as well as in a group therapy setting.

Case Transcript

Counselor: Before we check-in and talk about how the past week went would you mind filling out this very brief scale? It is called the Outcome Rating Scale, or ORS, and it is used to monitor your overall sense of well-being. We can use this to track your progress and to make sure you are getting the most out of our time together.

Client: Okay, I don't mind filling it out [client completes form and hands it back to the counselor].

Counselor: Thank you, I am going to take a quick look at it to see if I have any questions for you [counselor reads the form]. I see that you marked yourself somewhere at 50% on the line that lists social, work, and school relationships, but marked yourself at almost 100% on the other areas. It sounds like you've had some struggles in this area this past week.

Client: Yeah, I'm still feeling like I'm not making any improvements with my anxiety in social situations.

Counselor: I can see that you are feeling discouraged by this lack of progress, was there a specific time that was particularly challenging in the past week?

Client: Yeah, I tried the exposure assignment that we spoke about in our last session and I tried saying hi to two people while on campus for my classes. I ended up saying hi to a guy that I have two classes with. He didn't say anything back to me, he didn't even look up at me when I greeted him.

Counselor: This took a lot of courage for you to do this.

Client: Yes, but I felt really stupid and didn't want to even try talking to a second person after that.

Counselor: Okay, should we put this as an agenda item to talk about today?

Client: For sure, I really want to feel less anxious on campus and in my overall social encounters.

Note how this process gives the client an avenue to indicate significant opportunities to identify which psychosocial spheres have been problematic for them over the past week. This deliberate feedback process can be particularly useful for clients who are less assertive about their needs, difficulty in their daily life, and treatment goals. The ORS process can be used to align each session with a goal that is consistent or in some way related to the client's overall treatment goals. Counselors can highly benefit from the use of this scale to monitor treatment outcomes, for clinical purposes, or for reimbursement purposes.

Cognitive Behavior Therapy Outcomes Measures

Of all the therapeutic approaches, CBT seems most compatible with various evaluation and assessment measures. CBT constructs allow counselors to monitor quantifiable thoughts and behaviors such as depressive thinking and the number of days in the past week that an individual felt depressed. Besides also contributing to improved outcomes and quality of care, a second reason for CBT counselors to use ongoing assessment with formal measures is that it can increase understanding of the mechanisms of suffering and therapeutic change (Persons, 2007). There are a number of formal Cognitive Therapy measures that are sensitive to changes in the client's functioning that occur between each session. Among others, these include the Beck Depression Inventory, the Beck Hopelessness Scale, the Panic Belief Questionnaire, and the Beck Anxiety Inventory (Beck & Steer, 1990). Other Beck scales include the Beck Cognitive Insight Scale, the Beck Scale of Suicidal Ideation, the Dysfunctional Attitude Scale, the Clark-Beck Obsessive-Compulsive Inventory, and the Beck Youth Inventory. These scales are used to assess anxiety, depression, anger, disruptive behavior, and self-concept in adolescence and children. For information about the Beck scales listed visit www.beckscales.com. Another common measure, SUDS (Subjective Units of Distress Scale) is a client self-rating measure of their anxiety and distress on a 1–100 scale that counselors can monitor from session to session (Wolpe, 1969).

When it comes to research applications of treatment monitoring in CBT practice, several studies have reported the use of formal theory-based measures. For example, Kuyken (2004) monitored Beck Hopelessness Scale scores from session to session among depressed clients. He found that if hopelessness levels did not improve within the first four sessions, the Beck Hopelessness Scale predicted poor treatment outcomes. Persons (2007) notes a number of similar studies.

Schema Assessment

Most simply stated, a schema is an individual's self-view and world-view. There are various methods of assessing schemas. From a Cognitive

Therapy perspective, schemas are typically assessed and identified during the interview process (Beck, 2015). Young describes several methods for assessing schemas (Young, Klosko, & Weishaar, 2003). During the initial interview, the counselor elicits presenting problems and symptoms and attempts to formulate a connection between specific symptoms, emotion responses, problems, and maladaptive schemas.

Another method of schema assessment was developed by Alfred Adler, who used early recollections to understand a person's view of themselves, others, and the world around them. Accordingly, schemas are a similar psychological construct to what Adlerian Psychology counselors refer to as lifestyle or style of life (Adler, 1956). Lifestyle, as well as schemas, can be assessed with a semi-structured interview that includes eliciting a client's early memories. This process is done by asking the client: "What is your earliest memory?" or, "Think back as far as you can and tell me the first thing you remember." An early recollection must be distinguished from a report. An early recollection is a single, specific event that is personally remembered by the individual, whereas a *report* can be an event that occurred more than once or in which the client was told about the event by a friend or family member, or by seeing it in a photo or home video. In most cases, five to eight memories are obtained from early and middle childhood. From these memories the counselor searches for themes related to the client's view of self (that is, "I am inferior, defective, and vulnerable") and the client's view of the world ("The world is dangerous, inconsistent, and unfair"). These views can be summarized and interpreted to uncover the individual's lifestyle themes or schemas (Eckstein, Baruth, & Mahrer, 1992). CBT counselors can benefit by incorporating early recollections in their CBT assessment process to gain insight into the client's schema dynamics. Read more about the use of early recollections in Clark (2002) and about the incorporation of CBT and Adlerian Psychology practice in Sperry and Sperry (2013).

During the course of inquiry about life events and symptoms, the counselor seeks to develop hypotheses about themes in the client's story. Issues of autonomy, worthiness, connectedness, reasonable expectations, and realistic limits are probed to ascertain if any of these present significant problems for the patient. Freeman identified the utility in inquiring about "critical incidents" by asking the client to describe a situation or incident that they consider indicative of their problem (1992). The clinician listens for specific precipitating or trigger events, patterns indicative of various schemas, and specific emotional, behavioral, and cognitive responses. As themes and patterns materialize, the counselor formulates them in schema language; that is, view of self and view of the world and others. Because schemas are predictable and recurring phenomena they can be "triggered" in the interview through imagery, by discussing upsetting events, or by reviewing the clients patterned response to not getting what they want in various situations.

In addition to the clinical interview, various schema inventories are available including the *Life History Assessment Forms*, the *Young Compensation Inventory*, the *Young Parenting Inventory*, the *Young-Rygh Avoidance Inventory*, and the *Young Schema Questionnaire*. Imagery assessment is an additional method of schema assessment. See Cf. Young et al. (2003) for a description of these inventories.

Culturally Competent CBT Assessment

As mentioned throughout this book counselors are expected to work effectively with individuals from various cultures, ethnic groups, nationalities, social classes, religious groups, sexual orientations, gender identities, disabilities, and ages. The idea that diversity can be addressed in a single graduate course has been replaced with a paradigm that diversity and cross-cultural information and training is integrated throughout the course progression and practicum and internships (Magyar-Moe et al., 2005).

Pamela Hays's (2016) Culturally Responsive CBT (CR-CBT) approach provides a useful framework for conducting a strengths-oriented, culturally responsive approach to CBT assessment and outcome assessment. Cultural assessment includes understanding and assessing the client's psychological factors and cultural factors that influence well-being and problems. Hays also recommends that counselors avoid challenging core cultural beliefs but rather draw on the client's cultural strengths when developing more adaptive ways of thinking. This approach emphasizes collaboration over confrontation. Cross (2003) identified that culture is often a resource for healing and active coping interventions that are already in the client's life, such as prayer or social support systems.

"Pay-For-Performance" Paradigm Approaching

Besides the counseling profession prioritizing multicultural competency and awareness, there is a major shift facing mental health counselors and other healthcare providers in the United States regarding reimbursement. This is being considered to drive down healthcare costs and also to raise the quality of care which will result in improved client satisfaction. The goal of "pay-for-performance" is to positively reinforce efficiency and optimal treatment outcomes. Currently, the healthcare system is a "fee-for-service" payment structure that rewards practitioners for billing clients and insurance companies for expensive procedures and services regardless of the client benefitting from the services. The new system will provide counselors and other healthcare providers with reimbursement or even bonuses for meeting or exceeding certain benchmark outcomes in the treatment process.

Legislators and healthcare leaders have invested a significant amount of effort in implementing this paradigm and healthcare professionals are preparing for this significant change and expectation that services must lead to improvements in the client's well-being. This systemic change will force counselors to provide counseling services that lead to lasting change and will likely encourage them to provide evidence-based interventions such as CBT.

Assessing Strengths and Protective Factors

The influence of client strengths and protective factors in counseling practice is particularly important in CBT practice because counselors endeavor to assess for a balance of strengths and resources as compared to only considering weaknesses, problems, deficits, and pathologies, as other mental health professionals often do. We believe that counselors are responsible for seeing the potential, strengths, and abilities of the clients who we serve. Assessment processes that monitor strengths, abilities, protective factors, and resources provide a fuller picture of a client who is also part of a family system, culture, community, and overall society. Hays (2016) recommends assessing strengths throughout the session and asking the client to identify strengths towards the end of the initial session. The counselor can list observed strengths and protective factors if the client is unable to identify any in themselves.

Protective factors are psychological, social, biological, spiritual, and/or environmental processes that influence the prevention of an adverse life stressor, improve it more quickly, or reduce its impact (Gitterman, 2001). How individuals cope with the challenges of life is influenced by their utilization of the protective factors in their lives. Protective factors are any variable that can influence positive outcomes among clients receiving clinical services. These factors can be internal to the client such as attitudes, motivation, and optimism; or external factors such as community resources, support systems, and access to healthcare. Next, CBT supervision and the Cognitive Therapy Rating Scale are discussed.

CBT Supervision

CBT supervision is a supervisory approach that incorporates CBT processes throughout the process. Students and trainees require effective, focused CBT supervision. This process typically involves agenda setting, the trainee applying CBT principles to themselves, ongoing encouragement throughout the process, homework assignments for the supervisee, role-play counseling practice, supervisor feedback from the trainee, and ongoing assessment of CBT competence. Milne et al. (2010) reviewed 24 studies of CBT supervision and concluded that competent CBT supervision includes providing supportive feedback, observing the supervisee's work (e.g., via videos or two-way mirrors), and using various methods of teaching (role-playing, modeling of techniques, readings, reviewing videos, and utilizing didactic instruction).

Newman (2010) described the supervisory skills and responsibilities of a proficient CBT supervisor:

1. Take ultimate professional, ethical, and legal responsibility for the clients under the care of the supervisees. Monitor cases regularly, take confidential notes, and review and sign the supervisees' clinical notes promptly.
2. Be available for regular supervision sessions (e.g., weekly), and provide for supervisory coverage in the event of being unavailable to the supervisees.
3. Establish clear goals and objectives for clinical supervision. Make the process of supervision clear and predictable, rather than mysterious.
4. Give supervisees feedback on a regular basis, including providing supervisees' sessions with their clients or otherwise directly observe their work. Evaluate the supervisees' progress in constructive ways that will encourage them to advance and grow as professionals, but be prepared to identify supervisees who may require special remediation in order to ensure their ability to provide a reasonable standard of care to their clients.
5. Promote the professional development and autonomy of supervisees, yet balance this goal with being available for consultation (and perhaps direct participation) in complicated, critical, or dangerous clinical situations that the supervisees face with their clients.
6. Be a role model for ethical behavior, professionalism, and expert clinical problem solving. Respect the supervisees' boundaries, and use the power imbalance in the supervisory relationship wisely and compassionately.
7. Emphasize the importance of the therapeutic relationship, and behave in a collaborative and benevolent manner with supervisees.

Cognitive Therapy Rating Scale

The Cognitive Therapy Rating Scale (CTS) is the most-used measure of competency and implementation of CBT (Young & Beck, 1980). CBT supervisors utilize this measure to provide supervisees feedback about various CBT competencies. The CTS is also used in the Cognitive Therapy certification process.

The CTS includes 11 categories of processes and competencies described below (Newman, 2013):

1. *Setting an agenda.* When done effectively, the agenda is set at the beginning of the session and collaboratively focuses on specific treatment targets.
2. *Feedback.* Competent CBT counselors elicit feedback during and at the end of each session. This allows the counselor to see if the client fully understands information being discussed and also is a method to make changes if the counselor's interpersonal style or treatment strategies need to be modified to better help the client.
3. *Understanding.* Competent CBT counselors utilize therapeutic empathy to display an understanding of the client's "internal reality" by observing non-verbals, verbal communication, and interpersonal process.
4. *Interpersonal effectiveness.* Competent CBT counselors seek to provide encouragement and support, as well as to instill hope in their clients. Highly effective therapy should include warmth, genuineness, and a sense of caring with boundaries in a professional manner.
5. *Collaboration.* Competent CBT counselors engage the client in a collaborative process in each session. This can be done by providing options such as allowing the client to pick their seat in the counselor's office or by asking if the client is comfortable with the counselor taking notes during the session.
6. *Pacing and efficient use of time.* Competent CBT counselors effectively manage therapy time. They deliberately focus treatment tasks and monitor if they are moving too quickly or slowly based on the needs of individual clients.
7. *Guided discovery.* CBT counselors assist clients in the process of considering various perspectives, learning from experiences, and coming to new realizations through thought-provoking questions.
8. *Focusing on key cognitions and behaviors.* A competent CBT counselor is quickly able to assist clients in examining and modifying maladaptive thoughts and behaviors as therapy progresses.
9. *Strategy for change.* CBT counselors are able to write proficient case conceptualizations that inform treatment plans that are tailored to the unique needs of clients.
10. *Application of cognitive-behavioral techniques.* Competent CBT counselors implement effective CBT techniques with confidence and ease and even prepare and debrief the client regarding the techniques being used.
11. *Homework.* Proficient CBT practice includes action-oriented practices such as homework to target treatment goals. Homework assignments are clearly explained with a deliberate rationale.

Concluding Note

This chapter reviewed assessment and evaluation processes that can be incorporated into CBT practice. The chapter started with a review of the empirical support of CBT among various clinical populations. Second, the chapter emphasized the importance for counselors to incorporate outcome assessment in their daily counseling practice to monitor clinical improvements and the therapeutic relationship, which was followed by monitoring and evaluating clinical outcomes. Third, the "pay-for-performance" paradigm was discussed. Fourth, culturally competent CBT assessment was reviewed, followed by a discussion of assessing strengths and protective factors in counseling practice. Finally, the chapter reviewed CBT supervision and evaluation of CBT practice through the Cognitive Therapy Rating Scale.

References

Adler, A. (1956). *The individual psychology of Alfred Adler.* New York, NY: Harper & Row.

Aubuchon-Endsley, N., & Callahan, J. (2009). The hour of departure: Predicting attrition in the training clinic from role expectancies. *Training and Education in Professional Psychology, 3,* 120–126.

Beck, A. (2015). Theory of personality disorders. In A. Beck, D. Davis, & A. Freeman (Eds.) *Cognitive therapy of personality disorders* (3rd ed., pp. 19–62). New York, NY: Guilford.

Beck, A. T., & Steer, R. A. (1990). Manual for the Beck Anxiety Inventory. San Antonio, TX: Psychological Corporation.

Beck, J. (2011). *Cognitive behavior therapy: Basics and beyond* (2nd ed.). New York, NY: Guilford Press.

Clark, A. J. (2002). *Early recollections: Theory and practice in counseling and psychotherapy.* New York, NY: Brunner-Routledge.

Cross, T. L. (2003). Culture as a resource for mental health. *Cultural Diversity and Ethnic Minority Psychology, 9,* 354–359. Retrieved from http://dx.doi.org/10.1037/1099-9809.9.4.354

Duncan, B., Miller, S., Parks, L., Claud, D., Reynolds, L., Brown, J., & Johnson, L. (2003). The session rating scale: Preliminary properties of a "working" alliance measures. *Journal of Brief Therapy, 3,* 3–12.

Eckstein, D., Baruth, L., & Mahrer, D. (1992). *An introduction to life-style assessment* (3rd ed.). Dubuque, IA: Kendall-Hunt.

Freeman, A. (1992). Developing treatment conceptualizations in cognitive therapy. In A. Freeman & F. Dattilio (Eds.), *Comprehensive casebook of cognitive therapy* (pp. 13–26). New York, NY: Plenum.

Garfield, S. (1994). Research on client variables in psychotherapy. In A. E. Bergin & S. L. Garfield (Eds.), *Handbook of psychotherapy and behavior change* (pp. 190–228). New York, NY: Wiley-Blackwell.

Gitterman, A. (Ed.) (2001). *Handbook of social work practice with vulnerable and resilient populations.* New York, NY: Columbia University Press.

Hannan, C., Lambert, M., Harmon, C., Nielsen, S., Smart, D., & Shimokawa, K. (2005). A lab test and algorithms for identifying clients at risk for treatment failure. *Journal of Counseling Psychology, 50,* 155–163.

Hays, P. A. (2016). *Addressing cultural complexities in practice: Assessment, diagnosis, and therapy* (2nd ed.). Washington, DC: American Psychological Association.

Hollon, S. D., & Beck, A. T. (1994). Cognitive and cognitive-behavioral therapies. In A. E. Bergin & S. L. Garfield (Eds.), *Handbook of psychotherapy and behavior change* (pp. 428–466). New York, NY: Wiley-Blackwell.

Khanna, M. S., & Kendall, P. C. (2010). Computer-assisted cognitive-behavioral therapy for child anxiety: Result of a randomized clinical trial. *Journal of Consulting and Clinical Psychology, 78,* 737–747.

Kuyken, W. (2004). Cognitive therapy outcome: The effects of hopelessness in a naturalistic outcome study. *Behaviour Research and Therapy, 42,* 631–646.

Lambert, M. J., Morton, J., Hatfield, D., Harmon, C., Hamilton, S., & Reid, R. (2004). *Administration and scoring manual for the outcome questionnaire-45.* Orem, UT: American Professional Credentialing Services.

Lambert, M. J., & Ogles, B. M. (2004). The efficacy and effectiveness of psychotherapy. In M. J. Lambert (Ed.), *Bergin and Garfield's handbook of psychotherapy and behavior change* (5th ed., 139–193). New York: Wiley.

Lambert, M. J., Whipple, J., Hawkins, E., Vermeersch, D., Nielsen, S., & Smart, D. (2001). The effects of providing therapists with feedback on patient progress during psychotherapy: Are outcomes enhanced? *Psychotherapy Research, 11*(1), 49–68.

Magyar- Moe, J. L., Pedrotti, J. T., Edwards, L. M., Ford, A. I., Petersen, S. E., Rasmussen, H. N., & Ryder, J. A. (2005). Perceptions of multicultural training in predoctoral internship programs: A survey of interns and training directors. *Professional Psychology: Research and Practice, 36,* 446–450. Retrieved from http://dx.doi.org/10.1037/0735-7028.36.4.446

Miller, S., & Duncan, B. (2000). *The outcomes rating scale.* Chicago: Author.

Miller, S., Duncan, B., Brown, J., Sorrell, R., & Chalk, M. (2006). Using outcome to inform and improve treatment outcomes: Making ongoing, real-time assessment feasible. *Journal of Brief Therapy, 5,* 5–23.

Miller, S., Duncan, B., Sorrell, R., & Brown, J. (2005). The partners for change outcome management system. *Journal of Clinical Psychology, 61,* 199–208.

Milne, D., Resier, R., Aylott, H., Dunkerley, C., Fitzpatrick, H., & Wharton, S. (2010). The systemic review as an empirical approach to improving CBT supervision. *International Journal of Cognitive Therapy, 3,* 278–294.

Mours, J. M., Campbell, C. D., Gathercoal, K. A., & Peterson, M. (2009). Training in the use of psychotherapy outcome assessment measures at psychology internship sites. *Training and Education in Professional Psychology, 3,* 169–176.

Newman, C. F. (2010). Competency in conducting cognitive-behavioral therapy: Foundational, functional, and supervisory aspects. *Psychotherapy: Theory, Research, Practice Training, 47,* 12–19.

Newman, C. F. (2013). *Core competencies in cognitive-behavioral therapy: Becoming a highly effective and competent cognitive-behavioral therapist.* New York, NY: Routledge.

Orlinsky, D., Ronnestad, M., & Willutzi, U. (2004). Fifty years of psychotherapy process-outcome research: Continuity and change. In M. Lambert (Ed.), *Bergin and Garfield's handbook of psychotherapy and behavior change* (5th ed., pp. 307–389). New York, NY: Wiley-Blackwell.

Persons, J. (2007). Psychotherapists collect data during routine clinical work that can contribute to knowledge about mechanisms of change in psychotherapy. *Clinical Psychology: Science and Practice, 14*, 244–246.

Reis, B., & Brown, L. (1999). Reducing psychotherapy dropouts: Maximizing perspective convergence in the psychotherapy dyad. *Psychotherapy: Theory, Research, Practice, Training, 36*, 123–136.

Shadish, W. R., Matt, G. E., Navarro, A. M., & Philips, G. (2000). The effects of psychological therapies under clinically representative conditions: A meta-analysis. *Psychological Bulletin, 126*, 512–529.

Sperry, L., Carlson, J., & Kjos, D. (2003). *Becoming an effective therapist*. Boston: Allyn & Bacon.

Sperry, L., & Sperry, J. (2013). Psychotherapy and psychopathology: Cognitive-behavioral and Adlerian strategies. In T. Plante (Ed.), *Abnormal psychology through the Ages Volume II* (pp. 191–205). Santa Barbara, CA: Praeger Publishing.

Whipple, J., Lambert, M., Vermeersch, D., Smart, D., Nielsen, S., & Hawkins, E. (2003). Improving the effects of psychotherapy: The use of early identification of treatment and problem-solving strategies in routine practice. *Journal of Counseling Psychology, 50*, 59–68.

Wierzbicki, M., & Pekarik, G. (1993). A meta-analysis of psychotherapy dropout. *Professional Psychology: Research and Practice, 24*, 190–195.

Wolpe, J. (1969). *The Practice of Behavior Therapy*. Oxford, United Kingdom: Pergamon Press.

Wright, J. H., Wright, A. S., Salmon, P., Beck, A. T., Kuykendall, J., & Goldsmith, J. (2002). Development and initial testing on multimedia program for computer-assisted cognitive therapy. *American Journal of Psychotherapy, 56*, 76–86.

Young, J., & Beck, A. T. (1980). *Cognitive Therapy Scale: Rating manual*. Unpublished manuscript, University of Pennsylvania, Philadelphia.

Young, J., Klosko, J., & Weishaar, M. (2003). *Schema therapy: A practitioner's guide*. New York, NY: Guilford Press.

Chapter 8

Pattern-Focused Therapy in Everyday Counseling Practice

Let's consider the realities of professional counseling practice today. It is increasingly changing and much different than it was 10 years ago, and it is expected to change even more so in the near future, particularly for clinical mental health counseling. Several factors account for this change, but three stand out: the course of therapy will be brief, sessions or therapeutic encounters will be shorter, and the context for it will change. Instead of the usual 12–20 sessions as the norm, the typical course of treatment will more likely to be four to six therapeutic encounters. Instead of 50-minute sessions, the length of the therapeutic encounter will last for 15–30 minutes. Probably the most significant change is the prediction that much of counseling practice will occur in integrated primary care settings. Here, the counselor will function as part of a team, which includes physician, nurse, and the counselor in the role of behavioral health specialist. While at first this may seem alien to mental health counselors, those who have looked into this prospect—such as members of ACA's Interest Network for Integrated Care—are quite enthused. Why? For starters, integrated care is more compatible with counseling's focus on strengths and prevention and not just pathology. For another, there is little or no need to seek authorization for treatment or provide extensive documentation for counseling services. Finally, working as a salaried member of a team beats competing with other mental health professionals for HMO panels and insurance reimbursement.

These anticipated changes will require significant changes in how counselors are trained and practice. There is little doubt that counselors will be expected and required to practice new or significantly revised treatment approaches. This chapter describes a new approach that has been developed and used successfully to train graduate counseling students at Florida Atlantic University, particularly in the clinical mental health counseling program. While it was briefly described in Chapter 5, this chapter provides a more in-depth description of Pattern-Focused Therapy with an extended case example that illustrates this approach.

Pattern-Focused Therapy: Overview

Pattern-Focused Therapy is a brief therapeutic approach for easily and effectively identifying and changing an individual's maladaptive pattern of thinking, feeling, and behaving to a healthier and more adaptive pattern. It accomplishes this by replacing non-productive thoughts or interpretations and behaviors that underlie the maladaptive pattern with more adaptive ones. Other modalities such as behavioral rehearsal, cognitive restructuring, exposure, skill training, reframing, and interpretation can be employed as adjunctive treatments.

This form of therapy and counseling emphasizes patterns. Pattern is the predicable, consistent, and self-perpetuating style and manner in which individuals think, feel, act, cope, and defend themselves (Sperry, Brill, Howard, & Grissom, 1996; Sperry, 2006). Patterns can be maladaptive or adaptive. Maladaptive patterns tend to be inflexible, ineffective, and inappropriate, as well as to cause symptoms, impairment in personal and relational functioning, and chronic dissatisfaction (Sperry, 2010). If such a pattern is sufficiently distressing or impairing it can be diagnosed as a personality disorder. In contrast, an adaptive pattern reflects a personality style that is flexible, appropriate, and effective, and is reflective of personal and interpersonal competence (Sperry & Sperry, 2012).

The clinical value of this approach is threefold. First, it has much wider applicability than most other CBT approaches. For example, it can be used with almost every client presentation and diagnosis. The exceptions are acute psychosis and greatly impaired cognition, such as dementia (McCullough, 2000). Second, it does not require that individuals have the capacity for insight, a capacity that is assumed in CBT (and other) approaches that emphasize cognitive change strategies such as cognitive restructuring or disputation. In this regard it is a "cognitive and behavioral replacement" treatment approach rather than a "restructuring" approach. This means that it is easier and quicker to substitute or replace a problematic thought or behavior with a more useful thought or behavior than to slowly and meticulously dispute or restructure it. As the client shifts to healthier thoughts and behaviors, the underlying pattern shifts to a healthier and more adaptive one. Third, this focused treatment approach is relatively easy to learn and master, particularly with effective supervision.

Pattern-Focused Therapy: Origins and Components

Pattern-Focused Therapy was developed by Len Sperry (Sperry, 2016b). It is derived from four sources: the pattern focus in Biopsychosocial Therapy, the questioning strategy of Cognitive Behavioral Analysis System of

Psychotherapy (CBASP), specific questions from Motivational Interviewing (MI), and clinical outcomes measures. Both CBASP and MI are considered to be empirically supported treatments by the Society of Clinical Psychology of the American Psychological Association.

Biopsychosocial Therapy is an integrative approach that incorporates biological, psychological, and sociocultural factors in planning and implementing psychological treatment. It emphasizes a therapeutic process that focuses on pattern identification, pattern change, and pattern maintenance (Sperry, 1988, 2000, 2006).

Cognitive Behavioral Analysis System of Psychotherapy is a psychotherapy approach that focuses on identifying and changing hurtful thoughts and behaviors with more helpful ones.

From it a specific questioning sequence has been derived that consists of processing nine steps (McCullough, 2000, 2015).

Motivational Interviewing is a counseling strategy for helping individuals discover and resolve their ambivalence to change. Specific techniques involve seeking permission, rating importance, and rating confidence (Miller & Rollnick, 2012).

Clinical Outcomes Measurement. The assessment and monitoring progress in counseling, including the therapeutic relationship, is the fourth crucial component (Sperry et al., 1996; Sperry, 2010).

Pattern-Focused Therapy: Basic Premises

Pattern-Focused Therapy is based on four premises. The first is that individuals unwittingly develop a self-perpetuating, maladaptive pattern of functioning and relating to others. Subsequently, this pattern underlies a client's presenting issues. The second premise is that pattern change is an essential component of evidence-based practice. The third premise is that effective treatment involves a change process in which the client and counselor collaborate to identify the maladaptive pattern, break it, and replace it with a more adaptive pattern. At least two outcomes result from this change process: increased well-being and resolution of the client's presenting issue (Sperry & Sperry, 2012). The fourth premise is that *replacing* non-productive thinking and behaviors with more productive ones is likely to effectively and quickly lead to more therapeutic change than might otherwise occur with directly *restructuring* cognitions or *modifying* behavior.

Pattern-Focused Therapy: Therapeutic Process and Phases

This form of psychotherapy and counseling emphasizes patterns. Pattern-Focused Therapy begins with establishing a collaborative relationship and educating the client in the basic premises of this approach. Central to the assessment and case conceptualization process is the identification of the maladaptive pattern, and then planning treatment that focuses on pattern change. Other key factors considered in planning treatment are level of readiness for change, severity, skill deficits, and strengths and protective factors.

A basic therapeutic strategy in the change process is to analyze problematic situations reported by clients in terms of their maladaptive pattern. Clients are first asked to describe the situation and their resulting interpretations (thoughts) and behaviors. Then they are queried about their expected outcome in contrast to the actual one that resulted.

As the counseling process begins, clients inevitably report that they did not achieve their expected outcome. Parenthetically, a marker of subsequent therapeutic change is that clients increasingly experience noticeable change, as a result of shifting to a more adaptive pattern. They are then asked about their interpretations and if each *helped or hurt* them in getting what they expected. If the latter was the case, they are asked what alternative interpretations would have helped them achieve. Their reported behaviors are analyzed as to whether the behavior helped or hurt in achieving their expected outcome. If not, the focus is on identifying alternative behavior that could achieve that end. Finally, the client's level of motivation and confidence to change their maladaptive pattern are assessed and therapeutically processed.

A hallmark of third wave approaches is sensitivity to the therapeutic relationship. This approach places a high value on the development and maintenance of an effective and growing therapeutic relationship. Accordingly, near the end of each session the client rates the therapeutic relationship on the Session Rating Scale (SRS). The results are shared, compared to previous session ratings, and counselor and client discuss how their working together might be improved (Sperry, 2016a, 2016b).

The counseling process and counseling strategy and sequence can be summarized as:

Counseling Process

- Identification of presentation, precipitant or triggers, and predisposition: psychodynamics, family or system dynamics, values, strengths, and protective factors
- Functional assessment and pattern identification
- Case conceptualization incorporating pattern and protective factors/strengths
- Implementation of strategy for pattern change and maintenance

Counseling Strategy and Sequence

- Specify maladaptive pattern as context for processing a specific concern/situation
- Elicit the situation: beginning, middle, and end
- Elicit thoughts/interpretation of the situation
- Elicit behaviors: words, actions, and paralanguage
- Elicit what client desired/wanted to happen
- Identify what actually happened
- Ask if client got the desired outcome
- Seek permission to review situation and how it might have turned out differently
- Ask if client's interpretation(s) helped or hurt in getting desired outcome; if say hurt, ask what alternative interpretation(s) would have helped
- Ask if client's behavior(s) helped or hurt in getting desired outcome; if say hurt, ask what alternative behavior(s) would have helped
- Ask how important it is to change maladaptive pattern (1–10 scale) and process;
- Ask how confident they are to change that pattern (1–10 scale) and process.

A Typical Session in Pattern-Focused Therapy

Here is a four-step snapshot of how the counseling process typically develops and proceeds in this approach. The four steps are:

1. For every session, but particularly in the early meetings, a strong therapeutic relationship is established and maintained utilizing various relationship-enhancing strategies common among third wave approaches, including "seeking client permission" and related MI questions.
2. Simultaneously, each session—after the first one—begins with a brief review of progress on treatment goals since the last session with the Outcomes Rating Scale (ORS). Client's ratings are discussed in relation to the client's maladaptive pattern and the goal of shifting to a more adaptive pattern.
3. Then a questioning-processing sequence (Sperry, 2016b) is utilized to analyze the client's behaviors and interpretations in a specific problematic situation, in terms of whether they help or hurt the clients in achieving their desired outcome. This is related to the maladaptive-adaptive pattern.
4. Near the end of the session, mutually agreed-upon between-session activities (homework) is set. Then the MI "importance" and

"confidence" questions and answers are processed. The effectiveness of the therapeutic relationship in that session is assessed with the Session Rating Scale (SRS), and processed for how the counselor could be more responsive.

In a 15-to-20-minute session, one problematic situation is processed, whereas two might be processed in a 40-to-45-minute session. Or, employing another cognitive-behavioral intervention such as behavioral activation of role-playing (behavioral rehearsal) might occupy part of the time.

The following case examples illustrate how this approach is used in everyday counseling practice.

Pattern-Focused Therapy in Action: The Case of Jason

This is an actual case involving a college student working with a counselor at a university counseling and psychological services center. Clients are typically seen here for an average of 10–15 individual sessions. The counselor is a student in the second internship course of his graduate program. He utilizes Pattern-Focused Therapy with its distinctive blend of CBASP, Motivational Interviewing, and focus on shifting from a maladaptive to a more adaptive pattern.

This section includes background information and a brief case conceptualization. It is followed by two transcriptions from the third and fourth sessions. As noted below, only part of the session is included. Commentaries on both sessions are provided.

Background

Jason[1] is an 18-year-old single male college student who reports experiencing debilitating social anxiety and increasing social isolation. Lately, there have been increased demands on him to be more socially involved, such as being asked to join a student club and an upcoming verbal class report. While he can tolerate most solitary and family activities, he reports experiencing considerable anxiety in situations involving others he does not know well, particularly those in his classes and his dormitory. Being around others has been anxiety producing since childhood but his anxiety levels have increased dramatically since he is away from home at college. He describes his mother as more emotionally supportive and less demanding and critical than his father. His mother took him out of public school in first grade and subsequently home schooled through high school. As a result, he has had minimal contact with others until moving into the freshman dormitory. He is self-referred for counseling at the university counseling center and this is his first experience of therapeutic counseling.

CBT Case Conceptualization

Jason's increased social isolation and anxiety symptoms appear to be his reaction to demands for increased social involvement. Throughout his life, Jason has feared unreasonable demands and criticism, and isolated himself and avoided situations to be safe. When circumstances require it, he will minimally and conditionally relate to others. As a result, he lacks some basic relational skills and has a limited social network. His reaction and pattern can be understood in light of a demanding, critical, and emotionally unavailable father and the teasing and criticism of peers. His family history of anxiety and panic disorder may biologically predispose him to social anxiety and social isolation, as does the underdevelopment of relational skills. This pattern is maintained by his shyness, limited social skills, and social isolation. Therapy goals included reducing anxiety symptoms, increasing interpersonal and friendship skills, and establishing a supportive social network in his dormitory. Pattern-Focused Therapy addresses his maladaptive pattern while social skills training focuses on increasing relational skills. Jason meets DSM-5 criteria for social anxiety disorder and avoidant personality disorder.

Transcription—Session 3

For teaching purposes the following transcript is abbreviated and highlights only the way in which the Pattern-Focused Therapy approach is practiced, particularly with regard to the third step: the questioning sequence of PPT (described in the "A Typical Session in Pattern-Focused Therapy" section). Here, only one problematic interpretation (cognition) and one behavior are processed and related to Jason's maladaptive pattern of avoidance and isolation to be safe. It should be mentioned that Jason's treatment plan also includes the CBT intervention of exposure, which is also processed in this session but is not transcribed. Note that SUDS is used in this session. It stands for Subjective Units of Distress Scale and is a common measure in the behavioral orientation for the self-rating of distress and discomfort on a 1 to 100 scale, with 90–100 representative of being so psychologically and physiologically overwhelmed that an individual cannot concentrate or cognitively process; they can only react.

Counselor: In our last session we discussed your pattern of avoidance and isolation to be safe and you agreed that the price you've paying for feeling safe is high [Yeah.] So let's review a recent

	challenging situation and come up with alternatives that allow you to feel safer but also allow to grow in the process. Does that make sense?
Jason:	It does.
Counselor:	So can we review your assignment from your last session? [Sure.] It was to make eye contact with someone and greet that person. Is that right?
Jason:	Yeah. I went to a convenience store Tuesday night, and as I went through the checkout line, I said hello to the clerk and asked her how she was doing.
Counselor:	Okay, so what were your interpretations or thoughts right then?
Jason:	My first thoughts was "I'm not normal because I am here alone." My SUDS was at least 90.
Counselor:	Okay. So your interpretation was "I'm not normal because I am here alone." Let's also look at your behaviors. What did you do in that situation?
Jason:	While in the store, I kept my head down the entire time and looked at the floor, except when I looked at the clerk and made eye contact with her.
Counselor:	What else did you do?
Jason:	I just kept my head down and didn't talk to anyone except when I said "hi" and asked her how she was doing. I probably said it very softly.
Counselor:	Did the clerk respond?
Jason:	Yes she said she was doing fine. But then I couldn't think of anything else to say so I looked back down and was quiet, nervously quiet.
Counselor:	So your behaviors in this situation were to keep your head down and look at the floor and not to talk to anyone except when you greeted the clerk.
Jason:	Yes.
Counselor:	So, what did you want to happen?
Jason:	To go to the store and get a few groceries and toothpaste without any stress.
Counselor:	And what actually happened?
Jason:	I got my stuff but my SUDS was about 85 or 90. I was able to make eye contact with the grocery clerk and ask her how she was doing.
Counselor:	Did you achieve your desired outcome then?
Jason:	Sort of. I was able to make eye contact with the clerk and speak to her, but I wasn't able to talk to anyone else or even look at anyone else and I still experienced a lot of stress.

Counselor:	It sounds like you may have actually had two desired outcomes. One was to get groceries without experiencing any stress. Another was to be to make eye contact and greet a person while in the store. Is that accurate?
Jason:	I guess so. I was able to look at the clerk and ask her how she was doing. But I still experienced a lot of anxiety while in the store, and I couldn't think of anything else to say to the clerk.
Counselor:	Do you think that both going to the store and not experiencing any stress was a realistic desired outcome for you at that time?
Jason:	No, it really wasn't.
Counselor:	What might have been a more realistic desired outcome for you at that time?
Jason:	Probably make eye contact, say "hi" and ask how the person was doing while trying to tolerate my anxiety a little better.
Counselor:	That does sound more realistic. [Pause.] So, did you get it?
Jason:	I suppose so. But I wasn't able to think of anything else to say, and my SUDS was about 90 when I tried to talk. That bothered me a lot.
Counselor:	Okay, then, let's go back through your interpretations to see which ones were helpful and hurtful to you in getting the outcome of making eye contact with someone and greeting the person, while tolerating any anxiety. Your first interpretation was, "I'm not normal because I'm here alone." Do you think that thought was helpful or hurtful to you in this situation?
Jason:	Hurtful.
Counselor:	How was it hurtful?
Jason:	Because I kept my head down and didn't speak to anyone because they would look at me and think I was weird since I was alone.
Counselor:	Can you think of any thoughts, then, that you could replace the hurtful thought with that would be helpful to you in this situation?
Jason:	I am normal.
Counselor:	Good. How would that thought have been helpful to you?
Jason:	Well, if I kept telling myself that I was normal and not weird for being there alone much, and that it was okay to feel anxious, I may have been more likely to have kept my head up and made eye contact with someone. I probably would have been more likely to say hello to someone.
Counselor:	So telling yourself "I am normal and I am not weird for being here alone or feeling anxious" would have made it

	easier for you to keep your head up, make eye contact with others, and to talk to other people?
Jason:	Yes.
Counselor:	It seems, though, that in this situation you were able to do that. You made eye contact with the checkout clerk and greeted her.
Jason:	But I still felt a lot of anxiety, which really bothered me, and that made it harder to look up.
Counselor:	Do you think that your replacement thought would have made you feel less anxious, then, or help you accept the anxiety you felt?
Jason:	Probably. It would have been a lot easier for me.
Counselor:	So your interpretation "I am not normal because I am here alone" was hurtful to you because it made you keep your head down and not speak to anyone while you were in the grocery store, except when you spoke to the clerk, and then you still experienced a lot of anxiety, which made you feel more uncomfortable. If you replaced that interpretation, then, with "I am normal and I am not weird for being here alone, and it's okay to feel anxious" you would have experienced less anxiety or been more accepting of it, and you would have been more likely to keep your head up and speak to others. Is that right?
Jason:	Yeah.
Counselor:	Then let's move to your behaviors. One of them was to keep your head down the entire time, except when you made eye contact with the clerk. Do you think this was helpful or hurtful to you in achieving your desired outcome?
Jason:	Hurtful. I probably would have been more likely to make eye contact with other people and maybe even say hi if I didn't look down the entire time.
Counselor:	But you were able to make eye contact and speak to the clerk. So, how was it hurtful?
Jason:	While I was looking at the ground, I just kept thinking about how I wasn't normal and that I just wanted to leave.
Counselor:	So keeping your head down actually made you think more negatively?
Jason:	Yes. If I had my head up and looked at other people, I might have been distracted and not thought those things over and over again.
Counselor:	Then, what behavior would have been helpful to you in this situation?
Jason:	To keep my head up. I probably wouldn't have thought negatively as much and would have been more likely to

make eye contact with others and to even speak to people in the store.

Counselor: So in this situation, if you would have thought to yourself "I am normal and I am not weird for being here alone, and it's okay to feel anxiety" rather than "I'm not normal because I am here alone, and I shouldn't feel anxiety." And had you kept your head up instead of looking down you would have been more likely to get your desired outcome, which was to make eye contact and feel less anxious while feeling less anxiety and better tolerating greeting someone. Is that accurate?

Jason: Yeah, that is accurate.

Counselor: This situation and how you responded nicely captures your pattern of avoidance and isolation to be safe.

Jason: [pause] I see it.

Commentary

This transcribed segment of the session nicely illustrates the problematic situation that Jason reports along with a single interpretation and behavior. How the counselor processed these thoughts and behaviors as they relate to Jason's maladaptive pattern of avoidance and isolation to be safe are demonstrated in this segment.

Transcription—Session 4

This transcribed segment is from the beginning of session 4. It continues the process of pattern identification and pattern change begun in session 3. Recall that Jason's maladaptive pattern is to avoid and isolate himself from others that he does not know or trust in order to be safe. Near the beginning of this session, after briefly checking in with Jason, the counselor begins focusing on the maladaptive pattern utilizing the questioning sequence.

Counselor: So, let's continue discussing your old pattern of avoidance and isolation to be safe and work on the more adaptive pattern of connecting with others in a way in which you feel safer. So, how has it been since we met last?

Jason: Well, it's been okay, I guess. I went to the convenience store again yesterday.

Counselor: Good. And how did that go?

Jason: Well, I still felt anxious for being there alone, and I pretty much grabbed all of the stuff I needed and then headed straight for the checkout line.

Counselor:	Did you make eye contact or talk to anyone while you were there?
Jason:	Yeah, when I was picking out a few apples there was a lady restocking the fruit and she smiled at me.
Counselor:	And what did you do?
Jason:	I gave her a quick smile and then I looked down.
Counselor:	And what was your interpretation of that situation?
Jason:	That it was crazy that she was smiling at me, I mean, for a minute I couldn't figure out if she was smiling at me or at someone behind me.
Counselor:	What does that mean to you?
Jason:	That maybe she had confused me with someone else or maybe she was just smiling because that was part of her job or maybe she was smiling because she thought I looked like a loser at the grocery store all by myself.
Counselor:	And so these thoughts that were racing through your head at this time sound like they were really stressful to you. What was your SUDS level like right then?
Jason:	I would say probably around 80 or so. I was really sweaty and I couldn't believe she was actually smiling at me.
Counselor:	And how about after you smiled back and then walked away?
Jason:	It went down a lot. I was proud of myself for smiling back at her and so I felt a little better about being there alone.
Counselor:	That's wonderful. So by simply smiling back you eased your anxiety a little. How did it go in the checkout line?
Jason:	Better this week, I guess. I looked at the checkout girl and said "Hi." But this time I didn't look down right away. Instead I looked at the computer screen with my grocery total on it. She said "Hi. How are you today?" and smiled at me, and then I smiled back again! Right after that I looked down.
Counselor:	And what was going through your mind at that moment?
Jason:	I was like, whoa. She is actually looking at me right now and I have to think of something to do right away so I don't look like an idiot, fumbling around and stuttering like last time. I couldn't think of anything to say so I just smiled.
Counselor:	And how was your SUDS level?
Jason:	I would probably say around an 85 but when I walked out to the parking lot I was happy that I smiled and said "Hi." I felt better about having gone there, like maybe I had done a little better this week.
Counselor:	That is awesome! So you still experienced stress this time at the grocery store but when you kept your head up and

	smiled back at people, you felt better about it afterward. So this might fit in with the desired outcome we agreed on in our last session: that you would be able to greet and make eye contact with someone while you were there and tolerate the stress it would bring you. Is that right?
Jason:	Yeah, you're right. And then I felt better about it afterwards.
Counselor:	Do you think you could go back and do it again?
Jason:	Definitely.
Counselor:	That's great! It seems like you really made a lot of progress at the store. Good job! Would you like to go over the homework we have for this week?
Jason:	Sure. But, this one wasn't so good.
Counselor:	That's okay, it will help us for next time. This was when you were going to try and ask someone to go and see a movie with you, remember? Can you tell me about it?
Jason:	Well, I wanted to ask this girl I sit next to in my biology class if she wanted to go and see this indie film I had heard was playing on campus on Thursday. We were getting ready to leave at the end of the lecture and I grabbed my stuff and tried to talk to her, but it didn't work out very well.
Counselor:	Okay, well, what were your interpretations or thoughts in that situation?
Jason:	That she would think I was trying to stalk her or that I was some kind of freak. I was terrified that I would say the wrong thing or not say anything at all and then class would be over. Mostly I thought that I was not normal because I couldn't find the words to ask her.
Counselor:	So your interpretation was that you were not normal because you couldn't think of anything to say. That seems like a good interpretation for us to look at. What was your SUDS level for this thought?
Jason:	Almost a 90 . . . I was petrified.
Counselor:	Okay, well, what about your behaviors?
Jason:	Well, like I said, I grabbed all my stuff trying to find the words and I tried to look at her, which didn't last very long and then all I could say was "um, hey, do you like indies?" And she must not have heard me or something or I didn't say it very loud because she gave me a funny look and goes, "huh?" and then I looked down and said "nothing." I grabbed my bag and took off down the lecture hall to the doors.
Counselor:	So your behaviors in this situation were to speak softly, look down, grab your bags, and leave.
Jason:	Yeah. Pretty much how I thought it would go.

Counselor:	Well, we can review this in a minute. What was your desired outcome?
Jason:	To ask her if she wanted to see the independent film they were playing on campus.
Counselor:	And what actually happened?
Jason:	I didn't even ask her and I ran off. And my SUDS was at a 90 for about 15 minutes until I got back to my dorm room and could shut the door and calm down.
Counselor:	So, did you achieve your desired outcome then?
Jason:	No, of course not. I was so sweaty I had to take a shower and I stayed in my room all night on the computer.
Counselor:	Okay, well, then, let's go on to the next phase so we can see what might have made things different in the end. First, let's look at your interpretations and see which ones were helpful or hurtful to you in getting your desired outcome of asking someone to go see a movie. Your first interpretation was that "you were not normal because you couldn't think of anything to say in that moment." Do you think that this interpretation was helpful or hurtful in this situation?
Jason:	Hurtful.
Counselor:	How was it hurtful?
Jason:	Because it made me feel even more anxious and like I was going to fail again and then she would think I was weird and it would always be uncomfortable having to sit there in class with her after that.
Counselor:	Can you think of any thoughts that might have been more helpful instead?
Jason:	Um, well, that I am normal. Or at least I am not a freak.
Counselor:	Good, good. Now how would that have helped you?
Jason:	Well, I wouldn't have freaked out so much right before and maybe I would have been able to actually think of something to say since I wasn't so scared. I guess I would have been more likely to find something good to say and say it louder.
Counselor:	So telling yourself "I am normal and I am not weird for asking her if she likes indie films or for being anxious about it" would have made it easier for you to ask her.
Jason:	Yeah, I think so.
Counselor:	Well, you did ask her, even though she didn't hear you right away. Perhaps it was your anxiety that really bothered you and got you upset in this situation?
Jason:	Yeah, definitely.
Counselor:	Well, do you think your replacement thought would have made you less upset or stressed, or maybe help you accept those feelings?

Jason:	Probably.
Counselor:	So your first interpretation that you were not normal because you couldn't think of anything to say was hurtful because it actually made you anxious, which makes thinking of words difficult for anyone. If you replaced that thought with the one that says, "I am normal and it is okay to be anxious when asking someone to see a movie" you would have been more likely to be at a SUDS level that would allow you to think more clearly and find something to say, and then ask her. Is this right?
Jason:	Yeah.
Counselor:	Okay, well, let's move on to your behaviors. The first one was to grab your stuff right away. Was this helpful or hurtful in terms of getting your desired outcome?
Jason:	Hurtful . . . Probably because it looks like I just want to rush off.
Counselor:	So what might have been a better behavior?
Jason:	To take my time, and slowly gather up my books while I was thinking of how to ask her.
Counselor:	That's good, that would have given you a little more time to not be anxious and think of the words. What about speaking softly, did this help you or hurt you in terms of getting your desired outcome?
Jason:	Hurt, because she didn't hear me and then she gave me a funny look and I freaked out.
Counselor:	What might have been a better behavior?
Jason:	To speak louder and look at her so she could understand what I was saying.
Counselor:	Great, you are really good at this part. Then perhaps she might have said "yes, I like those movies" and you could then have asked her to go with you to see it. This would have prevented her from asking, "huh?" which made you even more anxious and led you to say "nothing" and leave.
Jason:	Yeah, I see.
Counselor:	So, in this situation, if you would have thought to yourself "I am normal and it is okay to be anxious when you ask someone to see a movie" instead of "I am not normal because I can't think of anything to say" and if you would have spoken louder and not grabbed up all your stuff and rushed off you would have been more likely to get your desired outcome of asking someone to see a movie with you. Is that accurate?
Jason:	Sure. Definitely.
Counselor:	Would you like to practice what this situation might look like if it happens again, this time with the new interpretations

	and behaviors? [Yes.] We'll role play it. I could be the girl in your class and you could practice asking me.
Jason:	I'll try.
Counselor:	Good, I think you can do it. Let's pretend we are sitting in class and it is almost time to leave. Everyone starts to pack up their belongings and you start to slowly put your books away. What are you thinking to yourself?
Jason:	That I am normal and it is okay to be anxious about asking someone to see a movie.
Counselor:	Good, and what are you doing?
Jason:	I am slowly putting away my books and then I look up and say, "hey, do you like indie films?
Counselor:	"Yeah—they're cool. Why?"
Jason:	"Well, because they're showing one in the old theater tonight about that news reporter in Iraq. Do you want to go see it with me?"
Counselor:	"Sure, what time is it?"
Jason:	"7:30. I could meet you out front if you like."
Counselor:	"That would be cool. Thanks."
Jason:	Okay. I see what you mean. I could carry on a whole conversation then. What if she says no?
Counselor:	Well, your desired outcome is to just get up the courage to ask someone to see a movie. There is a chance that that person might say no, but your desired outcome is to ask. I think the more practice you get at asking people, the more chances there are for them to say yes, don't you agree?
Jason:	Yeah, I mean, if she said yes then what would I say to her at the movie?
Counselor:	Well, this is something we can always work on in the future. I think you did great work today. Do you want to make an effort to try and ask someone to see a movie again? You don't have to ask the same girl, maybe try it with someone you know in your dorm?
Jason:	Yeah, that sounds like a good idea.
Counselor:	Okay! Well, I look forward to our next meeting.

Commentary

This transcribed segment begins by focusing on the maladaptive pattern and utilizes the questioning and processing strategy (step 3) to analyze Jason's problematic situation. The counselor also incorporates role-playing (behavioral rehearsal), a cognitive-behavioral intervention, to allow Jason to rehearse how he might act to achieve his desired outcome.

Pattern-Focused Therapy in Action: Case of Adriana

This is another actual case. It involves a young woman with a history of abuse and neglect who enters counseling in an intensive outpatient substance treatment program at the insistence of her parents. The program allows a maximum of 12 individual therapeutic counseling sessions. The counselor is a student in her first internship course in her graduate program. She utilizes Pattern-Focused Therapy with its distinctive blend of CBASP, Motivational Interviewing, and focus on shifting from a maladaptive to a more adaptive pattern.

This section includes background information and a full-scale case conceptualization that includes a cultural formulation and a very detailed treatment formulation. The transcription is from the sixth session. It illustrates how all four steps of PPT play out in actual counseling practice. The transcript lasted 35 minutes.

Background

Adriana[1] is a 22-year-old, single, mixed-heritage (Caucasian and Native Indian) female who currently resides with her adoptive parents. She comes to counseling at the insistence of her parents after they found her drinking alcohol and smoking marijuana in the backyard of their home. Given her ongoing use—since age 15—and its increasingly negative influence on her life, they gave her an ultimatum to go back for counseling if she wanted to continue living in the family home. She presented as mildly depressed and anxious during the initial assessment and stated that she could not stand the thought of being abandoned by her parents if she did not comply with their ultimatum. This is consistent with previous situations in which she responds with isolation and substance use when challenged by demands to achieve or the expectation to be more socially involved. For her, using substances "takes the sting away." She meets criteria for the following DSM-5 Diagnoses: Alcohol Use Disorder, Moderate; Cannabis Use Disorder, Moderate; Personal history (past history) of physical abuse in childhood; and Avoidant Personality Style.

CBT Case Conceptualization

Adriana presented as isolative and mildly depressed and anxious following her adoptive parents' ultimatum that she get counseling. Adriana has a long history of social isolation and substance use when she perceives situations to be threatening or demanding. Her pattern is to move away from others to be safe and avoid rejection and criticism. This is evident from early life when her biological father failed to provide a sense of safety, consistency, and caring, and continued later with criticism and high demands. Not surprisingly, an avoidant style is prominent. Her pattern and vulnerability can be understood in light of several factors. While there is no known family history or predisposition to substance use disorders, her ongoing use of substances appear to be her way of "self-medicating" the challenges to achieve and relate successfully with others. In short, she opted for a chemical solution in place of relational ones when she was unable to deal with such challenges.

Notable deficits in relational and coping skills account in part for this pattern. Her self-other schemas also play a part. She views herself as vulnerable and inadequate, while viewing others as critical, demanding, hurtful, and distrustful. As a result, she avoids close relationships and so reduces vulnerability to rejection. Other factors include a long history of childhood abuse by her biological father, as well as high demands for achievement, and criticism from her adoptive family. She also has some notable protective factors and strengths: she has strong alliance with her adopted father and she is intelligent, insightful, articulate, and reasonably motivated to change.

She identifies herself as Caucasian and Indian and is highly acculturated with no indication of acculturative stress. She believes that the root of her issues is because of her inability to utilize relational skills within interpersonal relationships and limited healthy coping skills. Both personality and cultural factors appear to be operative. Adriana's cultural dynamics will not likely negatively impact the therapeutic relationship, nor will treatment progress be dependent on cultural factors. The need for culturally sensitive interventions is not evident.

Given her relatively high level of functioning, a course of psychotherapy was mutually agreed. Basically, treatment will emphasize developing and maintaining a more adaptive pattern of connecting with others who are reasonably trustworthy such that she feels safer. The main first-order change goal is to decrease her mild depressive symptoms and anxiousness, social isolation, and substance use. The second-order change goal is to increase her capacity to relate more fully with others, especially those who are reasonably safe and trustworthy. In part, this will require that she develop needed relational and coping skills to facilitate such relationships.

Treatment will focus on the necessary shift from her maladaptive pattern to a more adaptive one. Treatment strategies will include providing support, skill building, and utilizing Pattern-Focused Therapy to replace maladaptive patterns and related thoughts and behaviors. Other interventions will include involvement in a psychoeducation/skill-building group and Schema Therapy to challenge her automatic negative thoughts and core schemas about trusting others and rejection-abandonment fears. In preparation for termination, a relapse plan will be established.

Treatment obstacles may include "testing" behavior; difficulties with self-disclosure; and fear of being criticized and negatively evaluated by the counselor. Treatment does not seem to depend on cultural factors. Given her protective factors and strengths, treatment prognosis appears to be relatively good.

Transcription

Counselor: I want to start the session by discussing the comparison of your ORS scores from last week's session (24) and today's scores (27). You seem to be doing well this week as your scores for individual well-being (5 to 6) and interpersonal well-being (4 to 6) are higher. What has changed from last week that contributes to the slightly higher scores for your well-being?

Adriana: My relationship with my parents has been getting better because I have been communicating my feelings more and also I signed up to start some classes over the summer to get back into school again. I've been trying some relaxation techniques that we spoke about too to help me relax more, like the breathing exercises.

Counselor: That's excellent that you are effectively communicating with your parents. I'm happy that you are starting school again too because I know how important this was to you.

Adriana: Yeah, it was time to get back into school and finish up some credits.

Counselor: Good, good . . . anything else that contributed to higher scores this week on the ORS?

Adriana: Um, no that's pretty much it. Um . . . I have been trying to be more social with others. To network a bit too. But I still feel a little hesitant to socialize with others.

Counselor: Okay, well we can discuss this further on how you can be more at ease when you do socialize with others. Is that okay with you?

Adriana: Yeah, that's cool we can talk about it.

Counselor: Okay let's start with you telling me a little bit about the situation last week when you were trying to socialize with others. How did that go?

Adriana: Last week one of my close friends invited me to an event sort of like a mixer to socialize and network with others. I'm trying to change my ways of avoiding others and agreed to go and see how it turns out. Otherwise, normally I would have declined the offer to go out and just stay home and be a homebody.

Counselor:	Okay, so you agreed to go to a mixer with your friend and how did it turn out for you?
Adriana:	So it was a mixer at a restaurant downtown and there were a lot of people there. It seemed to be a good turnout for the restaurant because a lot of people attended the event there. My friend and I got a table and we ordered dinner at the restaurant. She had other people there that she knew and called them over to our table and she introduced them to me and vice versa. But I noticed that when they sat down and joined us it was like I had nothing to say to them. I ended up not saying too much to them and when they asked me questions to try and talk to me or I guess just include me into the conversation I had short responses with them to end the conversation quick. I didn't even really notice I was doing that until my friend told me how I was acting at the mixer afterwards. I guess it comes natural for me to just sit back and be behind the scenes and quiet. It's just . . . I don't know . . . it's hard for me to trust people like that. I kind of just keep my business to myself.
Counselor:	Yes, I remember in the past when we discussed your difficulties in socializing at events because it is hard for you to trust others. How did you feel about not being able to socialize the way you want to at that mixer?
Adriana:	I definitely felt frustrated. It's like I know that I want to be able to get better at doing this by now but it's hard sometimes. I find myself isolating myself all over again when I try to socialize with people at events. I don't know why it's that way. It took a lot just to get me there.
Counselor:	Well let's look at it this way, you definitely made some progress because you actually attended the event with your friend whereas before you would have just stayed home instead.
Adriana:	Yeah, you're right. Before that's exactly what I would've done.
Counselor:	Did anything else happen that night? Or was it specific to that situation at the table with your friend and her associates.
Adriana:	Well a guy approached me and tried to talk to me, but I kind of just did the same thing and kind of pushed him away too. It's like I want to talk to guys too and get to know someone, but there I go again avoiding interactions with people. I was anxious and it was difficult to continue the conversation with him so once again I just kept it real short until the

conversation kind of just trailed off and came to an end and he walked away.

Counselor: What were you thinking in both situations with the friend's associates and the guy that approached you for conversation?

Adriana: Well when my friend's associates came over to the table and sat down to chat I was thinking "yeah this is awkward." And when the guy approached me I was thinking "okay I have nothing to say to this guy." Both situations were really out of my element because I'd rather just stay home and catch something on TV or just do something else at home.

Counselor: In both situations, it seems like you were trying to avoid interacting with new people.

Adriana: Yeah. I mean just like we spoke about before, I am trying to change that, but I still need to work on that.

Counselor: Yeah, it's a gradual process. We can discuss ways in which you can do things to help you become better at socializing with new people and not have to feel anxious and mistrustful of others.

Adriana: Yeah, that's true. I have a hard time seeing the positives sometimes.

Counselor: What were your behaviors in the situation, such as what did you say or do when you were at the event?

Adriana: Um, I kind of was short with people when they were trying to talk to me and I guess my facial expression didn't show enthusiasm to socialize with them at the restaurant.

Counselor: Okay so to avoid interactions with others at the restaurant you were very brief in your responses and your facial expression did not indicate that you were pleased to continue socializing with others.

Adriana: Yeah, that's pretty much it, that's all I did.

Counselor: So what did you want to get out of that situation at the restaurant?

Adriana: Well I just wanted to be able to socialize with people without being distant and anxious about interacting with them.

Counselor: Okay, so you want to be able to be more confident and less anxious about interacting with people that you do not know well. Is that correct?

Adriana: Yes, I just want to be able to do this without having such a hard time doing it, you know like socializing with new people.

Counselor: What actually happened at the restaurant?

Adriana: I just ended up not interacting the way that I want to learn how to interact with others. I was brief with people and I didn't show that I wanted to socialize with people. I was more comfortable with my best friend only because I've known her for many years, but when it comes to meeting new people I'm not as comfortable.

Counselor: It sounds like you didn't get the outcome that you wanted. What do you think?

Adriana: Yeah, I agree that it didn't turn out the way that I wanted it to. I wish that I could have just spoken to the people without being like that. I kind of feel bad too because I didn't want my friend to think that I was being rude to her friends. I don't know what they were thinking about the way I was acting, but it probably wasn't good.

Counselor: Did you let your friend know about how you felt and that you didn't mean to come off that way to her friends?

Adriana: Oh yeah when she brought it to my attention about how I interacted with them I let her know that. She said she understood, but still I kind of felt bad for doing that around her friends, you know.

Counselor: Don't beat yourself up about it because you did explain to your friend why you were behaving that way and you stated that she said that she understood as well.

Adriana: Yeah that's true it didn't turn out bad because my best friend did say it was okay. I guess maybe I just feel bad that I can't socialize like everyone else does.

Counselor: Well you're trying to do something about it and that's what counts. You may not be able to socialize and network the way you want now, but it's just a matter of not being able to do it yet. I have confidence that you'll gradually learn how to be more social in situations that require interaction with others you may not know well.

Adriana: Thanks. I appreciate you saying that.

Counselor: Let's look at this situation where you went to the event at the restaurant and weren't able to interact with others the way that you would like to socialize at these types of events. We can review your thoughts and behaviors and see if it could have turned out differently that night and possibly for future events as well. OK?

Adriana: Yeah, we can do that. I definitely need to learn how to change that.

Counselor: Your first thought was "this is awkward." Did it help or hurt you in getting what you wanted out of the interactions at the restaurant?

Adriana: It definitely hurt me because I already put it in my head that it was going to be awkward and look what happened, it ended up being awkward.

Counselor: Yes, this is true when you put negative thoughts in your head; you already expect the situation to turn out negative. It seems that you fulfilled what you were thinking of the situation.

Adriana: Yeah, you're right that's exactly what happened. I do that a lot too. I think negative about something and expect things to go wrong too. And I really want to change that too. I know that it's not good to think that way, but sometimes I can't help it.

Counselor: Okay, so what thought could you have had instead of thinking that interacting with them will be awkward that would help you get the outcome that you wanted?

Adriana: I mean I guess I could have just thought that it would not be awkward to talk to them . . . yeah I could have just thought that the interaction with her friends will turn out to go well instead of thinking that it is awkward.

Counselor: Yeah, that could definitely work in this situation with her friends and other situations where you are interacting with new people by thinking that the interactions are going to be positive.

Adriana: Also, I could think that this will be a good opportunity to network with other people.

Counselor: Right, that would be a good opportunity to network with people for opportunities that may be beneficial to you.

Adriana: Yeah, I need to start networking with people more because there may be opportunities that I'm missing out on.

Counselor: That's true you never know who you might meet as far as opportunities go. You may meet the right person who can help you pursue your goals further.

Adriana: Yeah, exactly.

Counselor: So let's move on to your second thought, which was that you had nothing to say when the guy approached you. Did that help or hurt you in getting what you want out of the situation?

Adriana: It hurt me because I ended up looking standoffish and, I mean, it possibly could have led to something else by getting to know each other, maybe possibly being able to date someone. You know, I would like to start dating but I have to work on being able to keep the conversation going and feeling more relaxed. I guess I just always have my guard up when it comes to trying to let people in. That just seems to be the way that it always goes.

Counselor:	Yes, if you were trying to get to know someone to possibly date then I could see how this hurt you in this situation. Do you think that you would be able to let your guard down just a bit to get to know other people?
Adriana:	Uh maybe I could, but I mean I'd have to practice that though, because I've been hurt in the past and that's why I keep that guard up against other people because I don't want that to happen again.
Counselor:	It seems that we can't control others hurting us, but is being hurt worth putting up a strong guard to prevent you from forming relationships with people?
Adriana:	Well I guess no it's not worth it because then I won't meet someone new.
Counselor:	Right, avoiding interactions with others will not lead to a new relationship with a guy because it will create distance.
Adriana:	Yeah, that's true. And I do that often too, distancing myself.
Counselor:	So what could you have thought instead of thinking that you have nothing to say to this guy to get what you wanted out of the situation?
Adriana:	I guess I could have just thought, okay, well I do have something to say with people instead of thinking I don't.
Counselor:	By thinking that you do have something to say, how would you have used that in the situation with that guy?
Adriana:	I mean, I guess I could have found some common ground between us to keep the conversation going. I guess I wasn't really paying attention to what we had in common because I was anxious and wanted the conversation to be over quickly.
Counselor:	Okay, that's great. Next time when you interact with others you can find common ground to make the conversation flow easier.
Adriana:	True. I can definitely do that in the future.
Counselor:	So let's review the new interpretations that you came up with. Your first new interpretation was to think that interactions with others will be positive and that it could be an opportunity to network with others. Your second thought was that you could think that you do have something to say when you interact with others. Do you feel that you can see yourself using these thoughts in future interactions with others?
Adriana:	Yeah, I can see myself doing it and I know it will require some practice though, but it can be done.
Counselor:	Right and it is okay that from time to time you may have negative thoughts, but to realize when you have them and how they impact the way you interact with others.
Adriana:	I'm seeing that more clearly now.

Counselor:	So let's move on to the behaviors. Did your first behavior, which was to be brief or short in conversation with others, did that help or hurt you in getting what you wanted in that situation?
Adriana:	That ended up hurting me.
Counselor:	And how did this hurt you?
Adriana:	Well I guess because by being short with them didn't necessarily help keep the conversation going to socialize with others and have a good time at the event.
Counselor:	So what could you have done differently to get to interact well with others in that situation?
Adriana:	I could have not been short with her friends when I was trying to interact with them.
Counselor:	Right, you could have continued the conversation instead of being short with her friends and that way you could have gotten to know them better and possibly hang out with her and her friends in the future.
Adriana:	Yeah, I definitely need to be more social to have fun at these events.
Counselor:	Your second behavior, which was having a facial expression that did not seem enthusiastic to interact with others, did that help or hurt you in getting what you wanted in that situation?
Adriana:	I could have just had a positive expression on my face when I was talking to her friends.
Counselor:	Right, and a more positive expression would let them know that you are interested in engaging in conversation with them and they would be equally pleased to continue the conversation with you.
Adriana:	Yeah, that's true. I need to gauge my facial expressions to know when I'm looking standoffish versus looking happy or more pleasant.
Counselor:	Do you see yourself doing that in future conversations by not being short with people and paying attention to your facial expressions?
Adriana:	Yeah, I think I can do this if I practice doing them.
Counselor:	Great. Can you see yourself practicing this more adaptive pattern in interactions between now and when we meet next? We can review your experiences then. Would that be OK?
Adriana:	Yes, I do.
Counselor:	So, how important is it for you to make those changes in your adaptive pattern? On a scale from 0 to 10, where 0 is not at all important, and 10 is extremely important, where would you say you are?
Adriana:	I'd say 9 or 10.

Counselor: And on that 10-point scale, how confident are you that if you will make some changes in it this week?

Adriana: That'd be a 6.

Counselor: Can you see yourself practicing this more adaptive pattern in interactions between now and when we meet next? [Yes.] We can review your experiences then. Would that be OK?

Adriana: Yeah, I can do that till we see each other next time. I definitely need to practice them. That's for sure.

Counselor: Okay, so let's take a few moments to complete the SRS so that I may gauge how the session was today.

Adriana: [Adriana fills out form and hands it back.]

Counselor: Okay, well I see that the scores (38) are pretty consistent with last week's (38), which are pretty high. Is there anything that you'd like to see differently in our sessions?

Adriana: No, I think you covered everything that we need to talk about during sessions. And, I do feel heard by you; and it is becoming easier to trust you.

Counselor: So glad to hear that. Thanks. [pause] Do you have any questions or concerns about this session and the technique we used?

Adriana: No.

Counselor: Okay. So when we meet next we can discuss your use of the new alternatives you learned in this session when you interact with others.

Commentary

This transcription illustrates all four steps of how PPT is typically practiced. This was the sixth of nine sessions. By the eighth session, both first- and second-order treatment goals had been attained so planning for termination began in the eighth session. A relapse prevention plan was made and the last session occurred a week later. Adriana had been in "client-centered" counseling previously, but had not profited from it. Adriana's successful outcomes can be attributed to her active engagement in the counseling process, a strengths-focused treatment plan that focused on pattern change, the counseling intern's positive expectation for client change and training in Pattern-Focused Therapy, an effective site supervisor, and feedback from her university-based internship seminar.

Concluding Note

The therapeutic approach described and illustrated in this chapter focuses on identifying and changing a maladaptive pattern to a more adaptive one primarily by *replacing* the non-productive cognitions (interpretations) and behaviors that underlie the maladaptive pattern. In the current era of accountability in healthcare, Pattern-Focused Therapy has considerable promise as an evidence-based practice, as well as a therapeutic approach that is relatively straightforward and easy to practice. It is the main thera-peutic approach taught in our graduate counseling program at Florida Atlantic University. Trainees learn this approach in simulated counseling encounters with direct coaching and feedback. They then apply it at their off-campus training sites, and review their case reports and session tran-scriptions with their site supervisor as well as in their university case seminar. At the end of their first practicum and their second internship semesters, their mastery of this approach is evaluated in a formal exami-nation. They are provided a standardized client (role-play) who presents with a specified diagnosis and situation for which they therapeutically process and are rubric-evaluated by two faculty.

We anticipate that increasingly professional counselors, particularly those in mental health settings, will be expected to provide documentation that they utilized interventions that are brief, effective, and outcomes-focused and appropriate for their clients. Quite likely they will utilize third wave approaches, perhaps even the one described and illustrated in this chapter.

Our hope is that this book has provided you a number of new insights and treatment options that you can incorporate in your everyday coun-seling practice, irrespective of your theoretical orientation. Rather than trying to persuade you to become a CBT counselor, although some of you may, our goal was to help you achieve optimal results with your clients using the powerful interventions described in this book.

Note

1 Names and identifying information of individuals have been changed to ensure privacy.

References

McCullough, J. (2000). *Treatment for chronic depression: Cognitive behavioral analysis system of psychotherapy*. New York, NY: Guilford Press.

McCullough, J., Schramm, E., & Penberthy, K. (2015). *CBASP as a distinctive treatment for persistent depressive disorder: Distinctive features*. New York, NY: Routledge.

Miller, W., & Rollnick, S. (2012). *Motivational interviewing* (3rd ed.). New York, NY: Guilford Press.

Sperry, L. (1988). Biopsychosocial therapy: An integrative approach for tailoring treatment. *Journal of Individual Psychology, 44*, 225–235.

Sperry, L. (2000). Biopsychosocial therapy: Essential strategies and tactics. In J. Carlson & L. Sperry (Eds.), *Briefly therapy with individuals and couples*. Phoenix, AZ: Zeig, Tucker & Theisen.

Sperry, L. (2006). *Psychological treatment of chronic illness: The biopsychosocial therapy approach*. New York, NY: Brunner/Mazel.

Sperry, L. (2010). *Highly effective therapy: Developing essential clinical competencies in counseling and psychotherapy*. New York, NY: Routledge.

Sperry, L. (2016a). Educating the next generation of psychotherapists: Considering the future of theory and practice in Adlerian Psychotherapy. *Journal of Individual Psychology, 72*(1), 4–11.

Sperry, L. (2016b). Pattern-focused psychotherapy. In L. Sperry (Ed.), *Mental health and mental disorders: An encyclopedia of conditions, treatments, and well-being* (3 vols, pp. 816–818). Santa Barbara, CA: Greenwood.

Sperry, L., Brill, P., Howard, K., & Grissom, G. (1996). *Treatment outcomes in psychotherapy* and *psychiatric interventions*. New York, NY: Brunner/Mazel.

Sperry, L., & Sperry, J. (2012). *Case conceptualization: Mastering this competency with ease and confidence*. New York, NY: Routledge.

Glossary of CBT Terms

ACCEPTANCE AND COMMITMENT THERAPY a third wave therapeutic approach developed by Steven Hayes that focuses on acceptance of internal states and commitment to behavioral change for achieving life goals.

ACTIVITY CHART a chart used for monitoring daily activities and mood states.

ALL-OR-NOTHING THINKING thinking that involves the extremes, with no middle ground.

ASSERTIVENESS TRAINING a behavioral intervention for increasing self-expression in difficult interpersonal situations.

ASSOCIATIONS FOR BEHAVIORAL AND COGNITIVE THERAPIES a professional organization for the advancement of human functioning, assessment, prevention, and treatment, as well as for the enhancement of well-being through the application of behavioral, cognitive, and evidence-based principles.

ANTECEDENT an activating event, precipitant, or trigger that precedes a targeted behavior, emotion, or cognition.

AUTOMATIC THOUGHTS ideas, thoughts, or images that arise as a response to a trigger or event.

BECK DEPRESSION INVENTORY a 21 multiple-choice question self-report inventory for ages 13 and above used to measure the severity of depression.

BEHAVIORAL ACTIVATION a behavioral intervention for activating individuals who have been inactive because of depression so they can once again experience satisfaction and pleasure.

BEHAVIORAL CONTRACTING an agreement between client and counselor that contains a list of behaviors to be followed or avoided in a specific situation.

BEHAVIORAL REHEARSAL an intervention for modifying or enhancing interpersonal skills through practice. In a counseling session, this practice typically occurs in the context of role-playing.

BREATH RETRAINING an intervention that involves learning to slow one's breathing rate that originates from diaphragmatic versus thoracic breathing.

BEHAVIORAL THERAPY a counseling and psychotherapy approach that focuses on identifying and changing maladaptive behaviors. It is also known as behavior therapy.

BEHAVIORAL ANALYSIS a type of assessment that focuses on the observable and quantifiable aspects of behavior. When it focuses on functions, it is called functional analysis. See also: functional analysis.

BELIEF MODIFICATION a cognitive intervention in which the individual examines or weighs evidence for a particular belief.

BIBLIOTHERAPY an intervention in which the counselor assigns between-session activities involving reading handouts, self-help therapy books, workbooks, and web-based materials.

BOOSTER SESSIONS therapy sessions periodically scheduled to assess the status and progress made after termination, as well as to provide a "boost" to ensure continuity in the change of behavior targeted.

CLASSICAL CONDITIONING developing conditional responses to previously neutral stimuli as a result of associations with innately evocative unconditional stimuli.

CONDITIONAL RESPONSE a learned response to a conditional stimulus as a function for its association with an innately evocative stimulus.

CONDITIONAL STIMULUS a previously neutral stimulus that, through association with an unconditional stimulus, produces a conditional response.

CONSEQUENCE an event that follows a behavior and influences the occurrence of some form of that behavior in the future.

COGNITIVE BEHAVIOR MODIFICATION (CBM) a technique that focuses on identifying dysfunctional self-talk in order to change unwanted behaviors.

COGNITIVE BEHAVIOR THERAPY (CBT) a structured present-focused approach of psychotherapy that helps the client to develop strategies to modify dysfunctional patterns of thought, cognitions, behaviors, and maladaptive emotions while resolving current problems.

COGNITIVE BEHAVIORAL ANALYSIS SYSTEM OF PSYCHO-THERAPY (CBASP) a third wave approach developed by James McCullough that utilizes situational analysis and replacement rather than modification of interpretations (thoughts) and behaviors.

COGNITIVE CONCEPTUALIZATION a core competency of CBT, helping both therapists and clients understand the origins, triggers, predisposing factors, and maintenance of problems.

COGNITIVE DISTORTIONS thoughts inaccurately perceived, resulting in a distorted perception of reality attributed to biased ways of thinking about oneself and the world.

COGNITIVE AND BEHAVIORAL REPLACEMENT an intervention for identifying maladaptive thoughts (interpretations) and behaviors and replacing them with more adaptive ones.

COGNITIVE DEFUSION an acceptance and commitment therapy intervention used to distance from one's internal experience, such as a self-defeating thought.

COGNITIVE DISPUTATION a component of cognitive restructuring that uses logic to help individuals understand the irrationality of their maladaptive thoughts.

COGNITIVE ERROR an error in thinking or cognition.

COGNITIVE RESTRUCTURING a cognitive intervention for identifying maladaptive thoughts and beliefs and modifying, restructuring, or disputing them so they become more adaptive.

COGNITIVE THERAPY a structured, short-term, present-oriented psychotherapy based on the premise that the way one thinks affects how one feels emotionally.

COGNITIVE THERAPY RATING SCALE a scale used to assess a therapist's specific strengths and weaknesses among various cognitive therapy competencies.

COGNITIVE TRIAD a pattern of thought that triggers depression and other emotional states, and in which one sees themselves, the world, and their futures pessimistically.

COLLABORATIVE EMPIRICISM a fundamental concept of CBT in which both the therapist and client become investigators by examining the evidence to support or reject the patient's cognitions. Empirical evidence is then used to determine whether particular cognitions serve any useful purpose.

COPING CARD a small, portable index card on which short cognitive and/or behavioral strategies and statements are written, to replace negative and untrue thoughts when one feels anxious, stressed, or angry, and/or when facing other overwhelming situations. This may include simple, truthful, realistic statements or reminders.

CORE BELIEFS unquestioned, rigid, persistent fundamental assumptions, which often go unrecognized, including thoughts, assumptions, and beliefs about oneself, others, and the world. Also referred to as "schemas."

COVER SENSITIZATION a procedure that aims to reduce maladaptive behaviors by pairing them with aversive events through imagery.

CUE EXPOSURE a procedure that is used to expose an alcoholic or drug addict to substance-related cues to extinguish conditional responses in real-life situations.

DESENSITIZATION TECHNIQUES behavior change methods for reducing an individual's emotional and behavioral response to feared situations by intentionally and gradually exposing the individual to the feared stimulus.

DIALECTICAL BEHAVIORAL THERAPY a third wave approach developed by Marsha Linehan that focuses on coping with stress, regulating emotions, and improving relationships. Initially used with suicidal clients and then with borderline personality disorder, it is now used with bipolar and substance use disorders.

DICHOTOMOUS THINKING polar-opposite thinking, also synonymous to "all-or-nothing thinking," in which a tendency to think in terms of best and worst are only considered.

DISTANCING a cognitive technique of learning to view one's thoughts more objectively and to treat them as hypotheses rather than facts.

DSM-5 the abbreviation for the *Diagnostic and Statistical Manual of Mental Disorders, Fifth Edition,* which is the handbook mental health professionals use to diagnose mental disorders in the United States.

DOWNWARD ARROW TECHNIQUE a series of questions used to help uncover an individual's core beliefs.

EMOTIONAL REASONING a cognitive process in which emotions are taken as evidence for the truth.

EMOTIONAL REGULATION TRAINING a behavioral intervention that helps individuals identify, accept, and manage their emotions. It is particularly effective for those with emotional dysregulation issues   that is, emotional responses that quickly change (labile) and are difficult to control.

EMPATHY TRAINING a therapeutic intervention useful for increasing an individual's capacity and skills for empathy.

EXPOSURE a behavioral intervention that is useful in treating various anxiety conditions, including phobias and panic. It works by exposing individuals to their feared objects, situations, or sensations.

EXTINGUISH to lessen a conditional response through the absence of the unconditional stimulus or through the absence of consequences.

EYE MOVEMENT DESENSITIZATION AND REPROCESSING (EMDR) an intervention for reducing trauma-based symptoms by visualizing the traumatic event while concentrating one of several types of bilateral sensory input, such as side-to-side eye movement.

FLOODING EXPOSURE prolonged and continued exposure to highly anxiety- provoking stimuli.

FUNCTIONAL ANALYSIS an analysis of the causal relations among cognitions, behaviors, emotions, and environmental and cultural contexts.

GUIDED DISCOVERY a fundamental concept of CBT in which the therapist elucidates behavioral problems and faulty thinking by designing new experiences that lead to the acquisition of new skills and perspectives. The patient is guided in discovering more adaptive ways of thinking and coping with environmental stressors by correcting cognitive processing.

HABIT REVERSAL an intervention for treating repetitive behavior disorders such as tics. It works by increasing tic awareness and developing a competing response to the tic.

HABITUATION decreased response strength or occurrence of a behavior as a function of repeated exposure to a stimulus.

HIERARCHY a process in exposure therapy where an individual lists behaviors and situations, ordered from least to most unpleasant.

HOMEWORK assignments and experiments to be implemented between counseling sessions. Automatic thought records or the active use of a coping card are examples of CBT homework.

IMPULSE CONTROL TRAINING a therapeutic intervention that aims to decrease involuntary urges towards a behavior.

INTEROCEPTIVE EXPOSURE a behavioral intervention that involves repeated and systematics exposure to feared bodily sensations. Commonly used to reduce panic symptoms.

INTERMEDIATE BELIEFS related attitudes, rules, and assumptions that follow from core beliefs.

INTERPERSONAL SKILLS TRAINING a behavioral intervention that encompasses a range of skills that promotes interpersonal effectiveness.

IRRATIONAL BELIEFS beliefs that are not supported or confirmed by the environment and lead to inappropriate or negative emotions.

MAGNIFICATION a cognitive distortion in which an individual views a problem or situation in an exaggerated and negative manner.

MENTAL FILTER a cognitive distortion in which an individual dwells on the negatives and ignores the positives.

MINDFULNESS awareness of one's internal states and surroundings without judgment while focusing on the present. The opposite of mindlessness.

MINDFULNESS-BASED COGNITIVE THERAPY a third wave approach developed by Segal, Williams, and Teasdale that combines cognitive therapy with mindfulness interventions. It is typically conducted in a group setting to prevent relapse of depressive episodes.

MINIMIZATION   cognitive distortions that inappropriately reduce the importance and significance of an event or emotion.

MOOD CHECK   an objective method of assessing a client's mood since the previous sessions for tracking purposes.

MOTIVATIONAL INTERVIEWING   a therapeutic intervention developed by William Miller that is used for helping individuals discover and resolve their ambivalence to change and eventually commit to change.

OPERANT BEHAVIOR   behavior that operated on the environment and is maintained by its consequences.

OVERGENERALIZATION   a course of thinking in which an individual applies one experience and generalizes to all experiences, including experiences that have yet to happen.

PATTERN   a description of an individual's characteristic way of thinking, feeling, responding, and defending self against others.

PATTERN-FOCUSED THERAPY   a third wave therapeutic approach developed by Len Sperry that identifies and replaces maladaptive patterns with more adaptive ones.

PRECIPITATING FACTORS   factors that cause and/or trigger the onset of a disorder, illness, accident, or behavioral response. Also called antecedents.

PROBLEM IDENTIFICATION   a solving methodology that includes eliciting, defining, and identifying the problem.

PROBLEM SOLVING TRAINING   a behavioral intervention that helps individuals build skills to cope with distressing situations.

PROGRESSIVE MUSCLE RELAXATION   a set of procedures for relaxing muscle tension, conducted progressively throughout the body.

PSYCHOEDUCATION   a psychological treatment method that provides individuals with knowledge about their condition as well as advice and skills for reducing their symptoms and improving their functioning.

PUNISHER   a consequence that causes a behavior to occur with less frequency.

RATIONAL BELIEFS   beliefs that support survival and happiness. The opposite of irrational beliefs.

RATIONAL EMOTIVE BEHAVIOR THERAPY (REBT)   a therapeutic approach developed by Albert Ellis in which irrational thoughts are disputed and replaced with rational thoughts.

RELAPSE PREVENTION   a therapeutic intervention used to assist an individual in maintaining treatment gains, including sobriety, and reducing relapse in the face of everyday stressors and high-risk situations.

REINFORCER   a response or consequence that increases or decreases the probability of a behavior occurring again.

RELAXATION TECHNIQUES   any method, process, procedure, or activity that helps a state of increased calmness, or an otherwise reduced level of pain, anxiety, stress, or anger.

ROLE-PLAY   an activity that consists of reenacting and imitating a role uncharacteristic of oneself. For instance, pretending to be in a specific situation.

SCHEMA   a set of beliefs about oneself and the world that an individual uses to perceive, process, and recall information.

SELECTIVE ABSTRACTION   a cognitive distortion that involves drawing conclusions based on one event or isolated detail, without taking into consideration the context.

SELF-EFFICACY   belief in one's capacity to bring about a desired outcome.

SELF-TALK   one's internal dialogue, which refers to silent monologues kept to oneself.

SELF-MONITORING   the process of monitoring and recording one's thoughts, behaviors, and emotions in a particular context.

SHAME-ATTACKING EXERCISES   an REBT homework assignment that is designed to forcefully and directly challenge one's sense of shame, in which an individual believes they will evoke some form of social ridicule or public disapproval. This is done by the individual engaging in a shame-producing behavior in a public setting.

SHAPING   the use of reinforcement to reduce aberrant behaviors and reinforce desirable behaviors.

SOCIAL SKILLS TRAINING   a behavioral intervention with a cognitive component that helps individuals develop or increase their social skills to facilitate healthier social interaction.

SOCRATIC QUESTIONING   a therapeutic method in which strategic questions are asked to facilitate discovery of errors in thinking, uncovering assumptions, and analyzing concepts.

STRENGTHS-BASED COGNITIVE BEHAVIOR THERAPY (SB-CBT)   a third wave approach developed by Christine Padesky to help individuals build positive qualities by emphasizing strengths and resilience in a CBT format.

SYSTEMATIC DESENSITIZATION   a behavioral intervention developed by Joseph Wolpe wherein relaxation is used as a counter condition to reciprocally inhibit the anxiety related to a feared object. At present, exposure has replaced systematic desensitization as the treatment of choice for panic and other anxiety symptoms.

THIRD WAVE OF COGNITIVE BEHAVIOR THERAPY   a group of therapeutic approaches that extend and deviate from traditional behavioral approaches (first wave) and cognitive approaches (second wave). They emphasize the therapeutic relationship, mindfulness, acceptance, and context. They tend to focus more on health and well-being and less on symptom reduction.

THOUGHT RECORD   a cognitive intervention clients use to examine the evidence both for and against the selected negative automatic thoughts. It involves recording descriptions of a given situation, automatic thought, cognitive distortion, resulting emotions, adaptive response, and outcome.

Index

Abandonment/Instability schema
46, 47
ABCDEF model of functional capacity
28, 37–38
ACA *Code of Ethics* 16, 134
Acceptance and Commitment
Therapy 10, 56–58; case example
57–58; history and overview
13–14; metaphor use 129; pattern
change 70; practice 57; similarity
to Adlerian Psychology 4; theory
56–57; as third wave Cognitive
Behavior Therapy 4–5
accountability movement in
healthcare 16
acculturation 126–127, 172
acculturative stress 126, 172
action (stage of change) 79–81
active listening 5, 25–26, 74
activierties: between-session 24; direct
session 23
adaptive interpersonal skills 101–102
adaptive pattern 58–60
ADDRESSING model 119
Adler, Alfred 12–13, 147
Adlerian Psychology 4, 12–13,
129, 147
Affective dimension, of ABCDEF
model 28
agenda setting 71, 151
agoraphobia, exposure therapy for 95
Alcohol Use Disorder 107–110, 171
alliance ruptures 78
all-or-nothing thinking 89
alternatives, generating in problem
solving training 105–107
anxiety: Acceptance and Commitment
Therapy 57–58; behavioral

activation 85; Behavior Therapy
10–11; case illustrations 114,
160–180; Cognitive Behavioral
Analysis System of Psychotherapy
15; cognitive disputation 88;
Dialectical Behavior Therapy 14;
exposure therapy 94–97; illness
57–58; mindfulness 103–104;
overcontrolled behaviors 65;
Pattern-Focused Therapy case
example (Adriana) 171–180;
Pattern-Focused Therapy case
example (Jason) 160–170; problem
solving training 106; relapse
prevention 108; as self-limiting 94;
thought stopping 113–114
Approval-Seeking/
Recognition-Seeking schema 46
art therapy 130
Asian-American culture and CBT 121
assertiveness: culturally focused CBT
122, 128, 133; interpersonal skills
training and 101–103
assertiveness training 122
assessment. *see* outcome assessment
Attention Deficit Hyperactivity
Disorder: impulse control training
100–101; social skills training
110–111
Autism, social skills training and
110–112
automatic thoughts 30–31, 38–39,
66–67, 77, 127, 131, 141
autonomy, in Motivational
Interviewing 54
avoidance: breaking cycle of
85–87; difficult-to-extinguish
behaviors 66; exposure therapy

94; overcontrolled behaviors 65;
Pattern-Focused Therapy case
example (Adriana) 171–180;
Pattern-Focused Therapy case
example (Jason) 160–170
awareness training, in habit
reversal 97
Axis I disorders 27
Axis II disorders 27

Bandura, Albert 11
Beck, Aaron 11–12, 16, 18, 87
Beck, Judith 70–71, 76, 78, 138
Beck Anxiety Inventory 139, 146
Beck Cognitive Insight Scale 146
Beck Depression Inventory 146
Beck Depression Inventory II (BDI-II)
27, 33, 37, 39
Beck Hopelessness Scale 146
Beck Scale of Suicidal Ideation 146
Beck Youth Inventory 146
behavioral activation 11–12,
31, 38, 84–88; definition 85;
description 85; illustration 86–87;
indications and contraindications
85; Pattern-Focused Therapy 160;
treatment protocol 85–86
behavioral deficits 65
Behavioral dimension, of ABCDEF
model 28
behavioral interventions, culturally
focused CBT 128
behavioral rehearsal 11, 31–32, 103,
107; interpersonal skills training
102–103; Pattern-Focused Therapy
156, 160, 170; problem solving
training 106
behaviorism 117
behaviors 65–66; behavioral
deficits 65; difficult-to-
extinguish 66; overcontrolled
65–66; overgeneralized 66;
undercontrolled 65
Behavior Therapy, history and
overview 10–11
Beitman, B. 68
beliefs: core 67; intermediate 66–67
bereavement 76
between-session activities 24
Biopsychosocial Therapy 58, 156–157
bipolar disorder 10, 47
body dysmorphic disorder, thought
stopping and 113

booster sessions 34–35, 40
borderline personality disorder:
Cognitive Behavioral Analysis
System of Psychotherapy 15;
Dialectical Behavior Therapy 14,
47; emotional regulation training
91; Schema Therapy 45, 47
Brief Acculturation Scale 126
bulimia nervosa, Dialectical Behavior
Therapy and 47

Cannabis Use Disorder 171
case conceptualization 29–30, 65;
case examples 38, 131, 161,
171–173; as core competency
in Cognitive Behavior Therapy
29–30, 151; in counseling process
158; cultural 116–118, 125, 131;
inaccurate 76–77; Pattern-Focused
Therapy case example (Adriana)
171–173; Pattern-Focused Therapy
case example (Jason) 161
Case Conceptualization: Mastering
this Competency with Ease and
Confidence (Sperry and Sperry) 131
case example: Acceptance and
Commitment Therapy 57–58;
Alcohol Use Disorder 109–110;
anxiety 114; Autism Spectrum
Disorder 111–112; behavioral
activation 86–87; borderline
personality disorder 91; Cognitive
Behavioral Analysis System of
Psychotherapy 53; Cognitive
Behavior Therapy (Jared) 36–40;
cognitive disputation 89; couples
counseling 93; cultural sensitivity
116, 131–134; depression 89;
Dialectical Behavior Therapy
48–49; emotional regulation
training 91; empathy training
93; exposure therapy 96–97;
habit reversal 98–99; hair-pulling
disorder 98–99; impulse control
training 100–101; Intermittent
Explosive Disorder 100–101;
interpersonal skills training
102–103; major depressive
disorder 86–87; mindfulness
104–105; Mindfulness-Based
Cognitive Therapy 50–51;
Motivational Interviewing 55–56;
Pattern-Focused Therapy (Adriana)

171–180; Pattern-Focused Therapy
(Casey) 60; Pattern-Focused
Therapy (Jason) 160–170; phobia
96–97; problem solving training
107; relapse prevention 109–110;
Schema Therapy 47; social skills
training 111–112; Strengths-Based
Cognitive Therapy 44–45; thought
stopping 114
case transcript: Outcomes Ratings
Scale (ORS) 145; Session Rating
Scale (SRS) 143–144
CBASP. *see* Cognitive Behavioral
Analysis System of Psychotherapy
chair dialogs, in Schema Therapy 47
change: client readiness for 54–55,
79, 158; mechanisms 68; stages of
79–81
children: Cognitive Behavioral
Analysis System of Psychotherapy
15; emotional regulation training
90; maladaptive schemas and
45–47
Clark-Beck Obsessive-Compulsive
Inventory 146
CLASS acronym 128
classical conditioning 10
client-centered counseling 180
client protective factor trifecta 19
clients: end-of-session feedback from
73; interrupting 77; non-motivated
78–79; patient *versus* 75–76; role
in counseling process 75
client values 17
clinical trials 5, 10
Code of Ethics, ACA 16, 134
cognition: automatic thoughts 66;
influence on psychological suffering
66–67; intermediate beliefs 66–67;
levels of 66
Cognitive Behavioral Analysis System
of Psychotherapy (CBASP) 51–53;
case example 53; history and
overview 14–15; in Pattern-Focused
Therapy 156–157; practice 52–53;
replacement 129; theory 51–52
Cognitive-Behavioral interventions
84–115
cognitive defusion 56–58
Cognitive dimension, of ABCDEF
model 28
cognitive disputation 6, 87–88,
87–89; definition 87; description

87–88; illustration 89; indications
and contraindications 88; treatment
protocol 88
cognitive interventions, culturally
focused CBT 129–131; art and
music therapies 130; cultural
strengths 129; homework 130–131;
most generous interpretation
technique 130; replacement 129;
stories and metaphors 129
cognitive map 22, 64
cognitive restructuring 87–89;
culturally focused 128, 129; social
skills training 111–112
Cognitive Therapy 87; cultural
explanation 127; history of 12–13;
relationship strains and ruptures 78
Cognitive Therapy Rating Scale (CTS)
150–151
collaboration 151; in Motivational
Interviewing 54; in Pattern-Focused
Therapy 59
collaborative empiricism 18, 25
commitment, consolidating 54
communication skills: culturally
focused CBT 128; interpersonal
skills training and 101–103
competencies, Cognitive Therapy
Rating Scale 151
competencies of Cognitive
Behavior Therapy 24–40; case
conceptualization and treatment
plan development 29–30; case
study illustration 36–40; formation
of effective therapeutic response
25–26; integrative assessment,
performance of 26–29; treatment
gains, maintaining 34–35;
treatment-interfering behaviors,
dealing with 35–36; treatment
outcomes, monitoring and
evaluating 33–34; treatment plan
implementation 31–33
competing response: in habit reversal
97–99; in impulse control training
100–101
computer-assisted therapy 138
conditional assumptions 67
conflict resolution: culturally focused
CBT 128; interpersonal skills
training 102
contemplation (stage of change)
79–81

"cookie cutter" therapy. 5–6
coping skills 107–109, 172
core beliefs 67
Core Competencies in
    Cognitive-Behavioral Therapy
    (Newman) 3, 24
counseling: ACA definition 9;
    consensus definition 3; phases
    70–73
counselors: approach to the
    therapeutic relationship 9;
    experience of 17; as "keepers"
    of the therapeutic relationship 3;
    myths about Cognitive Behavior
    Therapy 2–6, 7; role in counseling
    process 75; theoretical orientation
    and cognitive map 22
couples counseling 93
critical incidents 147
CTS (Cognitive Therapy Rating Scale)
    150–151
cultural assessment 120
cultural awareness 116, 118
cultural competence 9, 118, 120,
    125–126, 135
cultural dynamics: assessing
    120–121; personality dynamics and
    127–128
cultural explanation 127
cultural formulation 124–128;
    acculturation 126–127; case
    vignette 132; cultural explanation
    127; cultural identity 125–126;
    cultural versus personality
    127–128; definition 125; elements
    of 125–128
cultural identity 125–126
Culturally Responsive CBT
    (CR-CBT) 19; ADDRESSING
    model 119; assessment 148; case
    conceptualization 116–118, 125,
    131; case example 116, 131–134;
    description 116–117; DSM-5
    assessment of cultural factors
    123–124; RESPECTFUL model
    118–119
cultural strengths, recognizing and
    using 129
culture, influence of 13, 30

decentering 15
Defectiveness/Shame schema 46
Dependence/Incompetence schema 46

depression: Beck Depression Inventory
    146; behavioral activation
    85–86; Cognitive Behavioral
    Analysis System of Psychotherapy
    15, 51–53, 129; cognitive
    disputation 88–89; as cycle 85;
    Mindfulness-Based Cognitive
    Therapy 49–51; Pattern-Focused
    Therapy case example (Adriana)
    171–180; problem solving training
    106; Schema Therapy 45; thought
    stopping 113
desensitization, systematic 10–11,
    94, 95
destructive behavior, Dialectical
    Behavior Therapy and 14
developmental and pattern-focused
    assessment 27
diagnostic assessment 27
Dialectical Behavior Therapy 10,
    47–49; case example 48–49;
    emotional regulation training
    90; history and overview 14;
    mindfulness 104; practice 48;
    theory 47–48
difficult-to-extinguish behaviors 66
discrepancy, in Motivational
    Interviewing 54
dismantling 11
disputation: cognitive 87–89;
    culturally focused 128; Rational
    Emotive Behavior Therapy (REBT)
    6, 70
distress: rating subjective units of 11;
    SUDS (Subjective Units of Distress
    Scale) 146
distressing thoughts 112–114
distress sensitivity 26
distress tolerance, Dialectical Behavior
    Therapy and 48, 49
Distress tolerance dimension, of
    ABCDEF model 28
diversity issues 19, 116–135;
    Asian-American culture 121;
    Latino culture 121–122; LGBTQ
    culture 122
dropout rates 140
DSM diagnosis 27–29, 33, 123–124
Dysfunctional Attitude Scale 146

eating disorders: cognitive disputation
    88; Dialectical Behavior
    Therapy 14; mindfulness 104;

relapse prevention 108; Schema
Therapy 45
education: psychoeducation 24, 46,
48–49, 51, 69, 102, 172; relapse
prevention 108
elicitation phase, of CBASP
practice 52
Ellis, Albert 12–13, 18, 87
Emotional Deprivation schema 46
Emotional Inhibition schema 46
emotional regulation: Cognitive
Behavioral Analysis System of
Psychotherapy 51; Dialectical
Behavior Therapy and 48, 49;
empathy training 92; Schema
Therapy and 45, 46
emotional regulation training 90–91;
definition 90; description 90;
illustration 91; indications and
contraindications 90; treatment
protocol 90–91
empathy 32, 74, 151; Cognitive
Behavioral Analysis System
of Psychotherapy 51;
Mindfulness-Based Cognitive
Therapy 50; Motivational
Interviewing 54–55; therapeutic
relationship 18, 25–26
empathy training 92–93; definition
92; description 92; illustration 93;
indications and contraindications
92; treatment protocol 92–93
empirically supported treatments 139
enculturation 126
engagement 69
Enmeshment/Underdeveloped Self
schema 46
Entitlement/Grandiosity schema 46
Epictetus 12
escalators, phobia and 96–97
evidence-based practice: CBT as
16–18; defined 16; elements of
16–18; myths concerning CBT and
3–5; reimbursement 4–5; trend
toward 1
evidence-based practice elements
16–18; client values 17; counselor
experience 17; therapeutic
relationship 17–18
evocation, in Motivational
Interviewing 54
evolution of Cognitive Behavior
Therapy 10–16; first wave 10–11;

second wave 11–13; third wave
13–16
Experience dimension, of ABCDEF
model 28
explanatory model 127
exposure: culturally focused CBT 133;
gradual 94–96; imaginal 94–95;
interoceptive 94–95; overcontrolled
behaviors 66; virtual reality 94–95;
in vivo 94–96
exposure therapy 11, 94–97;
definition 94; description 94;
illustration 96–97; indications and
contraindications 95; treatment
protocol 95

Failure schema 46
fears, exposure therapy and 94–97
feedback: Cognitive Therapy Rating
Scale (CTS) 151; end-of-session
from clients 73; incorporating 141;
Outcomes Ratings Scale (ORS)
146; Session Rating Scale (SRS)
143–144, 158, 160
fee-for-service payment structure 148
fight-flight system 94
first-order change 13
first wave, history and overview
10–11
flooding 94–95
formative evaluation 139
functional assessment 28–29, 69
functional capacity, ABCDEF model
of 28
functional contextualism 56
Functional impairment dimension, of
ABCDEF model 28

gambling, impulse control training for
100–101
generalization phase, of CBASP
practice 52–53
generalization stage, of habit reversal
97–98
graded tasks, overcontrolled behaviors
and 66
guided discovery 32, 39, 133, 151

habit inconvenience review
97–98
habit reversal 11, 97–99; definition
97; description 97–98; illustration
98–99; indications and

contraindications 98; treatment
    protocol 98
habituation 94–95
hair-pulling disorder
    (Trichotillomania): case illustration
    98–99; habit reversal 97–99;
    impulse control training 100
Hayes, Steven 13, 56
Hays, Pamela 19, 116, 119, 123, 128,
    148–149
history of Cognitive Behavior Therapy
    9–19
homework 24; culturally focused
    130–131; engagement 69; in
    Pattern-Focused Therapy 159;
    review in counseling session 69
homicidal ideation 29
homosexuality 118
Horney, Karen 12
Horneyan model of psychology 12

if-then reasoning 66–67
illness anxiety 57–58
illustration. see case example
imagery: Acceptance and
    Commitment Therapy 57; Schema
    Therapy 47; Strengths-Based
    Cognitive Behavior Therapy 43
imagery assessment 148
imaginal exposure 94–95
implementation: CBT interventions
    76–79; premature 18; treatment
    plan 31–33
impulse control disorder: habit
    reversal and 97–98; impulse control
    training 100–101
impulse control training 11, 100–101;
    definition 100; description 100;
    illustration 100–101; indications
    and contraindications 100;
    treatment protocol 100
inactivity, breaking cycle of
    85–87
Individual Psychology 12
information, providing clients
    with 24
Insufficient Self-Control/
    Self-Discipline schema 46
integrated care 155
integrative assessment 26–29;
    developmental and pattern-focused
    assessment 27; diagnostic
    assessment 27; functional

assessment 28–29; risk
    assessment 29
intermediate beliefs 66–67
Intermittent Explosive Disorder
    100–101
interoceptive exposure 94–95
Interpersonal Psychotherapy 10
interpersonal relationships/behavior:
    Dialectical Behavior Therapy
    47–49; overgeneralized behaviors
    66; Schema Therapy 45, 46
interpersonal skills training 101–103;
    definition 101; description
    101–102; illustration 102–103;
    indications and contraindications
    102; treatment protocol 102
interrupting clients 77
interventions, Cognitive-Behavioral
    84–115; behavioral activation
    85–87; behavioral interventions
    128; cognitive disputation and
    restructuring 87–89; cognitive
    interventions 129–131; culturally
    sensitive/focused 123, 128–131;
    emotional regulation training
    90–91; empathy training 92–93;
    exposure 94–97; habit reversal
    97–99; impulse control training
    100–101; interpersonal skills
    training 101–103; mindfulness
    103–105; obstacles in
    implementing 76–79; problem
    solving training 105–107; relapse
    prevention 107–110; social skills
    training 110–112; thought stopping
    112–114
interview, diagnostic 27
in vivo exposure 94–96

Joffe Ellis, D. 18
justice, social 134–135

Kabat-Zinn, J. 15
Kleptomania 100–101

Lambert, M. J. 68
Latino culture and CBT 121–122
Level of Personality Functioning Scale
    (LPFS) 28–29
LGBTQ culture and CBT 122
Life History Assessment Forms 148
Linehan, Marsha 47–48
listening empathetically 93

maintenance (stage of change)
79–81
major depression 10, 86–87
maladaptive behaviors: as influenced
by one's "private intelligence" 12;
modifying or replacing 10, 58–60;
Pattern-Focused Therapy for
58–60
maladaptive pattern. see
Pattern-Focused Therapy
maladaptive schemas 45–46
marital distress, cognitive disputation
and 88
Marks, Isaac 11
MBCT. see Mindfulness-Based
Cognitive Therapy
McCullough, J. 14–15
medical problems with psychological
components 139
meditation 49–51, 104
Mental Status Examination (MSE) 27
metaphors 14, 43–44, 57–58,
129, 143
mindfulness 103–105; definition 103;
description 103–104; Dialectical
Behavior Therapy and 48, 49;
illustration 104–105; indications
and contraindications 104;
treatment protocol 104
Mindfulness-Based Cognitive Therapy
(MBCT) 10, 49–51; case example
50–51; history and overview 15;
practice 50; theory 49–50
Mindfulness-Based Stress Reduction
(MBSR) 15
Mistrust/Abuse schema 46, 47
mood check 72
mood disorders: Dialectical Behavior
Therapy 14; mindfulness 103–104
Mooney, Kathleen 16, 42–43
most generous interpretation
technique 130
Motivational Interviewing 54–56;
case example 55–56; interventions
to optimize readiness for change
80–81; non-motivated clients
78–79; in Pattern-Focused Therapy
157, 159; practice 55; theory
54–55
motivation of non-motivated clients
78–79
motivation stage, of habit reversal
97–98

music therapy 130
myths about Cognitive Behavior
Therapy 2–6, 7; downplay of
therapeutic relationships 3–4; rigid,
manualized from of treatment
5–6; use because of reimbursement
4–52–6

nail biting: habit reversal 98; impulse
control training 100
Narrative Therapy 129
Negativity/Pessimism schema 46
negotiation skills, improving with
empathy training 92
neo-Adlerians 13
neo-Freudians 13
Newman, Cory 3, 24, 25, 67–68,
119, 150–151

obsessive-compulsive disorder 10;
Clark-Beck Obsessive-Compulsive
Inventory 146; exposure therapy
95; Schema Therapy 45; thought
stopping 113
obstacles in implementing CBT
interventions 76–79;
early bereavement 76; inaccurate
case conceptualization
76–77; interrupting clients
77; non-motivated clients
78–79; relationship
ruptures 78
one-trial learning 66
ongoing assessment 139
open-ended questions 27, 37
OQ-45 142–143
oral-digital habits, habit reversal and 98
outcome assessment 139–140;
final 139; informal monitoring
of progress 140–141; OQ-45
142–143; Outcomes Ratings
Scale (ORS) 33, 37–39, 144–146,
159, 173; as Pattern-Focused
Therapy component 157;
Session Rating Scale (SRS) 33,
38, 143–144, 158, 160, 180;
training and use of outcomes
measures 142
Outcomes Rating Scale (ORS) 33,
37–39, 144–146, 159, 173
overcontrolled behaviors
65–66
overgeneralized behaviors 66

Padesky, Christine 16, 42–43
panic 10; exposure therapy 94–96; thought stopping 113
Panic Belief Questionnaire 146
paranoia, Pattern-Focused Therapy for 60
patient *versus* client terminology 75–76
pattern analysis 69–70
pattern change 70
pattern-focused assessment 27
Pattern-Focused Therapy 58–60, 155–181; basic premises 157; case example (Adriana) 171–180; case example (Casey) 60; case example (Jason) 160–170; clinical value of approach 156; counseling process, summary of 158; counseling strategy and sequence 159; origins and components 156–157; overview 156; practice 59–60; relapse prevention 180; theory 58–59; therapeutic process and phases 157–159; typical session 159–160
pattern maintenance 70
patterns. *see* Pattern-Focused Therapy
pay-for-performance paradigm 138, 148–149
permission seeking 60
personality: CBT model of 63–65; development of 64; theory of 63
personality assessment 69
personality disorder: behavioral activation 85; Cognitive Behavioral Analysis System of Psychotherapy 15; Dialectical Behavior Therapy 14, 47; emotional regulation training 91; empathy training 92; impulse control training 100; mindfulness 104; Schema Therapy 45
personality dynamics 127–128
Personal Model of Resilience (PMR) 43–45
phobias, exposure therapy and 94–97
physical abuse in childhood, history of 171
Piaget's cognitive-emotional development 51–52
pleasant activity scheduling, behavioral activation and 85–87

post-traumatic stress disorder: Dialectical Behavior Therapy 47; exposure therapy 95; Schema Therapy 45
precontemplation (stage of change) 79–81
predispositions, biological 64
premature termination 140
preoperational stage 51
preparation (stage of change) 79–81
problem-focus therapy: Behavior Therapy 10; CBT as 3, 10
problem-solving skills, improving with empathy training 92
problem solving training 105–107; definition 105; description 105–106; illustration 107; indications and contraindications 106; treatment protocol 106
processes, Cognitive Therapy Rating Scale 151
protective factors 149, 158, 172–173
psychiatric disorders, successfully treated with CBT 138
psychoeducation 24, 46, 48–49, 51, 69, 102, 172
psychological flexibility 56–57
psychological problems, successfully treated with CBT 138–139
psychopathology: CBT model of 63–65; theory of 63–64
psychotherapeutic process 65
psychotic symptoms, thought stopping and 113
PTSD. *see* post-traumatic stress disorder
public display, habit reversal and 98
Punitiveness schema 46

questioning-processing sequence, in Pattern-Focused Therapy 59–60

randomized controlled studies 139
Rational Emotive Behavior Therapy (REBT): cognitive disputation and 87; cultural explanation 127; disputation process 6, 70; example of rigid application to depressed client 5–6; history and overview 12–13; therapeutic relationship and 18
reciprocal inhibition 10–11

recollections, elicitation of early
    69–70
reflexive responses, reducing
reimbursement 4–5
reinforcement techniques 10
relapse prevention 107–110;
    definition 107; description
    107–108; illustration 109–110;
    indications and contraindications
    108; in Pattern-Focused Therapy
    180; treatment protocol 108–109
relational frame theory 13
relationship conflict, Cognitive
    Behavioral Analysis System of
    Psychotherapy and 15
Relationship Enhancement
    Therapy 92
relationship ruptures 78
relaxation training: social skills
    training 111–112; systematic
    desensitization 94–95
remediation phase, of CBASP
    practice 52
re-parenting 46
replacement 129, 133
resilience, Strengths-Based Cognitive
    Therapy and 42–44
resistance: client 26, 54–55; rolling
    with, Motivational Interviewing
    and 54–55
RESPECTFUL model 118–119
response prevention 95
restructuring, cognitive 87–89,
    111–112, 128, 129
risk assessment 29
Rogers, Carl 5, 18, 74
role-playing 32, 39, 150, 160,
    170; cultural sensitive therapy
    122, 133; emotional regulation
    training 91; interpersonal skills
    training 102–103; overcontrolled
    behaviors 66; Pattern-Focused
    Therapy 170; problem solving
    training 106; Schema Therapy
    46–47; social skills training
    111–112; use in counselor
    training 181
roles in counseling process 75–76
ruminative thought 31, 112

SB-CBT. see Strengths-Based
    Cognitive Behavior Therapy

schema: common themes 67;
    individual's cognitive 64; triggered
    in interview 147
schema assessment 146–148
Schema Therapy: case example
    47; Pattern-Focused Therapy
    and 172; practice 46–47; theory
    45–46
schizophrenia 10
Schizophrenia Spectrum
    Disorders 110
scratching, habit reversal and 98
second-order change 13
second wave, history and overview
    11–13
seeking client permission 159
Segal, Zindel 15, 49
selective abstraction 89
self-care, culturally focused CBT
    and 128
self-efficacy 30, 54–55, 66, 68, 133;
    Motivational Interviewing 54–55;
    relapse prevention 108–109
self-harm: Dialectical Behavior
    Therapy 14; relapse prevention 108
self-monitoring 31, 75, 111
self-other schemas 172
self-report inventories 27, 33
self-respect, maintenance of 102
Self-Sacrifice schema 46
Session Rating Scale (SRS) 33, 38,
    143–144, 158, 160, 180
sessions, number and length
    of 155
session structure 70–73; agenda
    setting 71; end of session 71, 73;
    homework review 72; initial part of
    session 71; middle part of session
    71; mood check 72; prioritizing
    agenda 72; summary and feedback
    73; update 72
simulation, in interpersonal skills
    training 102
situational analysis 52
skills, focus on teaching 23
skills training 11; for behavioral
    deficits 65; before cognitive
    disputation 88; interpersonal
    101–102
skills training group 48
skin picking: habit reversal 97–98;
    impulse control training 100

smoking cessation 55–56; relapse
prevention 108; thought
stopping 113
social anxiety: exposure therapy 95;
Pattern-Focused Therapy case
example (Adriana) 171–180;
Pattern-Focused Therapy case
example (Jason) 160–170; problem
solving training 106
social isolation: Pattern-Focused
Therapy case example (Adriana)
171–180; Pattern-Focused Therapy
case example (Jason) 160–170
Social Isolation/Alienation schema 46
social justice 134–135
Social Phobia, social skills training
for 110
social skills, improving: cognitive
disputation and restructuring 88;
interpersonal skills training 102;
problem solving training 105
social skills training 110–112;
definition 110; description 110;
illustration 111–112; indications
and contraindications 110–111;
treatment protocol 111
social support: culturally focused CBT
128; in habit reversal 98; in relapse
prevention 109
sociocultural competence 126
Socratic questioning 32; cognitive
disputation 87–88; culturally
focused CBT 133
Solution-Focused Brief Therapy 121
spending, compulsive 100
Sperry, Len 58, 156
Stop command 113–114
stories and metaphors 129
strengths, assessing client 149
Strengths-Based Cognitive Behavior
Therapy (SB-CBT) 42–45; case
example 44–45; history and
overview 15–16; practice 43–44;
similarity to Adlerian Psychology
4; theory 42–43; wellness
perspective 67
Strengths-Based Cognitive Therapy
practice steps 43–44; apply
Personal Model of Resilience
(PMR) 44; construct Personal
Model of Resilience (PMR) 43–44;
practice resilience 44; search for
strengths 43

stress: acculturative 126; mindfulness
for reducing 103–105
stuttering, habit reversal and 97–98
Subjective Units of Distress Scale
(SUDS) 11, 146, 161–163,
166–169
Subjugation schema 46
substance use/abuse: cognitive
disputation 88; Dialectical
Behavior Therapy 14; impulse
control training 100; mindfulness
104; Pattern-Focused Therapy
case example 171–180; relapse
prevention 107–110; thought
stopping 113
SUDS (Subjective Units of Distress
Scale) 11, 146, 161–163, 166–169
suffering: CBT factors that
influence 65–67; development
of 63–64; Dialectic Behavior
Therapy conceptualization of 14;
symptoms 64
suicidal ideation: Beck Scale of
Suicidal Ideation 146; Dialectical
Behavior Therapy 14, 47; risk
assessment 29
summative evaluation 139
supervision, CBT 149–150
supervisors 34
systematic desensitization 10–11,
94, 95

Teasdale, John 49
teeth grinding, habit reversal and 98
temperament, biological 64
termination of therapy 35, 140
theoretical premises of Cognitive
Behavior Therapy 22–24; direct
session activities 23; emphasis
on cognition and behavior 23;
homework and between-session
activities, use of 24; information
and psychoeducation, provision of
24; present and future, focus on 23;
teaching skills, focus on 23
therapeutic alliance. see therapeutic
relationship
therapeutic assessment 69
therapeutic processes, theory of 63
therapeutic relationship: in CBT
practice 73–74; emphasis in
Strengths-Based Cognitive Behavior
Therapy 3–4; evidence-based

practice element 17–18; forming effective 25–26; important factors 18; myths concerning CBT and 3–4; problem solving at expense of 3; rating in Pattern-Focused Therapy 59; relationship ruptures 78; role in professional counseling practice 18–19; Session Rating Scale (SRS) 143–144; stages 73

third wave Cognitive Behavior Therapy 42–60; Acceptance and Commitment Therapy 4–5, 56–58; Cognitive Behavioral Analysis System of Psychotherapy 51–53; counselor receptivity toward 9; Dialectical Behavior Therapy 47–49; history and overview 13–16; Mindfulness-Based Cognitive Therapy 49–51; Motivational Interviewing 54–56; Pattern-Focused Therapy 58–60; Schema Therapy 45–47; Strengths-Based Cognitive Behavior Therapy 3–4, 42–45; therapeutic relationship and 3–4, 9

thought stopping 112–114; culturally focused CBT 133; definition 112; description 113; illustration 114; indications and contraindications 113; treatment protocol 113

tics, habit reversal and 97–98

treatment: Cognitive-Behavioral interventions 84–115; course and length of 155; obstacles in implementing CBT interventions 76–79; stages of process 68–70; termination of therapy 35

treatment gains, maintaining 34–35

treatment-interfering behaviors, dealing with 35–36

treatment outcomes, monitoring and evaluating 33–34

treatment plan: development in Cognitive Behavior Therapy 29–30; implementation 31–33; update 34

treatment stages 68–70; engagement 69; pattern analysis 69–70; pattern change 70; pattern maintenance 70

trichotillomania (hair-pulling disorder) 97–100

12-step meetings 108–109

20/20: Consensus Definition of Counseling (Kaplan and Gladding) 3, 25

undercontrolled behaviors 65

Unrelenting Standards/ Hypercriticalness schema 46

update, in counseling session 72

virtual reality exposure 94, 95

Vulnerability to Harm or Illness schema 46

warning signs of relapse 108–109

wellness, from CBT perspective 67–68

Williams, Mark 49

"wise mind" 48

Wolpe, Joseph 10–11

Yalom, Irving 3–4

Young, Jeffery E. 45

Young Compensation Inventory 148

Young Parenting Inventory 148

Young-Rygh Avoidance Inventory 148

Young Schema Questionnaire 148

 Taylor & Francis eBooks

Helping you to choose the right eBooks for your Library

Add Routledge titles to your library's digital collection today. Taylor and Francis ebooks contains over 50,000 titles in the Humanities, Social Sciences, Behavioural Sciences, Built Environment and Law.

Choose from a range of subject packages or create your own!

Benefits for you

>> Free MARC records
>> COUNTER-compliant usage statistics
>> Flexible purchase and pricing options
>> All titles DRM-free.

REQUEST YOUR **FREE** INSTITUTIONAL TRIAL TODAY

Free Trials Available
We offer free trials to qualifying academic, corporate and government customers.

Benefits for your user

>> Off-site, anytime access via Athens or referring URL
>> Print or copy pages or chapters
>> Full content search
>> Bookmark, highlight and annotate text
>> Access to thousands of pages of quality research at the click of a button.

eCollections – Choose from over 30 subject eCollections, including:

Archaeology	Language Learning
Architecture	Law
Asian Studies	Literature
Business & Management	Media & Communication
Classical Studies	Middle East Studies
Construction	Music
Creative & Media Arts	Philosophy
Criminology & Criminal Justice	Planning
Economics	Politics
Education	Psychology & Mental Health
Energy	Religion
Engineering	Security
English Language & Linguistics	Social Work
Environment & Sustainability	Sociology
Geography	Sport
Health Studies	Theatre & Performance
History	Tourism, Hospitality & Events

For more information, pricing enquiries or to order a free trial, please contact your local sales team:
www.tandfebooks.com/page/sales

 Routledge
Taylor & Francis Group

The home of
Routledge books

www.tandfebooks.com